9.99 ✓

L 629.
2275
BRO

History of the
MOTORBIKE

This is a Parragon Book
This edition published in 2005

Parragon
Queen Street House
4 Queen Street
Bath BA1 1HE

A copy of the CIP data for this book is available from the British Library upon request.

The rights of Roland Brown to be identified as the author of this work have been asserted in accordance
with Section 77 of the Copyright, Designs and Patents Act of 1988.

Created, designed, produced and packaged by Stonecastle Graphics Ltd

Designed by Paul Turner and Sue Pressley
Edited by Philip de Ste. Croix

Printed and bound in China

ISBN: 1-40545-696-5

Photographic credits:

British Film Institute: pages 41(b), 56(t), 79(t), 79(bl, br), 104(t, cl, cr), 179(c)
Phil Masters: pages 42, 100(c), 112(b), 116(t, b), 118(bl), 119(t, b), 121(b), 138(tl, tr)
Andrew Morland: pages 24, 31(t, b), 35(t), 39(t, bl), 40(t), 46(b), 48(br), 51(t), 55(bl), 118(t)
Mortons Motorcycle Media Archive: pages 16(t, b), 17(b), 18(t, b), 19(t), 23(br), 26(b), 28(t), 30(b), 39(br), 41(t), 44(t), 49(t), 56(bl), 59(br), 67(t, c), 76(t), 89(tr), 98(c)
Garry Stuart: pages 8, 13(c), 15(bl), 21(t), 22(t), 27(t, b), 36(b), 38(t, b), 69(t, bl, br), 91(c), 98(b), 122(b)
Topham Picturepoint: pages 11(cr, br), 12(b), 13(t, b)

Roland Brown library/www.motobike.net (fees to Riders for Health); photos by:
BMW: pages 32(t), 37, 50(br), 70(t), 100(t, b), 114(t), 129(tr, cl)
Jason Critchell: pages 168(b), 170(t), 183(t, b)
Double Red: pages 178(c), 185(t)
Ducati: pages 54(t), 80(b, thanks Ludovica), 93(br)
Gold & Goose: pages 161(br), 186(tr), 189(tl)
Harley-Davidson: pages 14(l, r), 19(b), 20(t, b), 26(t), 28(b), 40(b), 57(t)
Honda: pages 51(c, b), 62(t), 64(t), 76(bl), 81(b), 105(bl), 112(t), 115(b), 120(t), 126(b), 127(t, c), 128(b), 129(cr), 137(b), 142(l), 143(cr), 150(t), 177(t), 191(c)
Milagro: pages 186(bl), 187(t)
Oli Tennent: page 177(b)
Others: pages 21(c, b), 33(b), 44(bl), 47(t, c), 52(t), 122(t), 132(b), 148(t), 150(c, b), 173(tr), 176(t), 179(t), 186(tl), 188(r), 189(cr), 190(l, r)

Photos © Roland Brown library/www.motobike.net, by:
Kevin Ash: page 95(t)
Roland Brown: pages 6, 10(l, r), 11(tl), 12(t), 15(t, br), 17(t), 22(b), 23(t, bl), 32(b), 33(t), 34(t), 35(b), 36(t), 59(t, bl), 71(c), 72(b), 74(t), 75(t), 77(b), 82, 83(r), 90(b), 93, 94(t), 95(b),
96(b), 97(bl, br), 98(t), 99(c, b), 102(b), 103(t, b), 107(t, b), 110(b), 111(b), 114(b), 115(t), 117(t), 118(br), 123(tl, tr), 129(tl, b), 131(t), 132(t), 133, 134, 135(bl), 136(bl), 137(t), 139,
141(b), 145(c), 146(b), 147(t), 148(br), 149(b), 152(bl), 153(t, b), 154(t, b), 155(t), 156(t) 157(b), 158(t, b), 159(t, c, b), 160(b), 161(tr, bl), 162(t), 163(t, b), 164(c), 165(b), 169(b),
170(br), 171(t), 172(t), 173(tl, b), 174(t, b), 175(tr, b), 176(bl, br), 178(t, b), 180(tr), 181(t), 182(tr, b), 184(t, b) 185(c, b), 186(br), 187(b), 188(l), 191(t, b)
Jack Burnicle: pages 92(b), 93(bl), 97(t), 99(t), 104(b), 106(t)
Jason Critchell: pages 94(b), 156(bl)
Phil Masters: pages 29(t), 30(t), 33(b), 46(t), 47(b), 49(b), 50(t, bl), 52(b), 53(c), 54(b), 55(t, br), 57(b), 58(b), 60, 62(b), 64(b), 66(t, b), 67(b), 68(t, b), 70(bl, br), 71(t), 72(t), 73(t), 75(b),
77(t), 78(t), 80(t), 83(l), 85(t, c), 87(t, b), 88(t, b), 89(tl, b), 92(t, r), 111(t), 113(t), 117(b), 120(b), 121(t), 127(b), 131(b), 141(t), 142(r), 143(b), 144(t, b), 148(bl), 155(b), 160(t), 161(tl),
164(b), 165(t, c), 168(t), 169(t), 170(bl), 171(b), 172(b), 175(tl), 179(b), 181(b), 189(b)
Gold & Goose: pages 48(t), 63(t, b), 74(b), 90(t, c), 124(c), 128(t), 130(t, b), 136(br), 140(bl, br), 143(cl), 144(c)
Mac McDiarmid: pages 91(b), 125(t, b), 138(b), 144(t), 149(t), 149(t, b)
Brian J Nelson: pages 4, 182(tl), 189(tr)
Dale Stenton: page 164(t)
Oli Tennent: pages 29(b), 44(br), 45(t, b), 46(c), 48(bl), 53(t, b), 56(br), 58(t, c), 65(t, b), 71(b), 72(c), 73(b), 74(c), 78(b), 80(c), 81(t), 85(b), 86(t, b), 91(t), 95(c), 96(t), 101(t, b), 102(t),
105(t, br), 106(b), 108, 110(t), 113(b), 123(b), 124(t), 124(b), 126(t), 136(t), 140(t), 143(t), 145(t, b), 152(t, br), 156(br), 157(t), 166, 180(tl, b)

Thanks to all those whose bikes are pictured!

History of the

MOTORBIKE

FROM THE FIRST MOTORIZED BICYCLES TO THE POWERFUL

AND SOPHISTICATED SUPERBIKES OF TODAY

ROLAND BROWN

p

Above: *Honda's fastest FireBlade yet – the impressive CBR1000RR – handled superbly thanks to its race-derived chassis.*

Contents

Introduction   6

1   Iron Horse   8
    1860s to the First World War

2   Boom and Bust   24
    1914–1939

3   Mobility and Freedom   42
    1940s and 1950s

4   Empire in Decline   60
    1960s

5   Superbikes Roar In   82
    1970s

6   Fire and Water   108
    1980s

7   Weekend Warriors   134
    1990s

8   Towards the Limit   166
    21st Century

Index   192

Above: Honda's CB750, regarded as the 'first superbike', heralded a new era of sophistication on its launch in 1969.

Introduction

'The motorcycle is a perfect metaphor for the 20th century. Invented at the beginning of the industrial age, its evolution tracks the main currents of modernity. The object and its history represent the themes of technology, engineering, innovation, design, mobility, speed, rebellion, desire, freedom, love, sex and death.'

It says much about motorcycling's current status that the words above were written by Thomas Krens of the Guggenheim Museum, curator of the hugely successful *Art of the Motorcycle* exhibition that opened in New York in 1998, and was later toured around the world. The humble motorbike, once feared and despised by so many, has become a respected art form and barometer of social trends.

The Guggenheim's collection of more than 100 bikes did a great job of illustrating how the motorcycle has evolved from a simple steam-powered bicycle into a sophisticated, streamlined piece of two-wheeled sculpture capable of travelling at three miles per minute. Or, in another embodiment, from a big, slow-revving V-twin built before the First World War into a big, slow-revving V-twin that looks equally old but incorporates an electronic engine-management system and various other carefully disguised modern features.

This book features several of those bikes plus many more to tell the story of the motorcycle. The landmark machines are all here, from Daimler's Einspur (generally accepted as the first model) to the Brough Superior; from Honda's CB750 four to the Harley-Davidson V-Rod. So too are many of the less well known but often equally fascinating machines that have entertained, empowered and sometimes infuriated riders along the way.

The history of the motorbike is the story of the people who have built and ridden them over the years, as well as the machines themselves. The way bikes are used has changed just as dramatically as their performance. Developed initially to provide a more practical alternative to the horse or bicycle, motorcycles became a great liberating force that expanded their riders' personal boundaries.

Then the rise of the cheap motor car stole that unique advantage and led to a decline in motorcycling's fortunes, firstly in America, and decades later elsewhere. Recently motorcycling has found new popularity in affluent societies as a leisure pursuit and lifestyle statement. Meanwhile riders in countries such as China, now the world's leading motorcycle producer, are discovering the benefits of practical mobility enjoyed elsewhere a century earlier.

Bikes and their uses might have changed a great deal over the years, but so many of the sensations surrounding them remain the same: freedom of the open road, comradeship of other riders, the thrill of performance unattainable by other road users. Oh yes, plus a sense of vulnerability and social alienation too, some might add. Motorcycles might occasionally be museum exhibits these days, but they'll always be out of the ordinary. To many riders that's part of the appeal, and will remain so as the history of the motorbike is rewritten in years to come.

Iron Horse
1860s to the First World War

Previous page: American firm Pope's Model L, built in 1913, was one of the finest of pre-First World War V-twins.

Below right: Gottlieb Daimler's Einspur had its saddle situated above the engine, which led to problems on its history-making ride in 1885.

Below: The Michaux-Perreaux was essentially a bicycle with the addition of a steam engine, which drove the rear wheel via twin belts.

Michaux-Perreaux (1869)

Engine:	Steam, single cylinder
Capacity:	304cc (22 x 80mm)
Maximum power:	N/a
Transmission:	Twin belts
Frame:	Tubular steel
Suspension:	Leaf-sprung saddle
Brakes:	None
Weight:	191lb (87kg) dry
Top speed:	9mph (15km/h)

The very first motorcycle ride was an exciting experience, despite being a slow and fairly brief one. Paul Daimler, aged 17, took an eight-mile (13km) round trip near Stuttgart in Germany on Einspur ('Single-track'), the creation of his engineer father Gottlieb. Reports indicate that his journey was enlivened when the hot engine set fire to the saddle, presumably making this the first, but not the last, example of a young motorcyclist riding as though his trousers were on fire.

Einspur is generally credited with being the world's first motorbike, following that brief journey on 10 November 1885, but in some ways it barely deserves that honour. For one thing, Daimler's wooden creation had four wheels, because on account of its very high saddle the bike was fitted with a pair of stabilizers like those used on children's bicycles. Like many parents since, Gottlieb Daimler was no motorcycle enthusiast. He had built the machine simply as a rolling test bed for his engine, and promptly abandoned Einspur to concentrate on the automobile production for which his name is still famous.

Daimler Einspur (1885)	
Engine:	Air-cooled inlet-over-exhaust two-valve single
Capacity:	264cc (58 x 100mm)
Maximum power:	0.5hp @ 600rpm
Transmission:	Single speed; belt final drive
Frame:	Wood
Suspension:	None
Brakes:	None front; shoe on wheel rear
Weight:	198lb (90kg)
Top speed:	7mph (12km/h)

In fact Einspur was not the first powered two-wheeler, because bikes had been built more than a decade earlier, but driven by steam rather than an internal combustion motor. Steam engines had been popular since early in the century. Large and heavy, they powered trains and luxury liners, as well as the steam carriages that had been in use since the 1830s.

Bicycles, on the other hand, had been a relatively late arrival. A simple two-wheeler called the draisienne or 'hobby-horse' had been invented in 1817 by a German called Carl von Drais, but this involved the rider in the tiring and potentially painful process of paddling along with his feet. It was not until 1861 that Frenchman Pierre Michaux and his two sons fitted a crank and pedals to the front wheel, creating a much more satisfactory velocipede, which was a success despite earning the nickname 'boneshaker' in Britain.

Michaux became Europe's largest velo manufacturer, his factory near Bar-le-Duc in eastern France producing more than 400 machines per year. Then he spotted another opportunity, and collaborated with an engineer named Louis Perreaux, who developed a lightweight steam engine that could power the velo. Steam was produced by a cylindrical multi-tube boiler, fired by alcohol fuel through a series of burners. The engine had a steel piston and cylinder, and two flywheels, which drove the rear wheel via belts on either side. Water tanks were fitted behind the boiler, and there was a steam pressure gauge in the rider's view, in front of the steering head.

This steam-powered bicycle was patented in 1868 and completed the following year. After pulling away under the power of conventional pedals, the rider introduced the engine with a regulator. Perreaux claimed to have reached a speed of 9mph (15km/h) on it. But despite its ingenuity, the Michaux-Perreaux was not a commercial success. The small boiler meant that the steam was quickly used up, limiting its range. And with its hot burners, steam and high pressure, the machine could not have been very safe.

Similar experiments were taking place at the same time on the other side of the Atlantic, where Sylvester Roper of Roxbury in Massachusetts built a steam-powered bicycle that also dated from 1869. Roper's machine used a chassis from the Hanlon brothers, who built boneshakers and demonstrated them at local fairs and circuses. It differed from its French contemporary by having a frame made from hickory wood rather than steel, and a lower-slung engine that had two cylinders instead of one, and which drove the rear wheel via rods and cranks, instead of belts.

Above left: Early Americans: the 1896 steam-powered Geneva (left) and petrol-powered Thomas of 1900, on display at the Guggenheim.

Above: Although regarded as the first motorbike, the tall Einspur required twin stabilizers to keep it upright.

Above: The Hildebrand brothers of Germany began by building a steam-powered bicycle.

Hildebrand & Wolfmüller (1894)	
Engine:	Water-cooled four-stroke parallel twin
Capacity:	1489cc (90 x 117mm)
Maximum power:	2.5hp @ 240rpm
Transmission:	Drive to rear axle
Frame:	Tubular steel
Suspension:	None
Brakes:	Friction spoon front; bar rear
Weight:	192lb (87kg)
Top speed:	28mph (45km/h)

Right: The world's first production bike was the 1489cc Hildebrand & Wolfmüller, built in 1894.

Above: Tricycles powered by engines from French firm De Dion-Bouton won many races in the last decade of the 19th century.

Familiar failings

Roper claimed his machine could be 'driven up any hill and outspeed any horse', but he too faced the problem of carrying sufficient water, and turned to four wheels for his future creations. Other engineers continued to experiment. In 1884 another American, Lucius D. Copeland from Arizona, produced a steam-driven bicycle based on the American Star, a reversed 'penny-farthing', with small front wheel and larger rear.

Copeland demonstrated his bike at fairs across America in an attempt to raise funds. He is reported to have built 200 machines in the world's first motorcycle factory a few years later, but initially found financial backing only after adding an extra wheel to produce a tricycle. Another steam bicycle was the Geneva, built by the Geneva Bicycle and Steam Carriage Co from Ohio. Similar to Copeland's device, it featured a solid copper boiler on one side of the front wheel, with the water tank and engine on the other, driving the front wheel by friction pulley. Performance was little better than that of a bicycle, range was poor and very few were built.

In France, Michaux and Perreaux also produced a three-wheeler with belt drive to the single front wheel. But the arrival of the internal combustion engine would soon make the steam-powered machines obsolete. Many alternatives to steam had already been considered, including clockwork, compressed air and hydrogen gas. A Frenchman, Etienne Lenoir, had driven six miles (10km) near Paris in 1862 in a four-wheeled vehicle powered by a hydrogen gas engine. In 1879, an Italian named Giuseppe Murnigotti patented a motorcycle powered by a twin-cylinder hydrogen gas engine, claiming a top speed of over 12mph (20km/h), but it was never built.

Instead it would be the four-stroke engine powered by petrol (or benzine, as it was then known) that would dominate both motorcycle and automobile production, and trigger the huge expansion in personal transport. The familiar four-stroke principle had been invented by French scientist Alphonse Beau de Rochas in 1862, and patented in revised form 14 years later by two Germans, Dr Nicolaus Otto and Eugen Langen.

Otto gave his name to the four-stroke cycle (of induction-compression-combustion-exhaust) on which modern four-strokes still operate. It was his assistants Gottlieb Daimler and Wilhelm

Maybach who developed the principle into a successful static engine, which ran on mains-supplied hydrogen gas. And it was Daimler who, having seen the engine's potential, left his job at the Deutz Engine Company and persuaded Maybach to join him in developing the engine for use in a vehicle. Instead of using gas fuel they decided on benzine, which at the time was used mainly for cleaning clothes.

The vehicle that Daimler and Maybach had in mind was a four-wheeled horseless carriage. The duo had no great interest in motorcycles. It was simply for convenience that, after spending the next two years developing an engine, they bolted it into a home-made wooden chassis that had two main wheels, plus two stabilizers that prevented it from leaning in bends. Even so, Einspur, generally accepted as the world's first motorcycle, was an impressive and influential piece of engineering.

Its powerplant was a 264cc single whose vertical cylinder had no fins and was cooled with the help of a powered fan. Its inlet valve was opened by piston suction, and sat above a cam-driven exhaust valve, in the layout that would be commonly used later and given the name inlet-over-exhaust (or ioe). Twin flywheels were enclosed in a cast aluminium crankcase. Ignition was by a hot tube, which projected into the cylinder and was heated by a bunsen-style burner. Carburation was a float device created by Maybach. The motor turned at 750rpm, very fast by previous standards, and produced roughly half a horsepower.

Daimler and Maybach bolted the engine into a wooden frame, based on that of a boneshaker bicycle, which they built in their garden shed workshop in Canstatt, near Stuttgart. Final drive was by belt, with a moveable pulley acting as a simple clutch. A handlebar twist control, as pioneered by Michaux-Perreaux, operated both this and the rear brake at the same time. Daimler later added a simple two-speed transmission, though its effect was limited because the bike had to be stopped to swap between ratios.

That was not a concern during Einspur's history-making first ride in 1885. Paul Daimler rode the eight miles (13km) from Canstatt to Unterturkheim and back, returning safely despite the minor fire caused by the saddle's location above the hot engine and burner. Despite the bike's promise, its creators were mainly interested in developing its engine for their horseless carriage.

Above: Early versions of the Motocyclette from the Paris-based Werner brothers placed the engine above the front wheel. The later 'new Werner' of 1901 would become the first with the engine located low, between the wheels.

Above: Indian built its first bike in 1901, pre-dating Harley-Davidson by two years. The 264cc single-cylinder engine replaced the seat tube, forming a stressed member of the frame. The humped rear mudguard held petrol and oil.

Left: The British-made Holden, which entered production in 1899, was the world's first four-cylinder bike. Its 1047cc engine featured two pairs of horizontal cylinders, each containing a single piston with a crown at each end. Exposed conrods drove the rear wheel via a crank.

Harley-Davidson (1903)	
Engine:	Air-cooled inlet-over-exhaust two-valve single
Capacity:	412cc (76 x 89mm)
Maximum power:	3hp
Transmission:	Single speed; belt final drive
Frame:	Tubular steel
Suspension:	None
Brakes:	None front; pedal rear
Weight:	198lb (90kg)
Top speed:	30mph (48km/h)

Above: Harley-Davidson's founders were, from left to right, Arthur and Walter Davidson, William Harley and William Davidson. They built their first bike in a small wooden shed in Milwaukee in 1903, and by 1910 were producing over 1000 machines per year.

Right: The first Harley-Davidson was powered by a 3hp inlet-over-exhaust engine, angled forward in a loop-style frame, with belt final drive. Performance was unspectacular, but the bike gained a reputation for strength. Just three Harleys were built in 1903 and 1904.

After Maybach had ridden it to test some modifications over the next few months, Einspur was abandoned before being destroyed by a fire in 1903. Existing machines are replicas.

At around this time British engineer Edward Butler was developing an alternative three-wheeled machine that he called the Velocycle, and which he had patented in 1884, a year before Einspur's arrival. Partly to avoid infringing Otto's patents, Butler used a two-stroke engine, with two horizontal cylinders, one each side of its single rear wheel. The determined Butler took several more years to raise the funds to build his first machine, which he renamed the Petrol-Cycle and tested in east London.

Unfortunately Butler became a victim of Britain's draconian speed limit, which restricted mechanized vehicles to just 4mph (6.5km/h) on open roads and half that speed in towns. He was dismayed to discover that the limit applied to his Petrol-Cycle, not just to steam-powered vehicles as he had imagined. Butler's backers concentrated on developing his engine for static and marine use, but he refused to give up and redesigned the machine with a four-stroke engine. It had a top speed of about 12mph (19km/h) and incorporated several innovative touches. But development was intermittent, and was eventually abandoned.

Another outstanding early machine was produced by Frenchman Félix Millet, who in 1889 unveiled a tricycle powered by a radial five-cylinder engine placed inside a wheel. A two-wheeled version soon followed, with its engine initially in the front wheel and then, after a redesign, in the rear wheel, the crankshaft supplying direct drive to the wheel. This probably became the first ever racing motorcycle when it was entered in the Paris-Bordeaux-Paris race in 1894. The event was abandoned shortly after its start, but the following year a Millet was leading the Paris-Orléans race when it crashed, ending up in a ditch.

The year of 1894 was a momentous one in motorcycle history, for in that January four German pioneers patented the Hildebrand & Wolfmüller, or H & W – the world's first production bike. Munich-based brothers Heinrich and Wilhelm Hildebrand had built a steam-powered bicycle several years earlier, and joined with compatriots Alois Wolfmüller and Hans Geisenhof to develop a large parallel twin four-stroke engine. This heavy device promptly broke the bicycle frame they fitted it into, so the quartet created a much stronger replacement, with the fuel tank between the four steel downtubes.

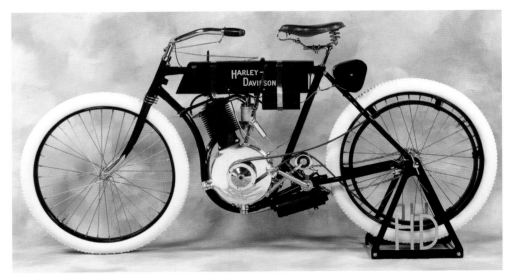

The H & W was an impressive machine, and the first to be called a motorcycle ('*motorrad*' in German). The 1489cc four-stroke parallel twin's cylinders lay horizontally, with its pistons driving the rear wheel via long connecting rods, in steam engine fashion. There was no flywheel, apart from the solid rear wheel itself; broad rubber bands were used to help the pistons on their return stroke. A timing device on the rear wheel regulated the opening of the exhaust valves; inlet valves were automatic (i.e. suction-operated).

Induction was by a surface carburettor, a set-up that effectively combines carburettor and fuel tank, as air passes over the surface of the fuel before entering the engine via a regulator. Ignition was by a simple hot platinum tube, as pioneered by Daimler. Power output was 2.5hp at 240rpm. There was a twistgrip throttle to control engine speed but no clutch, so each time the bike stopped it had to be bump-started.

Neat features included the liquid-cooled engine's water tank, which was built into the curved rear mudguard; and the use of a frame downtube to double as the oil tank. There was also an exhaust silencer in front of the motor. The H & W was innovative in its use of pneumatic tyres, which had been patented by Scottish vet John Boyd Dunlop in 1885. But the braking system was less sophisticated, comprising a simple spoon that pressed on the front tyre, plus a pedal-operated rear bar that scraped on the ground.

That sounds like a barely adequate way to slow a machine with a top speed approaching 30mph (48km/h), but such concerns did not put off eager would-be motorcyclists. With orders worth more than two million marks, the Hildebrand and Wolfmüller firm built a new factory for 1200 employees, in addition to a smaller plant where the bikes were assembled. After a successful demonstration in Paris, the *motorrad* was also licensed for production in France, where it was renamed the Petrolette. In May 1895 Alois Wolfmüller also took two machines to Italy, where he and an Italian rode them in the country's first motor race, a 62-mile (100km) return trip from Turin to Asti. They finished an impressive second and third, beaten only by a Daimler car.

After this promising start, problems were quick to follow. The two Petrolettes entered for the big Paris-Bordeaux-Paris race shortly afterwards both broke down, and flaws in the design became clear, many relating to the crude hot tube ignition. Starting was often difficult, and the lack of flywheel effect also made for erratic progress. Customers in both Germany and France

FN Four (1906)	
Engine:	Air-cooled inlet-over-exhaust eight-valve in-line four
Capacity:	412cc (48 x 57mm)
Maximum power:	4hp
Transmission:	Single speed, shaft final drive
Frame:	Steel twin downtube
Suspension:	Telescopic front; rigid rear
Brakes:	None front; drum and contracting band rear
Weight:	165lb (75kg) dry
Top speed:	40mph (64km/h)

Below: Belgian firm FN's sophisticated Four.

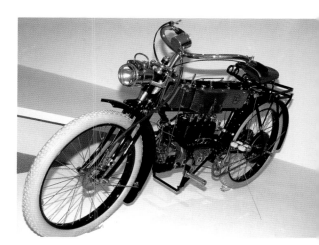

Above: FN's four-cylinder engine had four mica windows in its crankcase to reveal oil flow.

Left: America's Pierce Arrow four, dated 1911.

Early Racers

Motorcycle competition began in Continental Europe in the last decade of the 19th century. While speed restrictions caused problems in countries including Britain – where the limit was raised from 4mph (6.5km/h) to 12mph (19km/h) in 1896, and to 20mph (32km/h) in 1903 – French riders had few such problems. Races between cities became popular and events such as the Paris-Bordeaux-Paris were important for publicity and machine development. Distances were often well over 100 miles (161km), with bikes competing against cars and tricycles, including the increasingly fast and successful De Dion-Bouton trikes.

By the turn of the century the racing trikes were big, twin-cylinder devices producing up to 8hp, with fat tyres, drop handlebars and fearsome performance. But a crash at the Paris-Roubaix race in 1900 injured several spectators. The popularity of the 'mototris' faded as two-wheelers took over, led by the

Werner factory. The inter-city events suffered another blow in 1903 when the Paris-Madrid race was abandoned at Bordeaux following a string of bad accidents.

Racing began slightly later in America, where in 1901 Pennsylvania-based George Holley rode his single-cylinder bike to victory in what is thought to be the first ever American motorcycle road race, from Boston to New York. 'That was quite a ride,' recalled Holley, later famous for carburettor manufacture. 'Cobblestones, mud, sand, chickens and people, but the engine kept purring and I arrived right on schedule. Of course, with the layer of mud and dust on my face even my own mother wouldn't have recognized me!'

Several countries entered the inaugural Coupe Internationale, held in France in 1904, which followed the Gordon Bennett series of car races, and allowed three bikes per nation. Unfortunately the event was abandoned after the course was sprinkled with nails, causing

many punctures. The race was also controversial the next year, when Austria won after a French rider had been disqualified for changing a wheel. In 1906 the Puch-mounted Austrians won again on their home course, despite rival teams' complaints about sidecars full of spares patrolling the circuit.

The following year saw the first Isle of Man Tourist Trophy race. Mainland Britain still had a 20mph (32km/h) speed limit, and the law did not allow roads to be closed for speed events. There were no such problems on the Isle of Man, where Charles Collier, one of the brothers who had founded Matchless, won the single-cylinder event on a 500cc JAP-powered machine, averaging 38.5mph (62km/h) over the 158-mile (254km) course. Rem Fowler won the multi-cylinder class on a Peugeot-engined Norton V-twin, at a slightly lower average speed.

Above: Riders line up at the start line for the Isle of Man TT in 1914, the year in which Cyril Pullin rode a Rudge single with novel multi-speed transmission to win the Senior race.

Top right: Harry (left) and Charlie Collier were co-founders of Matchless and noted TT racers. Charlie won the very first TT race in 1907.

began to demand refunds. By early 1897 the operations in both countries had collapsed, and Hildebrand & Wolfmüller had gone into liquidation.

At around this time, another important landmark in motorcycle development occurred when the De Dion-Bouton firm of Paris announced that it was planning to sell its single-cylinder engine to other manufacturers. De Dion-Bouton had been founded in 1882, when Count Albert de Dion had gone into business with Georges Bouton, after admiring a model steam engine that Bouton had built. After producing several steam carriages and a tricycle, the duo turned to the internal combustion engine, and built a 138cc single-cylinder unit that revved to over 1500rpm, twice as fast as Daimler's Einspur motor.

That first engine produced just half a horsepower, but with its capacity enlarged to 185cc and its output increased by 50 per cent, the De Dion soon showed its potential. Tricycles powered by the little engine scored good results in several long-distance French races in 1896. And when De Dion-Bouton then began selling the motors to whoever wanted to bolt them into a modified bicycle frame, a new form of 'clip-on' motorbike was created, and the motorcycle industry exploded into life.

Over the next few years, dozens of firms, mainly from France, Germany and Britain, created bikes by bolting De Dion engines into frames in a wide variety of locations. The bottom bracket was taken up by the bicycle pedals, which were retained as 'light pedal assistance', or lpa as it was known, was still required on hills. But almost every other position was used for the engine, including above the front or rear wheel, to either side of the bike, and integral with the saddle tube – with widely differing effect on the balance and centre of gravity of the vehicles.

Rival firms moved quickly to produce engine units of their own. French competitors included Clement and Aster, while the best known of the foreign alternatives was Fafnir of Germany. De Dion's own design was also built under licence by companies including the Motor Manufacturing Company (MMC) from Coventry in England. Meanwhile many bicycle firms were taking the opportunity to expand into the booming market for powered two-wheelers. Leading British marques Excelsior, Matchless and Raleigh began in this way, as did Peugeot and René-Gillet from France, Bianchi of Italy and Motosacoche of Switzerland.

Eventually, in 1901, it was French firm Werner, founded by two Russian-born brothers living in Paris, that set the pattern that motorcycle design would follow for the next century and more. Michel and Eugéne Werner's first business was in cinema, and they built their first bike using a petrol engine originally intended to power a film projector. This was so promising that they abandoned the film projection work to set up a factory for their 'Motocyclette'. They sold more

Above: Glenn Curtiss became the fastest man on earth in 1907 when he rode his 4.4-litre V8 machine at 136.36mph (219.4km/h) over a measured mile at Ormond Beach in Florida. The Chicago Daily News *reported that: 'No such speed was ever made by anything but a bullet.'*

Scott 2-Speed (1912)	
Engine:	Liquid-cooled two-stroke parallel twin
Capacity:	532cc (73 x 63.5mm)
Maximum power:	3hp
Transmission:	Two-speed, chain final drive
Frame:	Steel twin cradle
Suspension:	Telescopic front; none rear
Brakes:	Stirrup front; shoe-on-sprocket rear
Weight:	200lb (91kg)
Top speed:	50mph (80km/h)

Left: Alfred Scott's two-stroke twins had many advanced features, including the telescopic front forks seen on this 1910 machine.

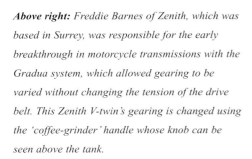

Zenith Gradua V-twin (1914)

Engine:	Air-cooled side-valve four-valve V-twin
Capacity:	550cc
Maximum power:	6hp
Transmission:	Gradua system; belt final drive
Frame:	Steel single downtube
Suspension:	Girder front; rigid rear
Brakes:	Stirrup front; contracting band rear
Weight:	Not known
Top speed:	50mph (80km/h)

Above right: Freddie Barnes of Zenith, which was based in Surrey, was responsible for the early breakthrough in motorcycle transmissions with the Gradua system, which allowed gearing to be varied without changing the tension of the drive belt. This Zenith V-twin's gearing is changed using the 'coffee-grinder' handle whose knob can be seen above the tank.

Below: Wolverhampton-based bicycle firm Sunbeam moved into motorcycle production in 1913 with this neat 349cc, 2.5hp single with enclosed 'oil bath' chain cases.

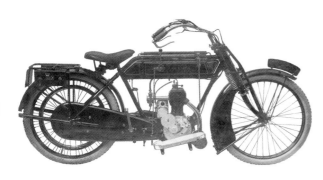

than 300 machines in 1898, even though the engine's location above the front wheel made for heavy steering and a oily rider.

By the turn of the century, MMC of Britain was building Werners under licence, and annual production had reached over 1000 units. In 1901 the brothers redesigned the Motocyclette with its engine placed low, between the wheels, creating the 'new Werner'. Although other manufacturers had tried this layout before, the Werners' success, and the French firm's efforts to protect its patent, have resulted in the new Werner being regarded as the machine from which most modern motorcycles are descended.

New firms join in

Still more European companies joined the rush to become motorcycle manufacturers, some of them carefully modifying their designs to get round the Werners patent. New marques included Ariel, Coventry Eagle, Royal Enfield, Singer and Riley from Britain; FN and Minerva from Belgium; Puch of Austria; Adler, Opel and NSU from Germany; and Terrot of France. Although the output of the Werner and other singles rose towards 3hp by the end of the century, the fairly light bikes still generally used slip-prone final drive belts instead of the heavier chains.

By this time, the motorcycle's popularity in Britain had been increased by the lifting of the law that limited speed to walking pace, and required someone to walk in front of the vehicle waving a red flag. The Emancipation Run from London to Brighton on 14 November 1896 celebrated the limit being raised to 12mph (19km/h) and the abandonment of the need to wave the flag. (The commemorative London to Brighton run for old vehicles still takes place annually.)

Even before the Emancipation Act was passed, Major Henry Capel Lofft Holden had been developing an exotic machine that would become the world's first four-cylinder motorcycle, and arguably the first superbike. Holden's engine had a capacity of 1047cc and arranged its cylinders in two horizontal pairs. Each pair of cylinders was joined, forming a pipe-like shape, and contained a single piston with a crown at each end. Two large gudgeon pins (one to each pair of pistons) extended through the cylinder walls to long, exposed connecting rods, which turned the rear wheel via a crank arrangement.

Circuit Racing Arrives

The year 1907 was a momentous one because it saw not only the first Isle of Man TT race, but also the opening of the world's first artificially built race circuit: Brooklands. The 2.77-mile (4.46km) banked, egg-shaped track near Weybridge in Surrey, south of London, was designed by Henry Holden, of four-cylinder bike fame, and constructed of concrete. Hugh Locke King, the circuit's owner, intended it both for racing and as a high-speed test track for British manufacturers.

Brooklands was created mainly for car use, and bikes did not race there in 1907. But the first of many motorcycle races there took place the following year, when the two-lap sprint was won by Will Cook on a 984cc NLG, built by North London Garages, at an average speed of 63mph (101km/h).

Charles Collier of Matchless finished third in that race and was involved in another famous Brooklands battle in 1911, when he took on the American star Jake de Rosier of Indian in a match race. De Rosier came out of Collier's slipstream to win the first heat. The American lost the second heat with a burst tyre, and won the decider when the Matchless' ignition failed. Collier gained some compensation shortly afterwards when he raised the lap record to 91.37mph (147km/h).

Indian also made a big name for itself in 1911 at the Isle of Man TT, where the American marque's three-speed racers shocked the British industry by taking first, second and third places in the Senior race, the first to be run over the famous Mountain course. Back home, de Rosier and Indian were leading lights in the sport of board-track racing, where motorcycles raced on steep wooden velodromes, sometimes battling at speeds of over 100mph (161km/h).

Board racing was exciting, popular and backed by the leading factories including Excelsior, Flying Merkel and Indian. The factory bikes were exotic and fast. Indian was the first to build a special eight-valve V-twin; Cyclone replied with an overhead-cam design.

Most had dropped handlebars, no silencing, and no brakes. Many had no throttle and ran flat-out, slowed only by a kill-switch. Riders wore little protective clothing and often crashed on the slippery, splintered tracks, the steepest of which, at St Louis, Missouri, was banked at 62 degrees.

Stars such as de Rosier, Charles 'Fearless' Balke and Charles 'Crazy Horse' Verrill were well paid but often injured. The motorcycle world was shocked when de Rosier died in 1913, following injuries received in a crash almost a year earlier. Two riders and six spectators had been killed in 1912 when a bike went into the crowd at Newark, New Jersey. Public resistance to the 'murder dromes' grew, and a few years later the uniquely thrilling sport of board racing had been abandoned.

The Holden revved to 420rpm, produced about 3hp and reached a top speed of about 25mph (40km/h). The prototype was reportedly quiet and fairly reliable, but prone to overheating, so liquid cooling was added, delaying the start of production to 1899. Unfortunately for Holden, by this time light motor cars had become available at comparable cost. This was the first – but by no means the last – time that an exotic motorcycle would fail to sell because it was too expensive.

Over in America, progress had been slow until the turn of the century, with many people's scepticism summed up by the comment from Colonel Albert Pope, the leading bicycle manufacturer: 'You can't get people to sit over an explosion!' Despite this, Pope's Columbia motorcycle, built in Connecticut in 1900, was one of the country's earliest production bikes.

The following year saw the arrival of Indian, a marque that would have a more lasting impact. George Hendee was a bicycle manufacturer and former racer who built machines called the Silver King and Silver Queen. He teamed up with Oscar Hedstrom, a Swedish machinist and fellow bicycle race enthusiast who was working in New York. Hedstrom had fitted a modified De Dion engine to a tandem bicycle that was used for pacing cycle racers at Madison Square Garden.

Above left: Harley-Davidsons racing on a board track, where speeds reached over 100mph (161km/h) and many riders crashed on the steep, often splintered, wooden surface.

Top right: The banked turns and wide concrete straights of Brooklands allowed very high racing speeds, and also made the Surrey circuit very useful for performance testing.

Above: This Harley-Davidson catalogue cover dates from 1913, by which time the Milwaukee firm's production had reached more than 5000 bikes per year. The cover picture's touring image is appropriate because at this time Harley declined to compete against rivals including Indian and Thor with a factory race team.

Below: This shot of one of the three original 1903 Harley singles shows the bike's sturdy construction and belt final drive.

At Hendee's request, Hedstrom designed a motorcycle that combined a diamond-frame bicycle chassis with a 264cc (16 cubic inch) single-cylinder engine that used his own cylinder barrel and crankcases. Hedstom angled the engine slightly backwards as a stressed member of the frame, replacing the seat tube. The humped rear mudguard doubled as a twin-section tank containing petrol and oil. A cylindrical case behind the front downtube held three rechargeable dry-cell batteries, which provided power for a spark ignition coil timed from the crankshaft.

Two examples of this first Indian are thought to have been built in 1901. The lightweight machine produced just under two horsepower, giving a top speed of about 30mph (48km/h). Pedals were provided for starting, and the bike used chain drive instead of the more common but slip-prone leather belt. Engine speed was regulated by a twistgrip on the right handlebar, which advanced or retarded the ignition timing. This mechanism reached the engine via a series of metal rods and joints, and sometimes broke when the handlebars were turned. But the generally well-built Indian became a success, and was followed in 1907 by the firm's first V-twin.

At around the time that Indian was beginning production, an important partnership was being formed when two Milwaukee-based friends, Bill Harley and Arthur Davidson, became interested in the internal combustion engine. The pair worked for the same engineering firm, Arthur as a pattern maker, Bill as a draughtsman. Initially they planned to power a small boat to save effort on their fishing trips. But both were also cyclists, and with the help of a German acquaintance who was familiar with the De Dion engine, they fitted a single-cylinder motor into a bicycle frame in an attempt to create a powered two-wheeler.

The first engine was not a success. But the duo persevered and in 1902 they had completed a production engine, helped by family and friends including Ole Evinrude, who advised on carburettor design and would later become famous in the marine world. Arthur Davidson had two elder brothers, Walter and William, who worked for the railways and were trained as a mechanic and toolmaker respectively. Both joined the new operation, encouraged by their Scottish-born father, who built the first factory, a small wooden shed with the words: 'HARLEY-DAVIDSON MOTOR CO' on its door.

The firm's first machine was ready for testing in 1903, the year that the Wright brothers made the first powered flight. The bike featured an inlet-over-exhaust single-cylinder engine, inclined forward in a loop frame, and produced about 3hp, good for a top speed of 30mph (48km/h). Final drive was by belt, and even this first model epitomized future Harley-Davidsons by being sturdy and rather heavy. It was a success, and production numbers rose from three bikes in 1903 to over 150 in 1907, and more than 1000 by 1910.

While Harley-Davidson and many other firms were producing singles in increasing numbers, other configurations were making an impression too. The most glamorous was the four-cylinder machine introduced by Belgian firm FN in 1904. Like several other motorcycle operations including Britain's BSA, FN was originally an armaments manufacturer that had begun building first bicycles, then single-cylinder motorbikes. But the Four, designed by Paul Kelecom, was much more sophisticated.

The 362cc in-line four had a notable advantage of smoothness over singles, as its inner and outer pairs of pistons moved in opposite directions, cancelling out primary vibration. Valvegear was familiar inlet over exhaust; the long one-piece crankshaft ran in a cast-iron crankcase, which contained four small mica windows that could be used to check oil flow. Final drive was by shaft, neatly enclosed in a frame tube.

Sophisticated and successful

The chassis was based on a twin-loop steel frame, with tubes running to each side of the engine. There was no rear suspension but the FN featured one of the first telescopic forks, in a system combined with a parallelogram linkage. The front wheel had no brake but the rear had two: a drum that was operated by the rider pedalling backwards; and a hand-operated contracting band acting on the outside of the drum.

When it was unveiled in 1904 the exotic Four caused a sensation, and it proved wrong those who thought it too complex by becoming a commercial success too. The engine was rated at 3.5hp and gave a modest speed of about 35mph (56km/h), because transmission was single speed until a two-speed gearbox and clutch were introduced in 1908. Engine capacity grew to 412cc and then to 491cc in 1911, increasing top speed to over 40mph (64km/h). The Four was updated and its engine enlarged again to 748cc just before the First World War, during which the occupied factory produced bikes for the Germany army.

America gained a sophisticated in-line, shaft-driven four of its own when Percy Pierce of Buffalo, New York, built a bike called the Arrow after returning from Europe with an FN. Pierce was clearly influenced by the Belgian machine, but the Arrow was no copy. Its 696cc motor had a side-valve instead of ioe layout, and the frame comprised large-diameter steel tubes which held fuel and oil. The Pierce Arrow had a top speed of 50mph (80km/h), and it was smooth as well as reliable enough to win several endurance events. But it was not profitable, and Pierce abandoned production in 1913.

An even more exotic American bike was the Curtiss V8, a stunning prototype which Glenn Curtiss built and rode to a claimed speed of 136.36mph (219.4km/h) on the hard sand of Ormond Beach in Florida in January 1907. The 4.4-litre (265ci) air-cooled V8, which produced 40hp at 1800rpm, had been designed to power an airship. The New Yorker rode it through a measured mile in 26.4 seconds to become 'the fastest man on earth', as he was widely known. But a broken drive shaft damaged the V8's chassis, preventing a return run, and Curtiss's speed did not gain official recognition.

Engineers on both sides of the Atlantic created a wide variety of motorbikes in the early years of the 20th century, among the most innovative being Alfred Angas Scott. The Yorkshire-based engineer's speciality was the two-stroke parallel twin, the first of which he built in 1904. Four years later Scott, one of 12 brothers, began production of an enlarged 333cc version with water-cooled cylinder heads.

Scott's two-stroke had a unique exhaust note, a soft purr that rose to a high-pitched yowl that became a trademark. His bikes were notable for advanced features including the world's first kick-start, and a two-speed gearbox that was also Scott's design. The chassis was equally clever, featuring a frame of straight, triangulated steel tubes and the novelty of telescopic front forks. A cylindrical fuel tank, painted in the factory's favoured purple colour with two silver bands, added to the distinctive look.

Scott himself rode to numerous victories in hillclimbs following the fine-handling twin's debut in 1908, and successfully updated his machine in subsequent years. Rivals resorted to campaigning to get the two-stroke handicapped (by multiplying its capacity by 1.32). Scott exploited this in his advertising, and also improved performance by increasing the actual capacity to 486cc and then to 532cc in 1912, by which time top speed had reached 50mph (80km/h). Isle of Man TT victories in 1912 and 1913 boosted the Yorkshire firm's profile still further.

Above: This Harley V-twin dates from 1913.

Below: Excelsior's Lee Humiston gave the Chicago firm publicity in 1912 with the first ever 100mph (161km/h) board track lap.

Below: Henderson's refined four was boosted in 1913, when Carl Stevens Clancy become the first motorcyclist to ride around the world.

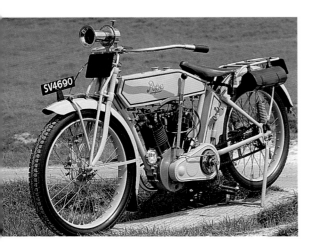

Top: *The Pope Model L's leaf-spring front and plunger rear suspension gave the 1000cc V-twin a comfortable ride by 1913 standards.*

Above: *American firm Flying Merkel's V-twins were notable for their orange paintwork and clever chassis. This Model V dates from 1911 and features a sprung rear wheel whose movement maintains constant drive belt tension. Alongside the 6hp Model V, Merkel offered a Model VS with larger, 7hp V-twin engine. Flying Merkel production ended in 1915.*

Transmission revolution

The 1908 Scott's two-speed gearbox was a notable improvement over single-speed alternatives. But the real breakthrough in motorcycle transmission came in the same year when Surrey-based Freddie Barnes, who had formed the Zenith firm three years earlier, invented the Gradua system. Until this point, riders had adjusted belt-driven bikes by changing the position of the crankshaft pulley that took the engine's drive to the rear wheel. The flaw of that system was that if belt tension was correct in high gear, it was too slack in low.

Barnes' Gradua system solved this problem using a long handle, nicknamed the 'coffee-grinder', which ran vertically up the right side of the motor. The bottom of the shaft was connected to both the crankshaft pulley and the rear wheel. When the rider turned the coffee-grinder, both the pulley and the spindle moved together, so gearing could be altered while the drive belt remained correctly tensioned.

Such was the Gradua system's advantage over single-speed engines that in 1911 Barnes won more than 50 hillclimbs, after which the organizing Auto-Cycle Union banned the geared bike from many events. Zenith capitalized on this by producing a new badge, featuring the word 'Barred' and the image of a motorbike behind the bars of a jail. Zenith carried on using the logo and retained a reputation for performance long after the Gradua had been superseded by Rudge's Multi-gear system, which used a similar variable belt without needing to move the rear wheel.

Gears became increasingly important as power outputs increased. Singles remained the mainstay of most manufacturers. But enlarging capacity in search of extra performance also added to vibration, which taxed the transmission and frames that were already suffering from the combination of rough roads and crude or non-existent suspension.

The simplest solution was the V-twin, as an extra cylinder could be fitted without too much trouble into the typical diamond frame structure. In the United States, particularly, the long distances and rugged roads led to a demand for more power, and the rearward incline of many bikes' single cylinders invited the addition of a forward one. Indian produced one of the first V-twins in 1907, by mounting two cylinders at 42 degrees on a common crankcase. A year later, the twin's ioe valvegear was updated with mechanical inlet valve as an option, although many riders preferred the limited – but trusted – suction-operated automatic inlet valve.

Other manufacturers were making their mark, too. One of the biggest was Excelsior, whose race bikes often got the better of main rivals Indian and Harley-Davidson. The Excelsior Supply Company began building bikes in Chicago in 1907, with a simple 438cc, 3.25hp single, and three years later introduced an 820cc V-twin model with cylinders spaced at 45 degrees. In 1911, the year that Excelsior was taken over by bicycle maker Ignatz Schwinn, this was followed by a 1000cc model.

The big Excelsior V-twin was a fast and impressive machine that was gradually developed in the following years. Racing was valuable for development and publicity. Stars including Joe Wolters and Jake de Rosier scored numerous wins on the Chicago-made bikes, and the firm gained publicity in 1912, when Lee Humiston recorded the first official 100mph (161km/h) lap, at a board track in Los Angeles.

In contrast the Henderson company, later to be united with Excelsior, produced sophisticated in-line four-cylinder bikes that became known more for long-distance ability than for speed. Brothers William and Tom Henderson built their first machine in Detroit in 1912, placing the pillion in front of the rider. Their 965cc, 7hp four adopted a more conventional arrangement the following year, when Carl Stevens Clancy gave the firm a boost by becoming the first motorcyclist to ride around the world.

Most American firms preferred the V-twin layout, however, including Massachusetts-based Pope, which also produced some notably refined machines. The American Cycle Manufacturing Company, which had been founded by Albert Pope, started in 1911 with a single, and the following year built a 1000cc V-twin with pushrod-operated overhead valvegear instead of the common inlet-over-exhaust. The Pope was powerful, fast at over 60mph (97km/h) and comfortable too, thanks to an advanced plunger-type rear suspension system.

Another firm famed for performance was Merkel, or Flying Merkel, as the machines were known after the first of Joseph Merkel's generally bright orange 1000cc V-twins was launched in 1910. These too had a clever rear suspension, a cantilever system similar to that later used by Vincent, plus a sprung front fork that further improved handling and comfort. Racers including the famous Maldwyn Jones scored many successes for Merkel over the next few years, leading to advertisements boasting that: 'If it passes you, it's a Flying Merkel'.

The other main manufacturer of V-twins was Harley-Davidson, whose first attempt was the Model 5D of 1909. This 811cc (50ci) unit adopted the 45-degree angle that Harley would retain, but the 7hp bike was unreliable and promptly withdrawn. Chief engineer William Harley persevered, and the firm returned two years later with the much improved Model 7D (Harley regarded 1904 as year zero, so 1911 was the seventh model year), which was more reliable and sold well.

For 1912 the V-twin was made available with a larger 989cc (61ci) engine, developing 8hp, and could be ordered with the option of a clutch (in the rear wheel hub), and with chain instead of belt final drive. Further improvements included a more sophisticated lubrication system, a new frame that gave a lower seat, and a sprung seat post – the curiously named 'Ful Floteing' system – for added comfort. The Model 10F of 1914 incorporated more advances: footboards, enclosed valve springs, a kick-starter, clutch and two-speed transmission. Harley was on its way. And, as that list of features confirmed, the motorcycle had come of age.

Harley-Davidson Model 10F (1914)	
Engine:	Air-cooled four-valve inlet-over-exhaust 45-degree V-twin
Capacity:	989cc (84 x 88.9mm)
Maximum power:	11hp
Transmission:	Two-speed, chain or belt final drive
Frame:	Steel single downtube
Suspension:	Girder forks; rigid rear
Brakes:	None front; expanding band rear
Weight:	310lb (141kg)
Top speed:	60mph (97km/h)

Below: Most Harleys in 1912 were singles.

Left: Harley's Model 10F V-twin from 1914 has footboards, two-speed box and acetylene lamp.

Below: Bikes were much used in the First World War. Here members of the British Army's 60th Signals Division prepare their bikes in 1912.

Boom and Bust
1914–1939

After the dramatic advances during the early years of the 20th century, the changes that occurred in motorcycle design and technology after the start of the First World War were more gradual. By 1914, the motorcycle's basic format of four-stroke petrol engine and steel chassis was firmly established, albeit with a variety of cylinder arrangements, and most of the main mechanical features had been introduced. Steam power, tricycles and other early devices had been abandoned; gearboxes, chain drive and suspension had become commonplace.

By contrast, the motorcycle industry experienced a turbulent time on both sides of the Atlantic. In Britain there was initially a rapid expansion, triggered by the growing numbers of engineering firms that had begun specializing as manufacturers of various components. Companies including JAP and Villiers built engines; Sturmey-Archer became known for gearboxes. Other companies concentrated on producing frames, wheels or suspension parts.

This led to large numbers of firms and individuals starting up as motorcycle manufacturers by assembling these components into bikes, and proudly displaying their own marque name on their bought-in petrol tanks. By 1914, the number of British motorcycle manufacturers had risen to more than 50, most of them based close to each other in the Midlands cities of Birmingham and Coventry, where the industry would continue to be centred for many years.

Sales were healthy, too, at least in Britain where the 1910 registration total of 36,000 had increased to 123,000 by 1914. Despite this, most of the smaller marques would soon go out of business. They could not compete with larger firms that had the resources to design and develop new machines, and to test them thoroughly on the road and in international competition. Firms such as Matchless, Sunbeam and Triumph thrived; many others faded away with the advent of the First World War.

The same period also saw a motorcycling boom in America, in sales and also in the number of manufacturers and the increasingly sophisticated machines they were producing. The country's size, often undeveloped roads and cheap gasoline combined to create a demand for extra horsepower, with the result that the large-capacity V-twin engine became popular. As in Europe, firms such as Thor, Spacke and Joerns-Thiem built engines for sale, while other specialists produced parts such as gearboxes and wheels.

In 1913 there were no fewer than 36 motorcycle marques spread across the States. Indian co-founder Oscar Hedstrom retired that year, leaving his old firm as the world's largest, with a record annual total of 32,000 bikes built at 'the Wigwam', its large factory at Springfield in

Previous page: Panther's 1934 250cc Model 70 used the firm's sloping single cylinder layout.

Above: The sturdy nature of Harley-Davidson's bikes made them well suited to military work in the First World War. Many V-twins were fitted with a sidecar carrying a machine-gun.

Right: In 1916, sisters Adeline and Augusta Van Buren rode Indian Powerplus V-twins the 5500 miles (8850km) from New York to San Francisco – via Pikes Peak, Colorado – to prove women could help the war effort as dispatch riders.

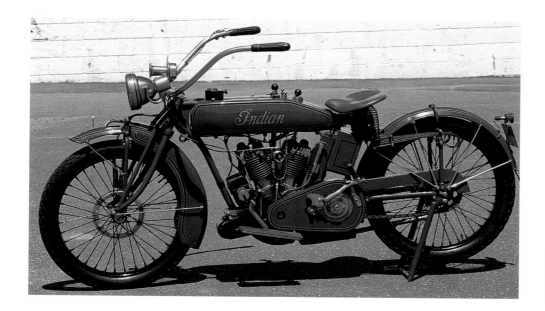

Indian Powerplus (1916)	
Engine:	Air-cooled side-valve four-valve 42-degree V-twin
Capacity:	988cc (79.4 x 100.8mm)
Maximum power:	18hp
Transmission:	Three-speed, chain final drive
Frame:	Steel single downtube
Suspension:	Leaf-spring front & (optional) rear
Brakes:	None front; drum rear
Weight:	410lb (186kg)
Top speed:	65mph (105km/h)

Massachusetts. Harley-Davidson was the leading challenger to Indian, the Milwaukee firm being known for robustness in contrast to its rival's reputation for speed. Other marques offering twins included Excelsior, the next biggest, plus Dayton, Emblem, Jefferson, Pirate, Iver-Johnson, Monarch and Reading-Standard.

Few people realized it at the time, but this would be a high point not only for Indian but for the whole American motorcycle industry. For it was also in 1913 that Henry Ford set up the world's first automobile production line at his factory in Highland Park, Michigan, further increasing the efficiency with which he could produce the Model T car, which was already a big hit following its introduction five years earlier. From now on US motorcycle firms would increasingly struggle to compete with Ford, whose car could be sold so cheaply that only the most enthusiastic rider could resist it.

The US bike firms' problems were not caused by lack of invention. While the efforts of European companies were inevitably concentrated elsewhere during the First World War, the Americans took over as world leaders in two-wheeled engineering, introducing a long list of significant features including the twist-grip throttle, starter motor, electric lighting, foot-operated clutch and drum brake on the rear wheel.

Indian's most famous model of this period was the Powerplus, which was launched in 1916 as a more powerful version of the firm's existing 42-degree V-twin. Designed by Charles Gustafson, Sr, it featured a side-valve layout instead of the ioe (inlet-over-exhaust) arrangement that Indian had used since its first twin in 1907. The 998cc engine produced 18hp, considerably more than the old Big Twin model, and had an impressive top speed of over 60mph (97km/h).

Chassis design was to Indian's familiar high standard, with optional leaf-spring rear suspension – an advanced feature at the time – plus a similar arrangement for the front wheel. Cable controls replaced the original model's complicated system of rods and linkages in 1918, by which time the Powerplus had become firmly established, helped by the exploits of the hard-riding Erwin 'Cannonball' Baker, who set a series of long-distance records.

Some of the smaller American firms adopted a variety of different engine and chassis features. Iver-Johnson and Reading-Standard used side-by-side (or 'flathead') valve layout, while Feilbach

Above left: Indian's Powerplus featured side-valve operation for its 998cc V-twin engine.

Below: Cyclone's innovative overhead-cam V-twins were powerful but unreliable.

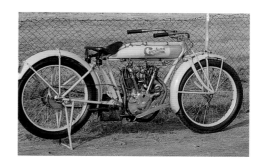

Cyclone (1916)	
Engine:	Air-cooled sohc four-valve 45-degree V-twin
Capacity:	996cc
Maximum power:	25hp @ 5000rpm
Transmission:	Chain final drive
Frame:	Steel single downtube
Suspension:	Leaf spring front & rear
Brakes:	None front, drum rear
Weight:	280lb (127kg)
Top speed:	85mph (137km/h)

Right: The amazing Wolseley Gyrocar, built in Birmingham in 1913, could remain stationary due to its huge, electrically driven gyroscope. Commissioned by Russian Count Peter Schilovski for military use, it ran successfully in tests. Only one was built before the First World War broke out in 1914, and the Count disappeared. After the war the car lay abandoned and Wolseley's directors decided to bury it intact, in case the Count returned. In 1938 it was exhumed to be displayed in the company's museum, but was scrapped in 1948.

Above: Two early women riders enjoying the luxury of a Harley and wicker sidecar.

and Peerless adopted shaft final drive, instead of chain. Manufacturers including Pope, Flying Merkel and Jefferson followed Indian in using sprung frames, instead of the old-style rigid rear ends. Various different front suspension designs were also used.

Arguably the most innovative marque, if not the most successful, was Cyclone, whose powerful V-twins made a big impact during their short time in production. Cyclone's 996cc V-twin, designed by Andrew Strand and built in St Paul, Minnesota by the Joerns Motor Manufacturing Company, was the world's first production roadster with overhead camshafts, which were driven by bevel shaft. The exotic 45-degree motor also contained lightweight conrods and a roller-bearing crankshaft.

Cyclone claimed a top speed of 100mph (161km/h) for its exotic machines, which were generally finished in bright yellow. That claim was ambitious but Cyclones were good for a genuine 85mph (137km/h) and their reputation was boosted by a string of race wins. Factory rider Don Johns was fast and spectacular, particularly because his bike's engine was 'ported' – vented to the open air through ports which opened when the pistons neared bottom-dead-centre.

This was thought to increase performance, and certainly made the flame- and smoke-belching Cyclone look fearsome, especially in night races. But the powerful V-twins suffered from reliability problems, and were too expensive to sell in sufficient numbers. By the end of the 1916 racing season Cyclone had abandoned production. With America fast becoming a nation of car owners, most of the other smaller motorcycle firms would soon follow.

Military machines

Over in Europe, motorcycle firms had become preoccupied with the First World War. In Britain, production of civilian bikes (and cars) was prohibited by the Ministry of Munitions from November 1916. Many civilian machines had already been commandeered for military use. Britain's War Office ordered large numbers of bikes, as the motorcycle had become a vital part of the military effort, replacing the horse as a means of communicating when telephones could not be used.

The most popular and commonly used bikes on the Allied side were the 3.5hp Triumph 500cc Model H, and the 2.75hp Douglas flat-twin. Douglas was a Bristol firm that had built trucks and cars before beginning motorcycle production, concentrating on flat twins with cylinders in-line with the bike. The little 2.75hp twin had capacity of 348cc and a top speed of not much more than 40mph (64km/h). But it lived up to its 'Lightweight' designation by weighing only 170lb (77kg), which aided manoeuvrability in difficult conditions.

Ironically Triumph, one of many marques with origins in the bicycle trade, had been founded back in 1902 by two Germans, Siegfried Bettmann and Mauritz Schulte. The firm's military machine, the Model H, was a 3.5hp, side-valve single that began the war as a single-speeder, before being uprated with a three-speed Sturmey-Archer gearbox. The reliable single earned the nickname 'Trusty Triumph', which would benefit the Coventry firm for many years afterwards. After the war the H would be modified by noted tuner Harry (later Sir Harry) Ricardo using a four-valve head and central spark plug to produce the outstanding Model R or Triumph Ricardo, with top speed increased to 75mph (121km/h).

American bikes were also used by the Allies, notably Harley and Indian V-twins, plus the Henderson four. All were sometimes fitted with sidecars, which could be used to mount machine guns. The Germans also made use of bikes, notably from NSU, Brennabor and Wanderer, plus Austrian-built Puch singles and twins. The Wanderer, a 600cc V-twin producing 4hp, was particularly popular.

Production of civilian bikes took some time to restart after the war ended in November 1918, partly due to shortages of coal and raw materials including iron, steel and rubber. Eventually the British industry recovered, with yet more small firms springing up to assemble machines using bought-in components. Motorcycle development gained from a leap in technology triggered by the war. This was particularly notable in metallurgy, as tougher steels plus strong and light alloys improved the performance and durability of engines.

Harder steels added strength to valve springs and camshafts, while the new alloys meant engine designers could specify pistons made from aluminium instead of heavier iron or steel, allowing increased engine revs and higher power outputs. Four-stroke engine design advanced alongside the improved materials. Side-valve layouts were commonly replaced by pushrod-operated overhead valves by the early 1920s, and shortly afterwards by overhead camshafts, normally operated by shaft and bevel gears.

Among the pioneers in this respect was Norton, an old firm that had risen to early prominence (boosted by Rem Fowler's TT win in the inaugural year of 1907) with side-valve singles and twins, notably the sporty 490cc Model 16H and the 633cc Big Four, a softly tuned, 4hp machine that was popular for use with a sidecar, the main form of family transport at the time. Founder James Norton was a former TT competitor who had become unwell with a heart condition that

Above: The 2.75hp model built by Bristol-based Douglas in 1923 had a 348cc side-valve flat-twin engine with cylinders in line with the bike. Similar Douglas models were much used by Allied dispatch riders during the First World War, when their light weight of about 170lb (77kg) aided manoeuvrability on rough ground.

Left: This 633cc Norton Big Four was built in 1937 but the name dated back 30 years to the Birmingham firm's original model of that name, which was powered by James Lansdowne Norton's first ever engine, and produced just 4hp. The dependable side-valve single remained in production until 1954.

Above: During the 1930s the Isle of Man TT was dominated by the 'unapproachable' Nortons. Scottish star Jim Guthrie won a total of six TTs.

required lengthy convalescence. His firm had suffered and gone into liquidation in 1913, but had been revived shortly afterwards as Norton Motors Limited.

The new firm was jointly run by Norton and Bob Shelley, brother-in-law of Dan 'Wizard' O'Donovan, a Brooklands-based racer and tuner. O'Donovan revamped the Model 16H to produce the Brooklands Special or BS, arguably the world's first production racer. The tuned 490cc single, still with side-valve layout, was sold with a certificate confirming that it had exceeded 75mph (121km/h) at Brooklands, or 70mph (113km/h) in slightly softer Brooklands Road Special (BRS) trim.

In 1922 Norton converted the single-cylinder engine to overhead-valve operation, with pushrods and rockers, to create the Model 18. The new bike performed well, as it proved by winning the Senior TT two years later. Sadly the white-haired 'Pa' Norton died in the following year, aged 56, after his heart condition had worsened.

The firm fought back, and took the 490cc single to its next stage in 1927, with the launch of the CS1, short for Cam Shaft Mk 1. The new engine, designed by Walter Moore, used a shaft and bevel arrangement to drive its overhead camshaft. Its 29hp output gave a top speed of 90mph (145km/h). The CS1 was raced successfully by Stanley Woods and others, and the following year was sold as a super-sports roadster. (Designer Moore later left for Germany's NSU, where he created a very similar motor that inspired the phrase 'Norton Spares Used'.)

By this time Norton had begun a lasting rivalry with BSA, whose full name of the Birmingham Small Arms Company revealed a background in gun manufacture. After turning to bicycle production in the 1880s, BSA had begun building motorcycles with engines from firms including Minerva of Belgium. The first all-BSA bike, a successful 499cc side-valve single, appeared in 1910, and was followed by a series of V-twins in the 1920s, notably the Model E, whose 770cc, 50-degree engine produced 6hp. The Model E was popular with family sidecar owners, and could be bought with a matching 'chair' in BSA's green and white paintwork.

In the mid-1920s BSA embraced mass-production methods to build large numbers of the Model B or 'Round Tank', a cheap and simple 250cc side-valve single that was popular with learners and delivery riders. Another successful single was the 'Sloper', designed by Harold Briggs and named after its angled-forward cylinder. Introduced in 1926 as the S27, with a notably quiet 493cc overhead-valve engine, the Sloper was later built with 350 and 600cc capacities, and remained popular into the 1930s. A similar layout had been adopted back in 1904 by Yorkshire firm Phelon & Moore, whose bikes were sold under the Panther name. The firm's first bike was a 500cc single whose sloping cylinder also acted as the frame tube. Panther would continue to build Slopers, with remarkably few changes, into the 1960s.

Sunbeam's classy singles

Another marque that thrived in the 1920s was Sunbeam, the Wolverhampton firm whose founder John Marston had built his first bike in 1912 at the age of 76. Sunbeam's motorcycles, like the bicycles that preceded them, became known for high-quality construction. The first, a 350cc single, incorporated a fully-enclosed drive chain that earned it the nickname 'Little Oil Bath'. The single also featured a multi-plate clutch, two-speed gearbox, and a cleverly designed quickly detachable rear wheel that facilitated puncture repair.

John Marston died in 1918, followed shortly afterwards by his son Roland, and the family was forced to sell the business to pay death duties. But Sunbeam thrived under its new owners, Nobel Industries (later to become chemical giant ICI). Riders including George Dance and Tommy de la Hay earned a string of victories in competitions including hillclimbs and the Isle of Man TT, beginning when de la Hay won the 1920 Senior race after Dance had set the fastest lap.

In 1922 Sunbeam won again through Alec Bennett, who was also riding a 500cc side-valve single known as the 'Longstroke' due to its 77 x 105mm engine dimensions. Team-mate Dance was almost unbeatable in hillclimbs and sprints for the next few years. Sunbeam's competition success would continue throughout the decade, notably with Senior TT victories by Charlie Dodson in 1928 and '29, although the firm would later pay the price for concentrating on racing to the detriment of roadster development.

An enterprising British firm that hit problems quicker than most was ABC, the All British (Engine) Company, whose sophisticated 398cc transverse flat-twin caused a sensation when it was unveiled in 1919. Talented young engineer Granville Bradshaw's bike featured overhead valves and a four-speed gearbox with car-style H-gate lever. The chassis was also cleverly designed, with tubular steel frame tubes splayed out to protect the engine's cylinders in a crash, plus suspension and drum brakes at both front and rear.

The ABC was built at Sopwith's former aircraft factory in Surrey, and also licensed for production by Gnôme et Rhône, also a former aero engine firm, in France. More than 40,000 orders were received, following positive press tests that reported lively acceleration and a 60mph

Opposite above: Norton's Model 18, introduced in 1922, featured the firm's first engine with pushrod-operated overhead valves instead of side valves. By the time this bike was built in 1937, the Model 18 had been restyled, and replaced as Norton's sportiest single by the overhead-cam CS1 and International.

Above: Royal Enfield was best known for V-twins when this bike was built in 1919. Its swept-back handlebars and girder front suspension were typical period features. Front and rear wheels were slowed by brakes working on dummy rims inside the main rims.

Above: BSA's Model E, introduced in 1919, was a 770cc V-twin that became successful due to its reliability and competitive price. Features include girder forks, no rear suspension, enclosed drive chain, dummy rim brakes, and tank-mounted plunger for manual oil supply.

BMW R32 (1923)

Engine:	Air-cooled side-valve four-valve flat-twin
Capacity:	494cc (68 x 68mm)
Maximum power:	8.5hp @ 3200rpm
Transmission:	Shaft final drive
Frame:	Steel twin tube
Suspension:	Leaf spring front; rigid rear
Brakes:	Drum front; rim rear
Weight:	269lb (122kg)
Top speed:	55mph (89km/h)

Right: BMW's first ever bike was the 494cc R32, built in 1923 and featuring the same layout of horizontally opposed twin-cylinder engine and shaft final drive that the German firm would be using more than 80 years later.

Below: The exotic Megola, built in Germany from 1922, was powered by a 640cc radial five-cylinder engine located in its front wheel. Both this Sport model and the softer Touring option came with twin rear-wheel brakes plus fuel gauge and rev-counter as standard equipment.

(97km/h) top speed, plus good handling and a smooth and comfortable ride. But teething problems caused a delay in production and the price rose from £60 to £160, causing most orders to be cancelled. A reputation for unreliable starting did not help, and Sopwith soon went into liquidation. Although French production continued for a while, fewer than 3000 bikes were built before the ABC story ended in 1923.

ABC's demise contrasted sharply with the lasting impact of another flat-twin of the same era: BMW's R32. After the end of the war, Germany's motorcycle industry had suffered along with the rest of that defeated country, with the economy in chaos, unemployment high and raw materials scarce. Nevertheless a number of German firms succeeded in building simple, lightweight bikes, based on engines such as the 174cc two-stroke single built by Bekamo of Berlin, or the 100cc two-stroke from DKW.

The Bayerische Motorenwerke, which had built BMW aircraft engines during the war, was one of many German firms that turned to motorcycle manufacture in the early 1920s. The first BMW bike was a simple motorized bicycle called the Flink, which was powered by a proprietary Kurier 148cc two-stroke engine, and was not a success. In 1921, BMW engineer Martin Stolle designed a 494cc flat-twin side-valve engine, designated the M2B15, which the Munich firm sold to other manufacturers including Victoria, Heller and Bison.

In 1923 engineer Max Fritz created the R32 by turning the flat-twin engine at 90 degrees, bolting on a three-speed gearbox and setting it in a triangulated, twin-tube steel chassis, with shaft final drive. Front suspension was by leaf spring working on a trailing-link fork; the rear end was unsprung. The motor produced 8.5hp, good for a top speed of about 55mph (89km/h), and the R32 was neatly finished and well built, with electric lighting and enclosed valvegear. It was launched at the Paris show and, although fairly expensive, it sold well and set the pattern for BMW roadsters that continues to this day.

Variety from Germany

Germany's other well-known manufacturer of flat-twins was Victoria, a former bicycle firm that built motorbikes using bought-in BMW motors, before hiring former BMW designer Stolle to create new powerplants of similar design and capacity. In 1928 Victoria added a range of single-cylinder models powered by British-built Sturmey-Archer engines ranging from 198 to 499cc. NSU, another German marque, preferred V-twins. The firm's 7hp 350cc twin scored top ten places in the TT in 1913. After the war NSU had some success with bigger V-twins, such as the 1000cc 18PS Sport, which was good for 75mph (121km/h).

Two-stroke bikes were also popular with German manufacturers, especially Zündapp and DKW. Founded by Danish-born J.S. Rasmussen, DKW began with small clip-on engines, and quickly progressed to small-capacity two-stroke bikes. By the end of the decade it was the world's largest manufacturer. As well as huge numbers of small bikes, DKW built larger machines such as the ZSW500, a 494cc water-cooled two-stroke parallel twin that was popular for solo and sidecar use.

Germany also produced the curious Megola, featuring a radial five-cylinder engine in its front wheel. Designer Fritz Cockerell's first prototypes housed the powerplant in the rear wheel, but he switched to the front to create the production Megola, which was first built in 1922. Each of the five air-cooled cylinders had a capacity of 128cc, giving 640cc in total. There was no gearbox or clutch; instead, while the motor and wheel turned forwards, the crankshaft spun at six times the speed in the opposite direction, balancing the driving forces.

The engine produced 10hp and revved to 3600rpm, turning the front wheel at 600rpm and giving the Megola a top speed of 60mph (97km/h). The chassis was almost as innovative as the engine, and featured a sheet-steel frame that gave an armchair riding position. The touring version of the Megola emphasized its two-wheeled car theme with integral footboards and legshields, plus a bucket-type car seat. There was no room for a front brake but the rear wheel had two, independently operated by hand and foot.

Alongside the laid-back touring Megola there was a Sport model, which had a conventional saddle and rigid rear end, though it shared the leaf-spring front suspension design. The Sport also had a more powerful, 14hp engine, and was timed at 90mph (145km/h) at Berlin's Avus circuit. Despite the Megola's curious layout it was reasonably successful. Approximately 2000 were sold before production ended in 1926.

Another unlikely machine of very different style was the long, Czech-built Böhmerland, probably the only bike ever designed specifically to carry three people – two on a low dual-seat, plus a third above the rear wheel. Albin Liebisch's machine, known as the Cechie in its home country, was powered by a conventional 598cc air-cooled, pushrod-operated single engine producing 16hp. This was normally fitted with a three-speed gearbox with hand change, but some models featured two gearboxes – the second one operated by either passenger!

The Böhmerland's length was increased by a large tool-box behind the rear wheel, which like the front wheel was a cast aluminium disc, lightened by cutaway sections. Three models were produced, the ultra-long 'Langtouren' (long tourer) and the relatively normal but still lengthy Jubilee, from which was derived a sportier Racer. Other features included twin fuel tanks either side of the rear wheel, and unusually bright two-tone colour schemes. Handling was very heavy but the bike was capable of 60mph (97km/h) and was reasonably reliable. It remained in production for 15 years from 1924, although only about 1000 were built during that time.

Neracar (1921)	
Engine:	Air-cooled two-stroke single
Capacity:	221cc (63.7 x 70mm)
Maximum power:	2.5hp
Transmission:	Chain final drive
Frame:	Pressed steel
Suspension:	Hub-centre front; rigid rear
Brakes:	None front; twin drums rear
Weight:	200lb (90kg)
Top speed:	35mph (56km/h)

Above: This Böhmerland had a rack over its rear wheel, but a seat could be fitted instead to carry two passengers without need for the sidecar.

Below: Carl Neracher's feet-forward Neracar was built in both two-stroke, as here, and four-stroke engined versions during the 1920s.

Above: Moto Guzzi's 498cc Condor single, introduced in 1938, was the Italian marque's first customer road racer. It was good for 100mph (161km/h) and very successful.

Below: Guzzi's Omobono Tenni won the Lightweight TT in 1937, setting a lap record on the way to the first all-Italian TT victory.

An equally curious contemporary was the Neracar, whose name was doubly appropriate because not only was it invented by an American named Carl Neracher, it was also 'near a car' in its design and level of weather protection. With a feet-forward riding position, motorcycling's first example of hub-centre steering, and its engine partly enclosed by pressed steel panels, the Neracar was a revolutionary machine. It entered production at Syracuse in New York in 1921, and in Britain the next year, built by luxury car firm Sheffield-Simplex at the former Sopwith factory in Surrey, previously home to ABC.

Early American-built bikes were powered by a 211cc aircooled two-stroke engine, later enlarged to 285cc for more performance, with drive taken directly from the engine's external flywheel via a friction arrangement. Later, British-built Neracars used more powerful Blackburne four-stroke engines with conventional gearboxes. Either way, the Neracar was efficient, comfortable, remarkably stable and reasonably inexpensive, if not particularly fast.

In 1926, Sheffield-Simplex introduced an upmarket De-Luxe model with rear suspension, an air-cushion bucket seat, adjustable windscreen and an instrument panel. But although the firm advertised numerous aristocrats among its customers, most motorcyclists preferred their bikes sporty and more conventional, and the luxurious machine was too civilized and unusual to sell in great numbers. By the end of that year, production of the Neracar had ended in both Britain and the United States.

Italy had not been among the leading countries during motorcycling's earliest years, but that nation's bike industry began to grow, especially when lightweight machines were freed from road tax in 1922. Numerous small bikes followed, along with larger machines from a manufacturer that would soon become famous: Moto Guzzi. The firm had come into being at the end of the First World War when two Italian Air Service pilots, Giovanni Ravelli and Giorgio Parodi, had devised a bike along with engineer and mechanic Carlo Guzzi.

Ravelli was killed in a flying accident but in 1921 the other two, backed by Parodi's wealthy father, set up a factory in Mandello del Lario, on the bank of Lake Como in northern Italy. Their first production machine, called the Normale, was a 498cc single with a horizontal cylinder, large external flywheel (soon nicknamed the 'bacon slicer'), unit-construction three-speed gearbox and magneto ignition. The bike was slim, low and fast, and Guzzi's reputation for performance grew when a prototype racing single won its second ever event, the Targa Florio in Sicily.

The soundness of Guzzi's horizontal single design was confirmed by sales success and many race victories in subsequent decades. Remarkably the firm, still based at Mandello, would produce the 500cc Falcone single into the 1970s, complete with bacon-slicer and identical cylinder dimensions of 88 x 82mm. Guzzi also introduced chassis innovations, notably with the 1928-model GT, which featured the world's first fully sprung frame. A special swingarm worked a pair of springs located under the engine in a box-like housing. Damping was provided by friction units either side of the rear wheel.

Other Italian marques rose to prominence in the 1920s, notably Benelli, which was founded by six Benelli brothers from Pesaro on the Adriatic coast, and produced its first bike in 1921. Tonino, the youngest brother, helped establish the firm with his racing exploits. A rival racing firm was Garelli, whose founder Adalberto Garelli had previously worked for Bianchi. Under his own name Garelli produced a 'split-single' two-stroke, featuring two parallel cylinders, and two pistons on one crankpin. The powerful two-stroke won many races, providing plenty of publicity for Garelli's roadsters.

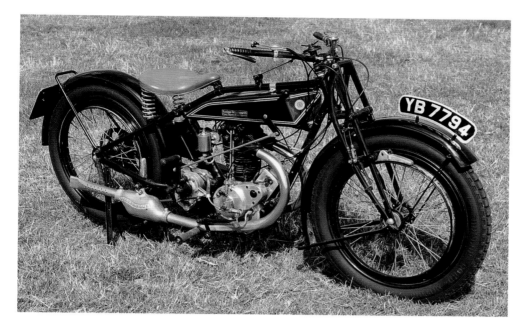

Left: Rudge was a leading exponent of four-valve technology in 1926, when this 500cc single was built. Graham Walker's victory in the 1928 Ulster Grand Prix led to the sportiest Rudge model being renamed the Ulster.

Below: The American Excelsior marque introduced its Super X in 1925, featuring unit-construction engine and gearbox. Its capacity of 750cc was unusual at the time, but became popular following the Super X's success.

Velocette's singular success

Britain's Velocette had also found success with a two-stroke, the 206cc single that the Birmingham firm, founded by John Goodman (a German-born engineer formerly called Johannes Gütgemann), had released in 1913. That model, enlarged to 250cc, remained popular after the war. But it was for four-strokes that Velocette became known, notably with the 350cc overhead-cam single, designed by John's son Percy, that was released in 1925. Alec Bennett won the next year's Junior TT by fully ten minutes. Bennett won again in 1938, and Freddie Hicks' victory the following year made it three out of four for Velocette.

Bennett's factory bike was a tuned version of the K model, and Velocette brought much of its performance to the street with the KSS, which was good for 80mph (129km/h). Even faster was the KTT, a hugely successful 'over-the-counter' racebike, which was launched in 1930. In 1932 the firm offered the KSS with a significant optional feature: a modern style positive-stop, foot-operated gearchange, as devised by development engineer Harold Willis and already fitted to the factory racebikes.

Another marque that achieved racing success through innovative engineering was Rudge, which had pioneered adjustable gearing with its belt-drive Multi system before the war, and had won the Senior TT in 1914. Rudge turned to chain drive and a three-speed gearbox in the 1920s, and became a leading exponent of four-valve cylinder heads, producing the 500cc single on which Graham Walker (the firm's sales manager, and father of TV commentator Murray) won the Ulster Grand Prix in 1928. Rudge called its sportiest roadster the Ulster in recognition, and retained the name for many years.

The Ulster was fast, with a top speed of over 90mph (145km/h), and featured an innovative braking system whereby the foot-pedal worked both front and rear drums, with the hand-lever also operating the front brake. Rudge's success continued into the 1930s, notably with a Senior and Junior TT double in 1931, but racing was very expensive and the motorcycle trade was suffering in the poor financial climate. The firm turned to selling engines under the name Python, but in 1933 the receiver was called in and the racing department closed.

Henderson KJ (1929)

Engine:	Air-cooled eight-valve inlet-over-exhaust in-line four
Capacity:	1301cc
Maximum power:	40hp
Transmission:	Three-speed, chain final drive
Frame:	Steel twin cradle
Suspension:	Girder front; none rear
Brakes:	Drum front & rear
Weight:	495lb (225kg)
Top speed:	100mph (161km/h)

Above right: The Henderson KJ, known as the Streamline, was a fast and sophisticated 1301cc in-line four, named after its streamlined fuel tank, which held an illuminated instrument panel. Introduced in 1929, it was short-lived because Excelsior-Henderson abandoned production two years later.

The poor financial climate was caused by the Depression that had hit America following the Wall Street Crash of December 1929. The impact was devastating in a US motorcycle market that was already drowning in a tidal wave of cheap cars. Already, the large number of bike firms that had sprung up in the boom years had been cut to a mere half-dozen, which relied heavily on exports and sales to US police forces. Even export demand was significantly down, in 1930 dropping to barely 10,000 from 38,000 ten years earlier.

The highest-profile casualty was Excelsior-Henderson whose boss, the 70-year-old Ignatz Schwinn, shocked the industry when in 1931 he suddenly abandoned motorcycle production and retired. Excelsior had become the third of the 'Big Three' American marques following the firm's acquisition by bicycle maker Schwinn in 1911. Six years later Schwinn had formed Excelsior-Henderson after buying Henderson, manufacturers of fast and glamorous in-line fours. The new company's Chicago factory had been famous as the largest in the world, complete with its own roof-top test track.

Excelsior continued to specialize in V-twins, notably the Super X of 1925, which boasted the novelties of 750cc capacity and unit construction (combined engine and gearbox). Aided by its

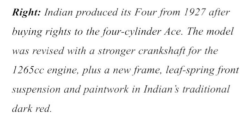

Right: Indian produced its Four from 1927 after buying rights to the four-cylinder Ace. The model was revised with a stronger crankshaft for the 1265cc engine, plus a new frame, leaf-spring front suspension and paintwork in Indian's traditional dark red.

The Record Breakers

The title of the world's fastest motorcyclist was hotly disputed in the years between the wars. A small group of riders pushed the limits of courage, ingenuity and mechanical strength to new heights as they raised the official two-wheeled record from its 1920 figure of 103.18mph (166km/h), held by America's Leslie 'Red' Parker on a Harley-Davidson, to over 170mph (274km/h).

Two early adversaries were Claude Temple of Britain and America's Bert Le Vack, who each rode thundering, hotted-up V-twins. Each set a record at around 108mph (174km/h) at Brooklands, before the scene moved to the long Arpajon straight, near Paris. Le Vack raised the record to 119.74mph (192.7km/h) only to be beaten soon afterwards by Temple, and then by Captain Oliver Baldwin on a Zenith-JAP. Back came Le Vack, who raised the record to 129.05mph (207.68km/h) on his JAP-engined Brough Superior in 1929.

Two weeks later Ernst Henne made his first successful attempt, recording 134.6mph (216.6km/h) on a partially enclosed BMW flat-twin whose 750cc supercharged flat-twin produced 75hp. Henne wore white overalls, a streamlined helmet – and, for some attempts, a conical tail strapped to his backside! Joe Wright twice took the record, the second time

breaking the 150mph (241km/h) barrier on a Zenith-JAP near Cork in Ireland in 1930. Then Henne began a series of four record-breaking runs, finally setting a speed of 169.14mph (272.2mph) on a closed section of autobahn near Frankfurt.

Britain's next challenger was Eric Fernihough, who in 1937 rode a supercharged, 1000cc JAP-engined Brough Superior to 169.7mph (273.1km/h) in Hungary. Italian Piero Taruffi went fractionally faster on a

Gilera, missing the record because he did not increase the old figure by the required amount. Any controversy was forgotten when Henne, his 500cc 'blown' (supercharged) BMW now fully enclosed following extensive wind-tunnel testing, raised the record to 173.67mph (279.49km/h). Back in Hungary, Fernihough replied with a 180mph (290km/h) one-way run on his Brough, but tragically crashed on the return run and was killed. Henne's record stood until 1951.

relatively lightweight chassis, featuring twin-cradle frame and leading-link forks, the Super X was too good for many larger-engined rivals in both oval racing and hillclimbing. Harley and Indian joined in with 750cc (45 cubic inch) models of their own, leading to the rise of Class C racing.

Henderson's four-cylinder machines had always been fast and sophisticated, and became even more so with the introduction of the Model KJ, known as the Streamline. Its 1301cc air-cooled ioe in-line four produced 40hp, giving a top speed of 100mph (161km/h), and the handsome Streamline's upmarket specification included leading-link front forks plus an illuminated speedometer set into the gas tank.

Such a high-end motorbike was always likely to struggle in the Depression. Indeed, founders Tom and William Henderson had long ago justified a price rise by admitting that: 'it would be impossible to continue production on the present high standard without an actual loss on every machine'. Schwinn was not prepared to do that, and Excelsior's similar lack of profitability left him with little alternative but to quit motorcycle manufacture.

Above: Ernst Henne's flat-twin record breaker has no fairing but features carefully shaped bodywork plus a tank pad for its near-prone rider. Henne also cheated the wind with a streamlined helmet, white overalls and, sometimes, a conical tailpiece of his own.

Harley-Davidson Model 61EL (1936)	
Engine:	Air-cooled ohv four-valve pushrod 45-degree V-twin
Capacity:	989cc (84 x 88.9mm)
Maximum power:	40hp @ 4800rpm
Transmission:	Four-speed, chain final drive
Frame:	Steel twin downtube
Suspension:	Springer forks; rigid rear
Brakes:	Drum front & rear
Weight:	515lb (234kg)
Top speed:	100mph (161km/h)

Above right: The Model 61E, known as the Knucklehead, was arguably Harley-Davidson's most important bike ever. The fast and stylish 989cc V-twin was launched in 1936, as the Depression was lifting, and gave the firm a decisive edge over old rival Indian.

Below: Los Angeles-based Al Crocker's overhead-valve V-twins were fast and light, but too expensive to sell in sufficient numbers.

Opposite below left: The British Excelsior firm's best-known model was the Manxman, a 250cc (and later 350 and 500cc) single with overhead camshaft driven by shaft and bevel gears.

Another luxurious four that had failed was the Ace, which had been designed by William Henderson after leaving the company he had founded. In 1922 the designer had been killed in a crash while testing a bike, and although the Ace was later updated, the firm went into liquidation and in 1927 was bought by Indian. The Springfield firm initially changed little, because the Four was a fine bike, with a smooth 1265cc motor, top speed of 80mph (129km/h) and good handling. Over the next few years the Four was rebranded as an Indian, produced with a traditional dark red paint option, and modified with a new twin-downtube frame and leaf-spring front suspension.

Indian's most important bikes during this period remained its V-twins, the large-capacity Chief and middleweight Scout, both of which were designed by Charles B. Franklin around 42-degree side-valve engines. The first Chief, launched in 1922, was derived from the Powerplus and featured a 998cc engine. It handled well and was good for 85mph (137km/h). But some riders wanted more cubes so a year later the motor was enlarged to 1213cc (74 cubic inches) to create the 'Big Chief'.

The mid-'30s Chief, complete with head-dress logo on the gas tank, was a good-looking bike, and could be ordered in a wide variety of colours because in 1930 Indian had been bought by Du Pont, the manufacturing giant that had connections in the paint industry. Indian listed 24 standard one- and two-colour schemes, plus the extra-cost option of any other colour from the Du Pont paint range.

The Scout, initially with a 596cc (37ci) engine that was bored-out to 745cc (45ci) in 1927, also earned a reputation for reliability. Among the best models was the 101 Scout of 1928, which featured improved handling from a new, lower frame. The 1934-model Sport Scout was another success, combining fine handling and a 750cc engine that responded well to tuning. It was stripped and used for hillclimbs, TT and endurance races, and Class C dirt-track racing.

But Indian had been badly hit by the Depression, and in 1933 had come close to bankruptcy after building a lowest ever total of just 1667 bikes. Inevitably Harley, too, struggled through the early 1930s. But crucially the Milwaukee firm pressed ahead with development of the bike that was arguably its most important ever: the Model 61E. Nicknamed the Knucklehead after the shape of its rocker boxes, the 61E was the first Harley whose V-twin engine used pushrod-operated overhead valves, instead of side valves. The motor also had a recirculating oil system instead of the crude total-loss system previously used.

Harley beats the Depression

The 989cc (61 cubic inches; hence the name) V-twin produced 37hp in basic Model 61E specification. The 61EL, with higher compression ratio, made 40hp and was good for a genuine 100mph (161km/h). A new twin-cradle frame, uprated spring front suspension, four-speed gearbox and Harley's first standard-fitment speedometer added to the appeal. The Model 61E was stylish and fast, and despite a few early problems (notably oil leaks and a frame that was barely strong enough) it quickly became popular. With the Depression easing by 1936, the Knucklehead's first year, Harley sold more than 1700 units and gained a lasting edge over old rivals Indian.

Harley's success with the Knucklehead contrasted with the fortunes of Al Crocker's more exotic V-twin, which debuted in the same year. Los Angeles-based Crocker was a leading figure in American motorcycling; a dealer, engineer and former rider with a passion for fast, light bikes. After building Indian-powered twins he had designed his own 500cc single for speedway racing, in collaboration with an engineer named Paul Bigsby, and then a roadgoing 998cc V-twin with cylinders at 45 degrees.

Crocker's classy V-twin produced 50hp from an overhead-valve motor with exposed valve springs. Its robust three-speed gearbox was cast integral with the frame, and used steel plates so that it could be aligned with the engine. Aluminium was used for parts including the gas tank, engine cases and footboards, reducing weight to 480lb (218kg). With a top speed of 110mph (177km/h) the Crocker was faster than Harley's 61E, as well as lighter. But it was also considerably more expensive, and fewer than 100 examples of this outstanding machine were built before Crocker abandoned production.

On the other side of the Atlantic, a similarly high-profile engineer and entrepreneur was having more success with an equally upmarket V-twin. George Brough boasted that his Brough Superior was 'made up to an ideal and not down to a price'. Nottingham-based Brough was the son of a motorcycle manufacturer and had a talent for publicity. Hence the Superior name, which led his father to comment: 'I suppose that makes mine the Inferior?' The initial Brough Superior,

Brough Superior SS100 (1925)	
Engine:	Air-cooled ohv four-valve pushrod 50-degree V-twin
Capacity:	988cc (85.5 x 86mm)
Maximum power:	45hp @ 5000rpm
Transmission:	Four-speed, chain final drive
Frame:	Steel single downtube
Suspension:	Girder forks; twin springs rear
Brakes:	Drum front & rear
Weight:	396lb (180kg)
Top speed:	100mph (161km/h)

Top: This 1932-model Brough Superior SS100 was owned by Lawrence of Arabia.

Above: George Brough, seated, was a great character as well as a fine rider and engineer.

Triumph Speed Twin (1938)

Engine:	Air-cooled ohv four-valve pushrod parallel twin
Capacity:	498cc (63 x 80mm)
Maximum power:	29hp @ 6000rpm
Transmission:	Four-speed, chain final drive
Frame:	Steel twin downtube
Suspension:	Girder front; rigid rear
Brakes:	Drum front & rear
Weight:	365lb (166kg)
Top speed:	93mph (150km/h)

Right: Triumph's Speed Twin changed motorcycling for ever following its launch in 1938. When production of civilian bikes restarted in the mid-1940s, following the Second World War, Triumph's main rivals would introduce parallel twins of their own.

Below: Business was generally slow for the American marques during the 1930s, but Harley could at least rely on orders from services including many police forces.

introduced in 1925, was a side-valve V-twin called the SS80, after its top speed of 80mph (129km/h). The subsequent overhead-valve SS100 came with a signed guarantee that it had been timed at over 100mph (161km/h) for a quarter of a mile.

Brough assembled bikes from bought-in parts including engines, and would accept only the best. Firms including engine manufacturer JAP produced 'only for Brough' parts. The initial SS100 used a 988cc JAP motor that gave 40hp; later bikes were powered by a similar-capacity unit from AMC (Matchless). Brough promised 'hands-off stability at 95mph' (153km/h), and called his bikes 'the Rolls-Royce of Motorcycles' following a comment of this nature in a magazine test. The luxury car maker was unimpressed until a director called at Brough's Haydn Road base to find workers wearing white gloves to avoid marking the show bikes they were building, after which all objections were dropped.

George Brough himself was a fine rider, and along with fellow Superior riders including Freddie Dixon and Bert Le Vack won many hillclimbs, sprints and races. The most famous owner was T.E. Lawrence (Lawrence of Arabia), who owned a string of Superiors, and died after crashing one in 1935, following a collision with a cyclist. Brough built numerous special models, including the long-distance Alpine Grand Sports and the SS100 Pendine, which featured low bars and tuned motor, and had a top speed of 110mph (177km/h). Fewer than 400 Broughs had been built when production stopped for good with the advent of the Second World War.

Another of the leading personalities of the 1930s was Edward Turner, a young engineer who was hired by Ariel boss Jack Sangster to design the ambitious Square Four – reportedly after Turner had drawn up the innovative engine layout on the back of a cigarette packet, then attempted to sell it to various manufacturers. Turner's design was essentially a pair of parallel twins with crankshafts geared together, sharing cylinder head, block and crankcase. The original 497cc unit was so compact that it could be fitted into the frame from Ariel's 500cc single.

Ariel's first Square Four, launched in 1931, used chain-driven overhead cams and a four-speed

Burman gearbox. The bike looked deceptive because its exhaust manifolds were integral with the cylinder head, so only two exhaust pipes emerged from the engine. In 1932 the motor was enlarged to 597cc, giving added performance that was especially appreciated by sidecar users. In this form the Square Four made 24hp at 6000rpm, and was smooth to its top speed of 85mph (137km/h), but suffered from problems including overheating of the rear cylinders. In 1936 Ariel introduced new 597cc 4F and 997cc 4G models, designed by Val Page, with pushrod valve operation, extra cylinder finning and a tunnel between the cylinders for cooling air.

By this time Turner had left to take over at Triumph, which had been bought by Ariel boss Jack Sangster. He announced his arrival with the Tiger 70, 80 and 90 models, cleverly restyled and renamed versions of the Coventry firm's range of 250, 350 and 500cc singles. Turner then launched the model that would be his greatest achievement, and arguably the most influential British machine of all time: the Speed Twin. The 498cc parallel twin engine, with pushrod valve operation and 360-degree crankshaft (pistons rising and falling together), produced 29hp. It was smoother and gave better performance than the majority of singles that then dominated motorcycle production.

The Speed Twin used essentially the same frame and forks as the Tiger 90 single, and was slightly lighter. It handled well, and had efficient drum brakes. *The Motor Cycle* magazine speed-tested the 'utterly delightful' Speed Twin at an impressive two-way average of 93.7mph (150.8km/h), with a one-way best of 107mph (172km/h), and enthused about its ample power and almost uncanny lack of noise. Boosted further by a competitive price barely higher than that of the Tiger 90, the Speed Twin was an immediate success, and inspired the other British manufacturers to design parallel twins of their own. Triumph launched a sportier version, the Tiger 100, in 1939. It had barely entered production when the outbreak of the Second World War halted further development, but motorcycling would never be the same again.

Above: Ariel took its 1000cc Square Four to Brooklands in 1936 to prove that its advertising boast of 'ten mph to a hundred in top' was true, with a timed demonstration. Pictured are designer Edward Turner (left), rider Freddie Clarke and service manager Ernie Smith.

Below left: The unlikely looking two-wheeled star of George Formby's No Limit *movie was his character George Shuttleworth's heavily patterned racer, the 'Shuttleworth Snap'.*

Bikes on Screen

Motorbikes have been appearing on film for almost as long as movies have existed, although rarely in a starring role. One early attraction for movie makers was the bike's potential for spectacular action, especially crashes. In

Love, Speed and Thrills (1915), Mack Sennett's sidecar chase sends numerous characters flying. The climax of Buster Keaton's *Sherlock, Jr* (1924) sees the hero, Keaton, leap onto the handlebars of his assistant's bike, only for the rider to be thrown off by a bump. Buster, perched on the bars, speeds through traffic junctions, over a collapsing bridge and under a tractor before hitting a pile of wood, flying unharmed through a window and saving the day.

The best-known early film featuring motorbikes is *No Limit* (1935), a romantic comedy starring George Formby and Florence Desmond. Formby plays George Shuttleworth, a chimney sweep who builds his own bike, the

'Shuttleworth Snap', and enters the TT. During practice the Snap's brakes fail, with the result that he breaks the lap record and becomes an instant star. As the race approaches, jealous rivals try to prevent him from taking part.

Director Monty Banks shot the film on location in the Isle of Man. As well as four Formby songs, it contains an improbably realistic action scene, when Shuttleworth runs out of fuel near the finish and has to push his bike home. Formby collapsed after the 15th take on a hot day, and a doctor was called. But *No Limit* was made for the general public, not motorcycle enthusiasts. Some Formby fans regard it as his best film, but there is little race action or authentic atmosphere.

Mobility and Freedom
1940s and 1950s

Above: As the British motorcycle industry enjoyed its boom years, the annual London show at Earls Court – seen here in 1955 – featured stands from many rival firms.

Previous page: The era's fastest and most glamorous streetbike was Vincent's Black Shadow, with its tuned 998cc V-twin engine.

Above: This 1951 advert boasts that the Triumph Twin has a 'reputation second to none'.

Right: Indian's 500cc Model 741 Military Scout proved its worth during the Second World War.

The main motorcycling trend of the 1940s and '50s was the rise of the parallel twin. Single-cylinder engines remained popular with many riders, but the pattern for two-wheeled design had been formed before the Second World War with the launch of Triumph's Speed Twin. Its pushrod-operated, overhead-valve, twin-cylinder engine layout would dominate the next few decades, as other British firms joined in, introducing bigger, more powerful engines and improved chassis.

Once the twins had arrived, most manufacturers adopted an approach of refinement rather than revolution. Gradually, specifications improved. Shorter-stroke engines with barrels made from aluminium instead of iron gave more revs and power. Telescopic front forks and twin-shock rear suspension replaced girder forks and crude plunger or rigid rear ends. Paintwork became more colourful, electrics more sophisticated, and features such as speedometers, dual-seats and pillion footrests were increasingly included.

The motorbike's image and function varied widely in different parts of the world. In post-war Europe the bike became increasingly popular as a means of transport, though in some countries the boom was short-lived. Motorcycling in Britain, in particular, enjoyed a 'golden age' in the 1950s, as the growing economy and desire for mobility led to a rapid rise in sales. But the situation was very different in the United States, where the motor car's grip tightened and the bike industry was depressed.

Most motorcycle manufacturers were kept busy in the early 1940s, as the war raged and factories concentrated on military production. Huge numbers of camouflage-painted machines emerged from the leading British factories, the majority of them simple 350 or 500cc side-valve singles such as BSA's M20 and Norton's 16H and Big Four. Both BSA and Norton later claimed to have built one in four of all bikes supplied to the Allied forces.

Triumph, whose factory at Meriden, near Coventry, was badly damaged by German bombing, produced not only motorcycles but stationary engines for pumps and generators. Other firms concentrated on lightweight bikes for use by airborne troops, notably Royal Enfield with its folding Flying Flea. Excelsior's Welbike was a compact 98cc two-stroke that fitted into a protective container for dropping by parachute.

Post-war expansion

The two surviving US manufacturers produced military models in their normal V-twin format. Indian's 500cc Model 741 Military Scout served with distinction, as did Harley-Davidson's 750cc WLA 45, which was supplied to Russian and Chinese forces as well as Americans, British and Canadians. After the war ended, many ex-military 45s were converted to civilian use, and helped establish Harley in foreign markets.

Germany also produced many military bikes, the most influential of which was DKW's RT125, a 122cc two-stroke single with top speed of just under 50mph (80km/h). As well as being built in vast numbers in its own right, the RT125 was widely copied after the war. BSA's Bantam, Harley-Davidson's Hummer, the Soviet Moska and Yamaha's first bike, the 1955-model YA1 'Red Dragon', would all be based on designer Hermann Weber's efficient and reliable machine.

Germany's best known military bike was BMW's R75 flat-twin, which led indirectly to one of Britain's most ambitious models of the post-war years: Sunbeam's S7. During the war Sunbeam had been bought by BSA, which had acquired some captured R75s from the British government. Sunbeam wanted to develop a flagship roadster along BMW lines, but considered a flat twin inappropriate, so designer Erling Poppe created a 487cc overhead-cam tandem twin powerplant, incorporating R75 features including shaft final drive.

The mist-green-coloured S7, launched in 1947, was a luxurious machine with balloon tyres and large skirted mudguards. Unfortunately the expensive, 25bhp Sunbeam was slow by 500cc standards, with a top speed of only about 75mph (121km/h), and didn't handle very well, due mainly to its weight and fat tyres. Its motor also used a lot of fuel and was unreliable, partly due to a tendency to overheat.

Sales were poor, and two years later Sunbeam introduced a sportier version of the tandem twin, the S8. This retained the original 487cc engine capacity and shaft final drive but was more conventional, with new telescopic forks, narrower tyres, and paintwork in Sunbeam's traditional black. Its engine gained performance with higher compression ratio and a new exhaust system, and was more reliable due to increased oil capacity and other improvements.

The S8's reduced weight and uprated chassis meant it handled better than the S7, too. The sportier model was much more popular than the original, which continued in updated S7 De Luxe form. But it would not be enough to save Sunbeam, which was eventually closed down by BSA in 1957 – after which the famous Sunbeam name was used only for scooters.

Another firm producing unusual twins was Scott, the Yorkshire marque that had built some of the most innovative machines of motorcycling's early years. In 1926, three years after founder Alfred Scott's death, Scott had introduced the Flying Squirrel, a 596 or 498cc two-stroke liquid-cooled parallel twin with more conventional layout that the firm's cylindrical-tanked early models. Production had continued through the 1930s and resumed after the war with few changes.

The Flying Squirrel offered a smooth 70mph (113km/h) cruising speed plus stability and a distinctive character, if not outstanding reliability. The struggling Yorkshire firm eventually went bankrupt in 1950. Scott was bought by an enthusiast named Matt Holder, who moved production to Birmingham, where small numbers would continue to be built right up until 1978.

Another firm building twins with limited success was Douglas, which had originally produced in-line flat twins and after the war used a BMW-style transverse cylinder arrangement, with a 350cc model called the T35. The last Douglas twin was the 1955-model 350cc Dragonfly, which featured a distinctive headlamp nacelle that merged with the fuel tank. The Dragonfly handled

Above: Many ex-military Harley WLA45 V-twins were converted to civilian use after the war.

Below: Sunbeam's S7 tandem twin featured distinctive paintwork and balloon tyres.

Sunbeam S7 (1947)

Engine:	Air-cooled sohc four-valve tandem twin
Capacity:	487cc (70 x 63.5mm)
Maximum power:	25bhp @ 5800rpm
Transmission:	Four-speed, shaft final drive
Frame:	Steel single downtube
Suspension:	Telescopic front; plunger rear
Brakes:	Drum front & rear
Weight:	435lb (197kg)
Top speed:	75mph (121km/h)

Above: Scott built two-stroke parallel twins for many years, and by 1947 had enlarged the Flying Squirrel's liquid-cooled engine to 596cc. The twin was smooth and torquey, but the Yorkshire firm lacked money for development.

Above: Sunbeam's S8 was notably slimmer and sportier than its S7 predecessor. Although more successful, it could not save the firm.

Right: The Douglas Dragonfly, introduced in 1955, was stylish and handled well, but its 350cc flat twin engine's performance was mediocre and production ended two years later.

well, thanks to its Earles fork chassis, and cruised smoothly at 60mph (97km/h). But it was too expensive to sell in sufficient numbers, and Douglas ceased all production in 1957.

While Sunbeam, Scott and Douglas struggled, the parallel (or 'vertical') twin cylinder layout, as pioneered by Triumph's Speed Twin before the war, was becoming more important. Triumph had already followed Edward Turner's original master-stroke with a hotted-up model called the Tiger 100 – its name highlighting the top speed of 100mph (161km/h). This became the marque's flagship when production at the Meriden factory restarted in 1946.

Along with higher compression ratio that helped increase its 500cc engine's peak output to a claimed 30bhp, the Tiger 100 featured silver paintwork and other new styling touches. The model enhanced Triumph's reputation for performance, and remained in the line-up throughout the 1950s, being updated with telescopic front forks in place of the original girders, and twin-shock rear suspension, instead of the early sprung-hub design.

BSA was quick to respond to Triumph's twin, and launched its own 500cc A7 twin in 1946. Designed by Val Page and Herbert Perkins, the A7 engine differed from its Triumph rival by having a single camshaft at the rear of the crankcases, instead of two at the side. The BSA unit was slightly less powerful and stylish than the Triumph, but impressively quiet, oil-tight and robust. It gained a little extra performance in 1949 with the launch of the A7 Star, complete with twin carburettors, increased compression ratio and 31bhp output.

Norton's first parallel twin was the Dominator Model 7, launched in 1949. Its designer, Bert Hopwood, had left Norton by the time the 29bhp Model 7 reached production. But his engine design, with a single camshaft in front of the cylinders, would be used for over two decades. Although the plunger-framed Model 7 handled reasonably well, it was overshadowed a few years later by the Dominator 88, with improved handling and reduced weight thanks to its Featherbed frame, borrowed from the Manx racing single.

The Manx had proved that single-cylinder machines were still competitive on the racetrack, most vividly when Geoff Duke won both the 500cc and 350cc world championships in 1951. The Manx was a post-war development of Norton's overhead-camshaft single, and was initially fitted with a single-tube 'Garden Gate' frame, and plunger rear suspension. The single's many race wins, often against more powerful multis, did much to maintain Norton's reputation for performance and quality.

Norton's Featherbed advantage

The most significant Manx development came in 1950 when Norton's race team boss Joe Craig adopted an innovative frame designed by Irish racer/engineer Rex McCandless. Its distinctive twin-loop cradle design gave much improved handling under racing conditions, as well as proving stronger and easier to manufacture. Duke's works team-mate Harold Daniell unwittingly christened the frame with his comment that the new bike felt like riding a feather bed.

The uprated Manx made a superb debut when it took the first three places in both Senior and Junior TT races in 1950. In later years the Manx was produced for sale both as the 500cc 30M and the 350cc 40M, with the larger model in particular being hugely successful. The lean and simple Manx, with its heavily finned engine, big silver tank and Featherbed frame, became established as the archetypal pure-bred single-cylinder racer.

Equally famous was its BSA rival the Gold Star, a roadster-based single that also notched up hundreds of victories in Isle of Man Clubman's events, short circuit races, and unofficial burn-ups on the road. The 'Goldie', especially the later 500cc DBD34 model, had an equally distinctive look based on its low, clip-on handlebars, and chrome-panelled petrol tank with a badge displaying a gold star in a red circle.

The Gold Star dated back to pre-war days, when racer Wal Handley had earned a Brooklands Gold Star award for lapping the banked Surrey circuit at over 100mph (161km/h) on BSA's 500cc M23 Empire Star. In the following year BSA produced a replica marketed under the name M24 Gold Star. The name signified that each machine had been built using polished internals and other special parts, which increased output to 28bhp, or 33bhp when tuned to run on alcohol.

After the war, BSA produced a competition single called the B32, which was initially for trials but made a useful racer. It was followed in 1948 by the 350cc ZB32 Gold Star, and a year later by the 500cc ZB34. Both were fast and came with a choice of camshaft, gears, compression ratio, fuel tanks, exhaust system and wheels. As with all Gold Stars, buyers received a certified dyno chart from their machine.

The Gold Star's arrival meant that the clubman racer had a bike that was keenly priced and ideally suited to both road and track. Gold Stars dominated the Clubman's TT in the early 1950s. Most famous of the line was the 1956-model DBD34, which incorporated race-proven modifications including steeper steering geometry, twin-shock rear suspension and a big Amal GP

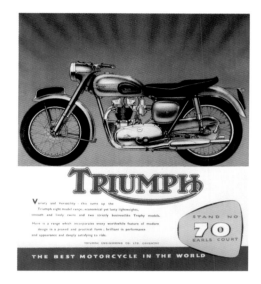

Top: Triumph's 'best motorcycle in the world' boast rang true in 1955, when the 650cc Tiger 110 featured telescopic forks and twin shocks.

Above: BSA relied on a more laid-back image in its 1955 advertising, which highlighted the range from 125cc Bantam to 650cc Golden Flash.

Left: This 500cc Norton Model 7 parallel twin, built in 1952, would be superseded a year later by the Featherbed-framed Dominator 88.

Above: Norton's Featherbed-framed Manx racing single, introduced to the works teams in 1950, was hugely successful and remained competitive for many years.

Below: BSA's DBD34 Gold Star was the ultimate single-cylinder sports bike of the late 1950s, with clip-on bars, revvy engine, close-ratio gearbox and top-class chassis components.

Below right: The most popular 350cc racer in the 1950s and '60s was the AJS 7R, known as the 'Boy Racer'. The ohc single won thousands of races around the world, at all levels.

carburettor that raised its 500cc engine's peak output to 42bhp. The DBD34 Gold Star was a true racer on the road: demanding, temperamental and extremely rapid.

Another firm producing rapid singles for road and track was Velocette, the Birmingham marque whose black-liveried racers had made a big impact before the war. In fact Velocette's most ambitious project of that era was a twin, the 500cc supercharged 'Roarer' debuted by Stanley Woods in the 1939 TT. When racing resumed after the war supercharging was banned, which put paid to the Roarer, but Velocette continued to record outstanding results with singles, notably the 350cc KTT production racer.

The ultimate KTT was the Mk VIII, which had been introduced in 1938 and remained competitive for many years. The 34bhp single was almost identical to Woods' TT-winning factory machine of that year, and was fast enough to take three more Junior TT wins after the war, ridden by Bob Foster and Freddie Frith. When the world championships began in 1949, Frith and Foster took the first two 350cc titles on works dohc or 'double-knocker' versions of the Mk VIII.

The overhead-camshaft singles earned Velocette's racing glory, but the bikes that made the money were the simpler, cheaper pushrod singles, notably the 250cc MOV and its derivatives the 350cc MAC and 500cc MSS. The MAC, in particular, was a long-running success, being produced from 1934 to 1960. Along the way it gained telescopic forks instead of girders, an aluminium cylinder head and barrel, and in 1953 a new, more sophisticated twin-shock frame to replace its original rigid (unsuspended) rear end.

Velocette was successful with its sporty singles, but failed spectacularly with its LE, or 'Little Engine', co-owner Eugene Goodman's ambitious attempt to provide a civilized commuter bike. The LE was powered by a 149cc liquid-cooled side-valve flat twin with modest 6bhp maximum output. It featured a pressed-steel frame, leg-shields, and shaft final drive. Top speed was just 50mph (80km/h), and acceleration was hindered by the high weight of 260lb (118kg).

The LE had some merits, being quiet, smooth, comfortable and practical. It also handled well. But its angular styling won few admirers, and the complex Velo was much more expensive than BSA's Bantam commuter bike. The LE sold very slowly, even after a capacity increase to 192cc

had improved performance and tempted many police forces to buy it. Velocette's huge investment was lost, and plans to halt production of the 350 MAC were abandoned.

One single that outlasted even the MAC was Royal Enfield's Bullet. The Bullet name had first been used in the early 1930s, following Enfield's introduction of a line of 500, 350 and 250cc models. In 1949 the firm launched a new 350cc Bullet, featuring a more compact engine with an alloy head. The bike was quick, reliable and handled well, and was joined three years later by a 500cc version. The Bullet was made in Britain until 1963, after which production continued in India, where the model had been built under licence for some time.

Another long-lived single was Ariel's Red Hunter, which also had its origins in the early 1930s, with the sporty NH350 and VH500 models. During the war the smaller Hunter was developed into a successful military bike, the W/NG. Red Hunter production later resumed and continued throughout the 1950s, helped by typical chassis updates, with the model by now being known more for practicality than performance.

Germany's manufacturers had widely differing fortunes after the war. DKW was split, with its original factory at Zschopau, in the Russian-controlled eastern part of Germany, becoming IFA and then MZ. Much of MZ's output was simple two-stroke singles, notably the ES250, introduced in 1956. Most had curious styling, but were reliable as well as cheap to buy and run.

DKW resumed production with a civilian version of its much-copied wartime RT125 single, which was updated over the years. By 1957 the RT250VS, also produced in 200 and 175cc capacities, featured Earles forks and twin-shock rear suspension. In that year DKW merged with Victoria and Express to form the Zweirad Union, which later also included Hercules. DKW's influence faded, and the name became little used.

Horex, a German marque that had been building bikes since 1923, resumed production after the war and was later best known for its stylish Imperator single. This was introduced in 1954 with a 398cc ohc engine producing 24bhp, and a sophisticated chassis incorporating twin-cradle frame and twin rear shocks. But the German market was in decline, and Horex production ended in 1957. Various enthusiasts tried to revive the Horex name, without lasting success.

BMW had been successful during the 1930s with side-valve flat twins including the 750cc R12 and R71, and had already produced more modern overhead-valve twins, notably the 600cc R6. When production belatedly resumed after the war it was with the R24, a 250cc single that sold well. By 1950 the flat twins were being built again, starting with the R51/2, a 500cc overhead-valve machine that was essentially the pre-war R51 with a few detail changes.

BMW quickly updated the design, producing a new 500cc engine for the R51/3, plus a 600cc model, the R67. Ironically, given that BMW had pioneered oil-damped telescopic forks before the war, the German marque's main 1955 change was the introduction of Earles forks, designed by Englishman Ernie Earles some years earlier. The 500cc R50 and 600cc R69 also featured twin-shock rear suspension, and remained in production until the end of the decade.

Rival German marque Zündapp had built a luxurious 800cc in-line four, the K800, in the 1930s, and was also a leading producer of flat twins. The KS601 'Green Elephant' became Germany's fastest roadster when launched in 1950, with a top speed approaching 90mph (145km/h). Its 597cc ohv engine was fitted in a new tubular steel frame with telescopic forks, plunger rear suspension and interchangeable wheels.

NSU concentrated on four-stroke singles, having begun after the war with the 98cc Fox, a 6bhp lightweight with a top speed of about 50mph (80km/h). In the early 1950s the 200cc Lux

BSA DBD34 Gold Star Clubman's (1956)	
Engine:	Air-cooled ohv two-valve pushrod single
Capacity:	499cc (85 x 88mm)
Maximum power:	42hp @ 7000rpm
Transmission:	Four-speed, chain final drive
Frame:	Steel twin downtube
Suspension:	Telescopic front; twin shocks rear
Brakes:	Drum front & rear
Weight:	384lb (174kg)
Top speed:	110mph (177km/h)

Below: The production version of Velocette's KTT Mk VIII, seen here on display at London's Earls Court Show in 1949, was a 348cc customer racebike based on world champion Freddie Frith's factory single of the same designation.

Bottom: Velocette's LE commuter bike won few friends with its angular looks, and was too heavy for its 149cc side-valve flat twin engine.

and 250cc Max offered increased performance, and NSU impressed on the racetrack with the powerful twin-cylinder Rennmax on which Werner Haas won the 250cc world championship in 1953 and '54. The final development of the Max was the Supermax, launched in 1956, by which time NSU was turning away from bikes in favour of car production.

The German firm did, however, continue high-volume production of its hugely successful 49cc two-stroke moped, the Quickly, of which more than a million were built before production ended in 1962. Few Europeans realized it at the time, but a more significant development of small-capacity bikes was going on in Japan, where a former car racer and piston ring manufacturer named Soichiro Honda had set up the Honda Technical Research Institute in a small wooden shed in Hamamatsu.

Honda began by attaching small two-stroke army-surplus engines to bicycles, and soon moved on to design a two-stroke engine of his own, completing the Honda Model A in 1947. The bike was simple and slow, but cheap and successful. Honda moved fast, enlarging the engine to 90cc, producing a three-wheeled vehicle, and in 1949 creating the first all-Honda machine, the 98cc two-stroke Model D, which was given the name Dream.

By 1950, the renamed Honda Motor Co was a thriving business employing 20 people, and Soichiro Honda had been joined by Takeo Fujisawa, the salesman who would help mastermind the firm's growth. The following year saw the 146cc Model E, Honda's first four-stroke. It produced 5bhp and was soon being built at a rate of 130 bikes per day – a Japanese record. The company grew even faster when Fujisawa arranged to sell the two-stroke Model E through bicycle dealers across Japan.

The first Honda that approached European quality was the Model J or Benly ('*convenience*'), a 90cc four-stroke single whose design owed much to NSU. It was launched in 1953 and sold well, but in the following year Honda almost went bust due to a combination of Japan's faltering economy, some ageing models, high wage demands and over-ambitious production. Honda survived, and benefited when the market downturn caused the demise of big rival Tohatsu and many of the other Japanese manufacturers that had emerged after the war.

Honda's most important success came in 1958 with the C100, known as the Super Cub. Powered by a fully-enclosed, 50cc four-stroke engine producing 4.5bhp, it was reliable, economical and practical thanks to its legshields, large wheels, big mudguards, well-padded seat

Above: Ariel's 1956-model Red Hunter 350 gave dependable, unspectacular performance.

Below: BMW's 500cc R50, introduced in 1955, handled well, thanks partly to its Earles forks.

Below right: The R51/2 of 1950 was essentially an updated 500cc pre-war flat twin. Like many bikes, it was often fitted with a sidecar.

Left: Victoria's Bergmeister, launched in 1953, was the German marque's first post-war four-stroke. Its 347cc transverse V-twin engine produced 21bhp, giving a top speed of 80mph (129km/h), and featured shaft final drive.

and good electrics. Backed by a clever advertising campaign based on the phrase 'You meet the nicest people on a Honda', the Super Cub became hugely successful in the United States, and established Honda in many other world markets.

Above: Honda's first four-stroke was the 146cc Model E, a three-valve single released in 1951.

By this time Europe was already familiar with the attractions of the scooter, which had been pioneered in Italy after the war by Vespa and Lambretta. Introduced by aircraft manufacturer Piaggio in 1946, the original Vespa ('*wasp*' in Italian) was created by an aircraft designer named Corradino d'Ascanio, and featured leg-shields for maximum weather protection. The enclosed two-stroke engine pivoted on the pressed-steel frame to provide rear suspension. The original 98cc capacity was increased to 150cc by 1954, but the chassis layout would remain almost unchanged half a century later.

The Vespa's main rival was the Lambretta, produced by Innocenti of Milan. The Lambretta looked very similar but mounted its shaft-drive two-stroke engine lower, in front of the rear wheel, which improved weight distribution. The Lambretta was updated in the 1950s but was never as popular as the Vespa. Many other firms also built scooters, notably Zündapp of Germany, whose Bella, introduced in 1953, handled well due partly to its large wheels.

Below: Boosted by its 'You meet the nicest people…' advertisement, devised by Honda's US agency Grays, the C100 Super Cub sold in vast numbers in the States and helped change many people's attitude towards motorcyclists.

Other Italian firms adopted a different approach to commuter machines. A Bologna-based electronics components firm called Ducati had begun two-wheeled production after the war with the Cucciolo ('*puppy*'), a 49cc four-stroke engine clipped onto a bicycle frame. The light and simple bike was a success, and Ducati expanded to build sportier machines after appointing a new chief designer, Fabio Taglioni, who adopted the desmodromic system, which uses cams rather than springs to close the valves.

Taglioni made his mark in 1955 with the 100cc Gran Sport, nicknamed the Marianna, whose single-cylinder engine used a shaft and bevel gears to drive its overhead camshaft, a Ducati trademark for the next two decades. The Marianna was successful in races such as the Giro d'Italia, and led to larger singles including the 175 Sport of 1957. The following year, a 125cc desmo Ducati won several grands prix and finished second in the world championship.

One of the best known Italian bikes in the years after the war was Moto Guzzi's Dondolino, or '*rocking-chair*', so nicknamed after its sometimes unstable high-speed handling. The 500cc

You meet the nicest people on a Honda. And the remarkable thing is the low cost of it all. Prices start about $215* Insurance is painless. Upkeep negligible. Honda's four-stroke engine demands 200 miles from a gallon of gas. And gets it. Plenty of drive. That's how you stay at the top of the class. World's biggest seller. HONDA

Above: Italian scooters were fashionable during the '50s, and were boosted by their association with celebrities such as movie star John Wayne, seen here with a Vespa.

Moto Guzzi Falcone Turismo (1958)

Engine type:	Air-cooled ohv pushrod two-valve single
Capacity:	498cc (88 x 82mm)
Maximum power:	19bhp @ 4300rpm
Transmission:	Four-speed, chain final drive
Frame:	Steel twin downtube
Suspension:	Telescopic front; horizontal springs and friction dampers rear
Brakes:	Drum front & rear
Weight:	368lb (167kg) dry
Top speed:	75mph (121km/h)

Right: Moto Guzzi's 500cc Falcone single changed little during 18 years of production. This Turismo model dates from 1964.

Dondolino racer, with its single horizontal cylinder in Guzzi style, was developed from the Condor of the mid-1930s, and itself led to the even more famous roadgoing Falcone ('*falcon*'). Introduced in 1950, the sporty Falcone cost half as much as the Dondolino and featured enclosed instead of exposed valves, and crankcases in aluminium instead of magnesium.

The Falcone made a fine roadster and also a successful racer, especially when boosted by Dondolino engine parts. In 1954 the original 23bhp model became the Falcone Sport and was joined by a Turismo version with higher bars and a detuned 19bhp engine. The Falcone remained in production through the 1950s with few changes. But Guzzi made its name with rapid racers, many of them shaped in a state-of-the-art wind tunnel at the firm's Mandello del Lario factory.

Guzzi's most successful racers were its horizontal singles, which won three 250cc world titles between 1949 and '52, and five straight 350cc championships from 1953. Potentially the greatest was the 500cc V8, introduced in 1956. Engineer Giulio Carcano's liquid-cooled, quad-cam, 90-degree V8 produced 72bhp, revved to 12,000rpm and was clocked at 178mph (286km/h) at the Belgian Grand Prix in 1957. But Guzzi, like most other Italian firms, quit racing that year before the mighty V8 had shown its full potential.

One of the Falcone's main rivals was Gilera's Saturno, a 500cc four-stroke single with more conventional vertical cylinder. The Milan-based marque introduced the Saturno as a racebike in 1940 and began full-scale production after the war. The Saturno, too, was built in Sport and Turismo models, the former benefiting from an aluminium cylinder head, higher compression and hotter cam that increased peak output to 22bhp.

While Gilera's fabulous fours were beating all in grands prix in the early 1950s, the Saturno also won races and remained a popular roadster. Early models had girder forks and Gilera's own rear suspension system, featuring horizontal springs in boxes above the swingarm. Later versions were updated with telescopic forks and twin shocks. But by 1959 demand for the Saturno had dropped, partly because it cost as much as a Fiat 500 car, and production ended.

One Italian firm that defied convention was Rumi, founded after the war by Bergamo-based friends Donnino Rumi and Pietro Vassena. In 1950 they launched two models, a Sport and a Turismo, powered by 125cc two-stroke parallel twin engines with cylinders angled horizontally forward. The leaner Sport, especially, was stylish and quick, with a top speed of just over 60mph

Left: Gilera's 499cc Saturno Sport made 22bhp and provided plenty of performance in 1950. Two years later the firm from Arcore, near Milan, had updated the single with telescopic forks and twin rear shocks, in place of this bike's girders and horizontal rear springs.

(97km/h). Rumi expanded the range with high-performance Junior and Bicarburatore ('*twincarburettor*') versions of the 125, and also built a small number of four-stroke V-twins before production ended in the 1960s.

Another entrepreneur who set out to satisfy Italy's post-war demand for personal transport was Count Domenico Agusta, the eldest of four brothers whose late father Giovanni had been an aviation pioneer. Domenico founded the Meccanica Verghera (MV) bike firm in the village of Verghera, outside Milan, and in 1945 launched his first bike, a 98cc two-stroke single that was known as the Vespa until complaints by scooter manufacturer Piaggio led to the MV being renamed the 98 2T.

The bike was a success and MV production expanded quickly, with improved models including the 125 TEL and its 1950-model successor the Lungo ('*riverside*'). This was a fine bike with 8.5bhp two-stroke engine, duplex cradle frame and swingarm rear suspension. In standard form it was good for 65mph (105km/h), and when tuned made an 80mph (129km/h) racer that took several class wins in the Milano-Taranto and Giro d'Italia.

Above: Ducati began motorcycle production in 1946 with the Cucciolo, essentially a bicycle powered by a 49cc four-stroke engine that produced just 1hp.

Agusta's glory years

MV also built outstanding small-capacity four-stroke singles, starting with the 175cc, overheadcamshaft CSTL that was released in 1953. By this time the firm had also begun its grand prix racing success, with Englishman Cecil Sandford's 125cc world championship win the previous year. Italian star Carlo Ubbiali went on to win five more 125c titles between 1955 and '60, plus three more in the 250cc class. In 1956, John Surtees won the first of his four 500cc titles for MV, beginning the Italian marque's long domination of the track.

Italy's Gilera and MV Agusta produced the fastest racebikes of the 1950s, but the era's fastest and arguably its greatest roadsters came from Vincent of Britain. The small firm from Stevenage in Hertfordshire, led by Philip Vincent and his Australian chief engineer Phil Irving, built small numbers of powerful, expensive V-twins that established an unmatched reputation for performance and high-quality engineering.

Philip Vincent had set up his bike business in 1927, and to gain credibility had bought the name HRD Motors from Howard Davies, a former TT winner whose bike-building firm had failed. Vincent-HRD's first bikes used engines from JAP, Rudge and Villiers. But after problems

Below: Rumi's 1954-model 125 Sport was light, agile and powered by an 8.5bhp air-cooled two-stroke parallel twin engine.

Vincent Black Shadow Series C (1949)

Engine:	Air-cooled ohv four-valve 50-degree pushrod V-twin
Capacity:	998cc (84 x 90mm)
Maximum power:	55bhp @ 5700rpm
Transmission:	Four-speed, chain final drive
Frame:	Steel spine
Suspension:	Girder front; twin shocks rear
Brakes:	Twin drums front & rear
Weight:	458lb (208kg)
Top speed:	125mph (201km/h)

Above: These riders are lining up at the start of the MotoGiro, one of the great long-distance Italian road races of the 1950s. The event has recently been revived as a test of endurance for both classic and modern bikes.

Right: Vincent's standard 1950-model V-twin, the Rapide Series C, developed 45bhp from its 998cc engine, and had the looks and handling to match its 110mph (177km/h) performance.

with JAP motors at the TT in 1934, Vincent and Irving designed their own 500cc high-cam single-cylinder engine. The 90mph (145km/h) Comet, released in 1935, was followed a year later by the firm's first V-twin, created by combining two cylinders at a 47-degree angle. The 998cc 45bhp Rapide thundered to 110mph (177km/h) but suffered from transmission problems.

After the war Vincent created the Series B Rapide, using a new 998cc unit-construction V-twin with cylinders at 50 degrees. The motor formed a stressed member of a compact and innovative chassis that incorporated diagonal twin rear shocks, and twin drum brakes on each wheel. The fast and sophisticated Rapide was joined in 1948 by the even more exclusive Black Shadow, whose tuned, black-finished, 55bhp engine gave a top speed of over 125mph (201km/h), recorded on a big Smith's speedometer calibrated to 150mph (241km/h).

American speed ace Roland 'Rollie' Free famously rode Vincent's race-spec Black Lightning to a record 150.313mph (241.89km/h) on the Bonneville Salt flats in Utah in 1948, wearing just swimming trunks and shoes to reduce wind resistance. Other Vincent heroics included George Brown's numerous sprint victories and records on bikes named Gunga Din, Nero and the supercharged Super Nero. Vincent updated the range in 1949 with the Series C models, featuring improved rear suspension and Girdraulic front forks instead of the original girders.

But the exotic V-twins were too expensive to sell in sufficient numbers, and by the early 1950s Vincent was in financial trouble. Production continued under receivership, and the firm diversified by assembling lightweight NSU bikes under licence. New Series D V-twins, the Black Knight and tuned Black Prince, featured all-enclosing fibreglass bodywork. But motorcyclists were not ready for such futuristic style in 1955. Sales were poor, and by the end of that year Vincent had abandoned production.

One of Vincent's rivals at the top end of the market had been Ariel's Square Four, which after the war had been built in 1000cc form only, the earlier 600cc version having been dropped. In 1949 the Ariel was revamped to create the Square Four 4G MkI, featuring a new all-aluminium engine. This was much lighter than the old iron unit, bringing weight down to a respectable 433lb (196kg) with plunger rear suspension, or even less with the rigid frame, which some riders preferred due to the plunger units' under-damped, rather vague feel.

Four-cylinder smoothness

As before, only two exhaust downpipes were visible, although the MkI emphasized its four-cylinder status with the words 'Square Four' on its timing cover. The Square Four produced 34bhp and was not dramatically fast, with a top speed of about 100mph (161km/h). Where the 'Squariel' scored was with its smoothness and its generous midrange torque, which gave effortless cruising ability and strong acceleration for overtaking.

In 1953 Ariel introduced the revamped 4G MkII. This was a stylish bike with a larger, rounded petrol tank and a further updated engine featuring four separate exhaust downpipes. Even in this final form the MkII's engine was prone to overheat in traffic, and handling was mediocre. Ariel deemed further redevelopment too costly and abandoned production in 1958.

The Ariel was not the only four-cylinder model during this time. The Danish-built Nimbus also had a long life, being produced with few changes from 1935 until 1959. The bike was an unlikely combination of sophisticated 746cc sohc in-line four-cylinder engine in a simple frame made from metal strips. A maximum output of 22bhp gave the Nimbus a top speed of about 75mph (121km/h). But few were sold outside Denmark. The other leading Scandinavian marque was Sweden's Husqvarna, which had produced motorcycles in small numbers since 1903. During the 1940s Husqvarna built mostly lightweight two-stroke roadsters, before focusing on the off-road competition bikes for which it became well known.

Like Nimbus, American firm Indian had continued to build in-line fours by developing the machine that it had inherited when buying Ace in 1927. In the early 1940s the Indian Four's 1265cc smooth-revving side-valve motor produced 40bhp, giving a top speed of 90mph (145km/h). But the Four was expensive, and remained prone to overheating of its rear cylinder. It was eventually dropped in 1943.

Indian's most dramatic updates to the Chief and Scout V-twins came in 1940, when the Springfield firm introduced the distinctive skirted fender styling for which the models are best known. In the same year the Chief gained new cylinder heads and barrels with larger cooling fins, plus a new frame incorporating plunger rear suspension in place of the old hard-tail. A mid-'40s Chief was heavy, at over 550lb (250kg), and not particularly fast, but very stylish and comfortable.

Ariel Square Four 4G MkI (1952)	
Engine:	Air-cooled ohv eight-valve pushrod square-four
Capacity:	997cc (65 x 75mm)
Maximum power:	34hp @ 5400rpm
Transmission:	Four-speed, chain final drive
Frame:	Steel twin downtube
Suspension:	Telescopic front; plunger rear
Brakes:	Drum front & rear
Weight:	433lb (196kg)
Top speed:	100mph (161km/h)

Above: Ariel's 1952-model Square Four MkI.

Above: The MkII 'Squariel' had four pipes.

Left: The Danish-built Nimbus combined a four-cylinder engine with crude steel plate frame.

Movie Mayhem

The movie that influenced motorcycling more than any other was *The Wild One*, released in 1954 and starring a young Marlon Brando. The riot at the biker gathering at Hollister in California on the July 4th weekend in 1947 had already resonated throughout the US motorcycle world. Sensationalized coverage in publications including the influential *Life* magazine, which pictured a drunken biker with a beer in each hand, horrified many people across America.

The American Motorcycle Association was also alarmed, and issued a press release stating that 'only one percent of motorcyclists are hoodlums and troublemakers', who would be 'outlawed' from its membership. This backfired by bringing together many of the biker gangs, who delighted in adopting the terms outlaw and one-percenter as their own.

Director Laslo Benedek's *The Wild One*, in which Brando's character Johnny clashes with the aggressive Chico, played by Lee Marvin, was loosely based on the events at Hollister. The movie brought the biker culture to a much wider audience, and had a lasting effect on the US public's attitude towards motorcyclists. Although tame by modern standards, *The Wild One* was violent and controversial enough to be banned for a period in some countries, including Britain.

The Wild One was the first big movie in which bikes were clearly identifiable, as previously machines had appeared with badges obscured. Brando's Johnny rode a 1950-model Triumph Thunderbird; Marvin's Chico a Harley-Davidson. Ironically, although Triumph agent Bill Johnson had attempted to halt production of the movie by writing to the

Motion Picture Association of America, the British marque's US sales were boosted by the exposure.

Above right: Brando and Mary Murphy are on a disguised Matchless here, but The Wild One's *two-wheeled star was Triumph's Thunderbird.*

Below: This 'Indian Brave' at the 1952 Earls Court Show is a British-built 248cc single.

In 1950 Indian enlarged the Chief's engine to 1311cc (80ci), fitted telescopic forks instead of girders, and specified a conventional right-hand throttle for the first time. The firm also attempted to compete with the British by building vertical twins, such as the 436cc Super Scout 249 and its successor the 250 Warrior, whose capacity was in fact 500cc. But these failed to save Indian. The famous 'Wigwam' factory built its last bike in 1953, after which Royal Enfield singles and twins were restyled and sold as Indians, without much success.

Right: This 1941-model Indian Four has been updated with a gearchange by foot instead of hand, plus telescopic forks from a later Chief.

Stateside struggle

The Springfield firm's failure to keep pace with rival Harley was one reason for its demise, but in contrast to booming Europe, the US motorcycling situation was depressed. Post-war demand for increasing mobility was centred on the car, not the motorbike. Fast and light bikes were being imported in increasing numbers from Europe. The US motorcycle scene was also suffering with an image problem, partly caused by growing numbers of bike clubs, such as Satan's Slaves, Road Rats and Gypsy Jokers. Members included Second World War veterans who were having problems readjusting to civilian life.

Harley soldiered on, and in 1957 introduced a significant new model in the shape of the 883cc XL Sportster, featuring overhead valves in place of the side-valve layout of its predecessor the KH. The Sportster gained performance with bigger valves, and was good for 100mph (161km/h). It also featured two-tone paintwork, telescopic forks, chrome-covered twin shocks and a single sprung saddle. The model was an instant hit, and would be successfully updated throughout the 1960s and far beyond.

Harley was badly in need of a high-performance twin because by 1957 the US market was proving fruitful for British firms. Triumph led the way, having established thriving agencies on both sides of the country: Johnson Motors on the West Coast and TriCor in the East. It was largely American enthusiasts' demands for extra performance and 'more cubes' that had led to the Brit manufacturers enlarging their parallel twin engines to 650cc. The leaders had predictably been Triumph, whose Thunderbird had been launched to great acclaim in 1950.

The original 'T-bird' was essentially a 649cc version of Triumph's popular Speed Twin. Its larger motor produced 34bhp, which was 4bhp up on the sporty 500cc Tiger 100's output. Although the top speed of just over 100mph (161km/h) was only a small improvement, the bigger motor had considerably more midrange punch. That helped the Thunderbird, which was barely heavier than the 500cc models, live up to Triumph's advertising claim that it was 'the most exciting motorcycle ever'. In 1954 Triumph unveiled a faster still 650, the Tiger 110, whose motor used hot cams, increased compression and a larger Amal carburettor to produce 42bhp.

BSA also had a popular 650cc model, the A10 Golden Flash, which had been rushed into production in late 1950 to compete with the Thunderbird. Despite its name and claimed 35bhp

Harley-Davidson XL Sportster (1957)	
Engine:	Air-cooled ohv four-valve pushrod 45-degree V-twin
Capacity:	883cc (76.2 x 96.8mm)
Maximum power:	40bhp @ 5500rpm
Transmission:	Four-speed, chain final drive
Frame:	Steel twin downtube
Suspension:	Telescopic front; twin shocks rear
Brakes:	Drum front & rear
Weight:	463lb (210kg)
Top speed:	100mph (161km/h)

Above: Harley's Sportster provided '50s cool.

Below left: Triumph's T-bird had lots of muscle.

Triumph Thunderbird (1957)	
Engine:	Air-cooled ohv pushrod four-valve parallel twin
Capacity:	649cc (71 x 82mm)
Maximum power:	34bhp @ 6300rpm
Transmission:	Four-speed, chain final drive
Frame:	Steel cradle
Suspension:	Telescopic front; twin shocks rear
Brakes:	Drum front & rear
Weight:	385lb (175kg)
Top speed:	103mph (166km/h)

BSA Road Rocket (1956)

Engine:	Air-cooled ohv pushrod four-valve parallel twin
Capacity:	646cc (70 x 84mm)
Maximum power:	40bhp @ 6000rpm
Transmission:	Four-speed, chain final drive
Frame:	Steel twin downtube
Suspension:	Telescopic front; twin shocks rear
Brakes:	Drum front & rear
Weight:	418lb (190kg)
Top speed:	105mph (169km/h)

Above right: BSA's quick and stylish 646cc A10RR Road Rocket was launched in 1954.

Above: The Matchless G12 De Luxe.

Below: The AJS Model 16MCS was an off-road competition version of the 1954-model 350cc single, but also made a capable roadster.

maximum output, the Flash was not a racy sportster but a dependable all-rounder that was often used with a sidecar. The Birmingham firm added some performance with the short-lived Super Flash, which was sold in the US in 1953, and then with the A10 Road Rocket, whose 646cc engine featured aluminium cylinder head, hot camshaft, high-compression pistons, and 40bhp peak output.

The Road Rocket was good for 105mph (169km/h) and sold well both in Britain and the States, as did its similarly styled replacement, the Super Rocket. The BSA group also earned some extra sales from its 650cc twin when Ariel, which had been taken over by BSA in 1944, launched its own model, the Huntmaster, closely based on the Golden Flash. A slightly revised 35bhp engine was combined with a new gearbox and frame in one of the British industry's more successful attempts at 'badge engineering'.

The master of that particular practice was AMC (Associated Motor Cycles), which had been formed when Matchless of Plumstead in south London had taken over Wolverhampton firm AJS in 1931. From then on, bikes were often sold under both Matchless and AJS names, with few differences apart from colour (typically red for Matchless, blue for AJS). Thus the original AMC 498cc parallel twin, launched in 1949, was both the Matchless G9 and AJS Model 20.

AMC followed the trend for increased capacity, enlarging the twin to 592cc to create the G11 in 1956, and three years later producing the 646cc G12, also sold as the AJS Model 31. In either guise it was a solid, reliable machine that handled well and was good for just over 100mph (161km/h). The G12 was also popular in De Luxe form, with uprated ignition and quickly detachable rear wheel. The sporty G12 CSR, with high-compression motor, siamesed exhaust and alloy mudguards, gave extra speed at the expense of vibration and unreliability.

The AMC empire also included Francis-Barnett and James, both of which had been successful before the war, and had later built Villiers-engined two-strokes before being taken over in 1947. Five years later Norton was also swallowed up by AMC, although production continued at Bracebridge Street in Birmingham, rather than moving to London (at least until 1962). Unlike AJS and Matchless models, Nortons retained a distinct identity. The marque belatedly joined the move towards increased capacity in 1956, when the Dominator 88's 500cc engine was enlarged to 597cc to create the Dominator 99.

Italy's All-Conquering Fours

The dominant racebikes of the 1950s were screaming 500cc fours from Italian factories Gilera and MV Agusta. The key figure was engineer Piero Remor, who had first designed a 490cc four-cylinder engine in 1923, and who in the 1930s had been involved with rider/engineer Piero Taruffi in building a supercharged four called the Rondine ('*swallow*'), on which Taruffi set several speed records.

Giuseppe Gilera, whose factory at Arcore near Milan was one of Italy's largest, had bought the Rondine project in 1936. Development of a supercharged 250cc four was abandoned after the war, when supercharging was banned by the FIM, but Remor used the engine as the basis for a dohc 500cc powerplant whose 55bhp output far exceeded those of singles including Gilera's own Saturno. Les Graham of AJS won the first

500cc world championship in 1949, but the following year Gilera's Umberto Masetti overcame his four's poor handling to win from Norton's Geoff Duke.

Duke gained his revenge in 1951 by winning on the slower but more agile Norton, but Masetti regained the title for Gilera in 1952. Duke was then signed by the Italian factory and won a hat-trick of championships between 1953 and '55. By this time Gilera had a new rival, because Remor had left for MV Agusta, taking chief mechanic Arturo Magni with him, and had designed a 500cc four for the Gallarate factory. This featured shaft final drive and a gearlever on each side of the engine, but after poor results it was redesigned with a more conventional layout.

Disaster struck when MV team leader Les Graham was killed at the TT in 1953. But the firm's fortunes changed with the signing of

John Surtees, who won the championship in 1956. Libero Liberati regained the title for Gilera in 1957 but at the end of that year the Arcore factory quit racing, largely for financial reasons, along with rivals Mondial and Moto Guzzi. That left the way open for Surtees, who added three more championships between 1958 and 1960, and especially for MV Agusta, who would rule the grand prix world for many more years.

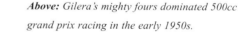

It was Triumph that ended the decade with the most significant arrival, when in 1959 the firm introduced a new high-performance, twin-carburettor version of its 649cc twin. Inspired by the exploits of Texan Johnny Allen, who in 1956 had ridden a Triumph streamliner to 214mph (344km/h) on the Bonneville salt flats in Utah, Edward Turner named the 46bhp twin the T120 Bonneville. The 'Bonnie' was an immediate hit, and its combination of performance, style and competitive price would prove irresistible for years to come.

Above: Gilera's mighty fours dominated 500cc grand prix racing in the early 1950s.

Below: At the 1954 Earls Court Show, James put the new 224cc Colonel alongside one of the firm's 225cc 2.25hp models from 1915.

Left: Triumph's original T120 Bonneville was launched hurriedly in 1959, complete with twin carbs and short-lived headlamp nacelle.

Empire in Decline
1960s

Previous page: *Bridgestone's sophisticated 350 GTR two-stroke twin used disc valve induction.*

Above: *By the early 1960s Soichiro Honda, the son of a Hamamatsu blacksmith, was on his way to becoming by far the most important figure in motorcycling history.*

Above: *This 247cc Honda C71 was built in 1960, two years after the model's introduction. Its 1957 predecessor the C70, Honda's first twin, had similar styling, with frame, front forks and big mudguards made from pressed steel.*

The British motorcycle industry began the 1960s on top of the world. The previous, increasingly affluent decade had ended with the UK manufacturers producing most of the best machines, and with a record number of over 350,000 registrations in Britain alone. Prime Minister Harold Macmillan's famous comment that 'You've never had it so good' seemed to apply particularly to a bike industry whose largest force, the BSA Group, posted record profits of over £3.5 million in 1960.

But already there were warning signs that the good times were drawing to a close. The 1950s had ended with the launch of two small, relatively inexpensive cars, the Austin Mini and Morris Minor. They and others would hit the UK motorcycle industry hard, just as Henry Ford's Model T had done in the USA decades earlier, and as the VW Beetle and Fiat's tiny Topolino were doing in Germany and Italy. Ordinary people now aspired to car ownership, and the motorcycle and sidecar combination that had provided British family transport for decades was regarded as distinctly second best.

Motorcycling was not helped by its downmarket image. In the US, Hell's Angels were making headlines for violence and lawlessness (although Honda's 'You meet the nicest people…' advertising projected a contrastingly wholesome impression). Britain's relatively harmless 'leather boys' preferred burn-ups between cafés. But their resultant accidents led to bad publicity, which was partly responsible for provisional licence holders being restricted to 250cc bikes in 1961. Many motorcycle dealerships, including the prestigious Kings of Oxford chain owned by Mike Hailwood's father Stan, began selling cars instead.

As early as 1960, many people realized that the biggest threat to the British motorcycle industry came from the east. In that year Edward Turner, head of the BSA Group's Automotive Division, visited several Japanese bike factories. His report to BSA's directors commented favourably that the Japanese firms had 'quality machine tool equipment, advanced techniques, scientific ability and keen commercial enterprise'.

By this time Honda's annual production of over 200,000 units exceeded the British industry's total. The large Japanese bike market was protected by import tariffs that were not reflected in Britain, where the market was much more vulnerable to foreign imports. Turner's report concluded that, rather than attempting to compete by building more and better small-capacity motorcycles, British manufacturers should concentrate their resources by building fewer different models. Turner and others believed that Japan's production of small bikes would be beneficial, as riders would graduate to larger British machines. For a while, some of them did …

Honda was already making an impression on motorcyclists outside Japan with a breathtaking arrival on the road-racing scene. Soichiro Honda had visited the Isle of Man TT back in 1954, while on a European trip to visit several car factories. In 1959 he returned with a five-man team of riders comprising four Japanese plus rider-manager Bill Hunt, the sales manager at Honda's recently established American office. Their bikes were 125cc parallel twins, inspired by the NSU Rennmax that had dominated the 250cc class before the German firm had quit racing in 1954.

Honda's inexperienced crew caused some amusement by arriving with knobbly tyres, better suited to ash-covered home tracks than the Mountain circuit. Even when these were swapped for Avons, Honda couldn't match the pace of the winning MV Agusta ridden by Tarquinio Provini, but top-12 finishes by all four Japanese riders won the team prize. For the 1960 TT, Honda's team included Australian Bob Brown, who finished fourth in the 250cc race. Hondas took sixth to tenth places in the 125cc event.

Even that success didn't prepare the motorcycle world for the 1961 season. Helped by MV's withdrawal to concentrate on the bigger classes, Honda's riders Mike Hailwood and Australian Tom Phillis dominated the season, winning the 250 and 125cc world championships respectively. At the TT, Hondas took the top five places in both races. Even allowing for the limited factory opposition, it was a brilliant effort that confirmed the arrival of a major new force.

By this time Honda was also building twin-cylinder roadsters, having begun in 1957 with the 250cc C70, which also owed much to NSU. The 18bhp parallel twin had chain-driven overhead camshaft and unit construction (combined engine and gearbox). It was rather ungainly, with a pressed steel frame and front forks, big mudguards and 16-inch wheels. Its successor, the C71, featuring an electric starter, was sold in small numbers in Europe in 1960.

Honda also built sporty and dual-purpose versions of some models, and it was the racier twins that helped establish the firm abroad in the early 1960s. First came the CB92, whose rev-happy and reliable 125cc engine gave a top speed of over 70mph (113km/h). With its flyscreen, low handlebars and big front drum brake, the little Honda looked the part too, though its pressed-steel frame and under-damped rear shocks did not match the aggressive image.

Increasingly sophisticated roadsters

The twin that did most to put Honda on the map was the 250cc CB72, whose twin carburettors helped give a maximum output of 24bhp and a 90mph (145km/h) top speed. Chassis layout was modern, with a tubular steel frame and telescopic forks in place of Honda's previous leading-link units. Many motorcyclists were still scornful of the revvy 'rice-burners', but Honda's successful racers and increasingly sophisticated roadsters were gradually making an impression.

Above: This lightweight Honda line-up from the early '60s features (from left) the standard 50cc C110 and the C110 Sport, both from 1961, plus the 55cc C115 model from 1963.

Below: Honda's 125cc CB92 twin reached Europe in 1961, proving that the Japanese firm could build stylish, quick, and reliable bikes.

Honda CB72 (1962)

Engine:	Air-cooled sohc four-valve parallel twin
Capacity:	247cc (54 x 54mm)
Maximum power:	24bhp @ 9000rpm
Transmission:	Four-speed, chain final drive
Frame:	Steel spine
Suspension:	Telescopic front; twin shocks rear
Brakes:	Drum front & rear
Weight:	337lb (153kg) dry
Top speed:	90mph (145km/h)

Above right: Honda's influential 247cc CB72.

Below: Yamaha's 246cc YDS-2 two-stroke twin.

Yamaha YDS-2 (1963)

Engine:	Air-cooled two-stroke parallel twin
Capacity:	246cc (56 x 50mm)
Maximum power:	25bhp @ 7500rpm
Transmission:	Five-speed, chain final drive
Frame:	Steel twin cradle
Suspension:	Telescopic front; twin shocks rear
Brakes:	Drum front & rear
Weight:	313lb (142kg) dry
Top speed:	90mph (145km/h)

Suzuki, too, was gaining ground. The firm had begun by building looms for weaving, before moving into motorcycle production in 1954 with a 90cc four-stroke single called the Colleda. Suzuki entered the grand prix world and was boosted in 1961 when Ernst Degner, star rider of the East German MZ team, defected to the West, taking the tuning secrets of two-stroke engine genius Walter Kaaden with him. The following year Degner won the first 50cc world title for Suzuki. New Zealand's Hugh Anderson and Germany's Hans-Georg Anscheidt won a total of seven more 50 and 125cc titles for Suzuki in the next few years.

Yamaha, whose parent company Nippon Gakki had long been a leading producer of musical instruments, had also begun building motorbikes in the mid-1950s, as a way of utilizing machinery that had manufactured propellers in the war. Yamaha's first bike, the YA-1 'Red Dragon', was one of several from different countries to be copied from German firm DKW's RT 125 two-stroke single. The YD-2, a two-stroke parallel twin, followed in 1957.

The models that launched Yamaha's reputation for rapid small-capacity two-strokes were the 250cc YDS-1 and especially its successor the YDS-2, which was exported successfully in the early 1960s. The YDS-2 produced 25bhp, was good for 90mph (145km/h), and captivated all who rode it. 'What a fantastic machine this is!' began the test in UK magazine *Motorcycle Mechanics* in 1963. 'The acceleration makes you gasp in sheer amazement because you only expect this sort of performance from a racing machine.' Yamaha's two-stoke racers were faster still, as they soon proved with the 250cc and 125cc world championships won by Britain's Phil Read and Bill Ivy.

Kawasaki, a giant corporation that built ships, planes and locomotives among other things, had also been manufacturing motorcycle engines since 1949, and had formed a firm called Meihatsu to sell them in the 1950s. Kawasaki set up its own motorcycle factory, and in 1961 built its first complete bike, the B7, a 125cc two-stroke single based on a Meihatsu. The following year Kawasaki took over Meguro, a marque that dated back to 1928, and had previously built the Rikuo, a copy of a side-valve Harley-Davidson V-twin. Kawasaki thus became an established manufacturer almost overnight, with a range from 50 to 500cc.

By no means all the Japanese manufacturers were thriving, however. In the mid-1950s there had been more than 80 bike firms, but by the early '60s only a handful survived. Olympus had abandoned bikes to concentrate on cameras, Hosk and Showa had been bought by Yamaha, and Fuji by Bridgestone. One of the biggest firms, Marusho, was known for high-quality Lilac 250cc and 125cc transverse V-twins. The firm went bust in 1961, returned with a BMW-style 500cc flat-twin three years later, but by 1967 had ceased production for good.

While Japanese firms had been making their bikes faster and more sophisticated during the late 1950s, Triumph had tried a different approach with its Twenty-One, named after its capacity of 21 cubic inches or 350cc. The 18bhp parallel twin, launched in 1957, was significant in featuring Triumph's first unit-construction engine and gearbox. And the Twenty-One also introduced the 'bathtub' – a sheet-steel enclosure of the rear wheel, intended to give scooter-like cleanliness. By no means all riders were impressed, especially when the bathtub was used on larger models including the 650cc Tiger 110.

Triumph's star of the 1960s was the T120 Bonneville. After a slightly troubled start (early models' crack-prone frames led to a stiffer twin-downtube design, which caused vibration and fuel frothing, cured by another new frame) the 'Bonnie' was successfully tweaked to keep it hugely popular throughout the decade and beyond. Its basic format of 649cc pushrod engine with twin carburettors remained, as did its key attributes of good looks and lively acceleration, backed-up by reasonable smoothness, reliability and handling.

If Triumph built what was widely regarded as the outstanding parallel twin engine of the 1960s, then Norton had the best chassis. The Dominator 99's Featherbed frame held a 597cc engine that was available in SS (Sports Special) trim, with twin carbs and higher compression. In 1961, the motor was enlarged to 646cc to power a US export model called the Manxman. The following year Norton created the Dominator 650SS, powered by a 646cc motor with SS

Above: Triumph's 1960-model T110 Tiger had controversial bathtub rear enclosure.

Left: Triumph's T120 Bonneville, here in 1961 form, was a star throughout the 1960s.

Triumph T120 Bonneville (1961)

Engine:	Air-cooled four-valve ohv pushrod parallel twin
Capacity:	649cc (71 x 82mm)
Maximum power:	46bhp @ 6500rpm
Transmission:	Four-speed, chain final drive
Frame:	Steel twin downtube
Suspension:	Telescopic front; twin shocks rear
Brakes:	Drum front & rear
Weight:	402lb (183kg) wet
Top speed:	110mph (177km/h)

Right: Struggling Norton produced one of its best ever bikes in 1962 with the Dominator 650SS, which combined a 49bhp parallel twin engine with Featherbed-framed chassis, and provided both speed and fine handling.

Below: Ariel gambled in 1960 by abandoning four-stroke production in favour of the futuristic Leader, featuring a 249cc two-stroke engine enclosed by pressed-steel bodywork. The gamble failed, and Ariel went bust.

Ariel Leader (1960)	
Engine:	Air-cooled two-stroke parallel twin
Capacity:	249cc (54 x 54mm)
Maximum power:	16bhp @ 6400rpm
Transmission:	Four-speed, chain final drive
Frame:	Pressed-steel
Suspension:	Trailing-link front; twin shocks rear
Brakes:	Drum front & rear
Weight:	310lb (141kg) dry
Top speed:	70mph (113km/h)

specification plus a new downdraft cylinder head developed from engineer Doug Hele's Domiracer competition bike.

The 650SS was a superb machine that produced 49bhp, had a top speed of almost 120mph (193km/h), and handled in finest Norton tradition. The 650SS did not match the Bonneville's sales, partly due to a higher price and also to Norton's generally lower production numbers. But the model was a success on road and track, being voted *Motor Cycle News*' machine of the year in 1962 and '63, and winning two major long-distance production races within months of its launch. Those achievements were overshadowed when in 1963 struggling parent company AMC closed the famous Bracebridge Street works, and moved Norton production to the Matchless factory in Woolwich, south London.

Another popular marque gained a new home for the wrong reasons in 1963, when Ariel production was moved from the traditional Selly Oak base to parent company BSA's factory at Small Heath, Birmingham. Ariel's problems dated back to the 1950s, when Edward Turner, the autocratic Triumph boss, had taken control of the BSA group's bike division. Rather than developing Ariel's assets, Turner seemed to regard the marque as a threat to Triumph. Development of an updated Square Four was abandoned, and in 1960 the small Ariel Competition Department was closed down, although trials ace Sammy Miller was beating all comers on his legendary HT Red Hunter single with the number plate 'GOV132'.

In 1960 Ariel also controversially abandoned production of roadgoing four-strokes including the Red Hunter and the 650cc Huntmaster twin, in favour of the Leader. This was an innovative machine powered by a 250cc, two-stroke parallel twin with angled-forward cylinders, designed by Val Page and owing much to the German marque Adler. Its chassis combined a pressed-steel frame, trailing link forks, further pressed-steel bodywork sections, and a dummy tank that could hold an open-face helmet.

Ariel's advertising slogan 'Tomorrow's Design Today' promised much, and the Leader offered smooth cruising, a 70mph (113km/h) top speed and light handling. But that was not enough to make it a lasting success, despite initially promising sales. The Leader's convenience and reasonable performance were offset by flaws including poor brakes, difficult starting, unreliable electrics and inaccessibility for maintenance.

Two-stroke troubles

Ariel attempted to broaden the two-stroke's appeal with more conventional models. The unfaired Arrow and its racer derivative the Super Sports Arrow (known as the Golden Arrow) were used with some success in club racing. But when sales dropped, Ariel had nothing else to offer. Moving production across Birmingham to Small Heath merely delayed the inevitable, and the last two-strokes were produced in 1965. BSA later revived the Ariel name for two disastrous commuter machines, the 50cc Pixie and three-wheeled Ariel-3, but the once proud 'House of the Horse' was effectively dead.

Perhaps Ariel's attempt to create a machine with motorbike performance and scooter-style convenience had simply been ill-timed. The UK two-wheeled scene was polarizing into two rival groups: the bike-riding, leather-jacketed rockers; and the mods, who rode scooters and wore tent-like parka jackets over smarter clothes; and preferred 'Mersey beat' pop tunes to rock. Bank holiday weekends in the mid-'60s saw battles between the two groups on the beaches of coastal towns such as Brighton and Southend.

Rockers tended to gather at transport cafés, the most famous of which was the Ace, near Wembley in north-west London. As many as 1000 bikes were sometimes parked outside the Ace, most of them British singles and twins that were tuned and otherwise modified to boost performance. Favoured sport of the 'café-race' crowd was the record run – 'record' as in gramophone recording – when a rider put a coin in the juke-box, rushed out to his bike and raced off in an attempt to complete a pre-set road course in time to hear the end of the song. Many didn't make it back at all.

Arguably the ultimate rocker bike of the era was the Triton, the unofficial blend of Triumph twin engine and Norton Featherbed frame that provided the best of British biking: the speed of the Bonneville or T110 with the handling of a Dominator or racing Manx. Tritons were constructed by individual riders and also by dealers, most notably by Dave Degens. The former Ace regular turned racer won numerous production events plus the Barcelona 24-hour race on Tritons. His Dresda firm also built more than 500 of the hybrids during the '60s, and would still be building them 30 years later.

Top: Rockers favoured low, clip-on handlebars and badge-covered black leather jackets.

Above: Bikes are lined up at Regency Square in Brighton, the south coast city that was a popular destination for rockers' runs.

Left: The ultimate 1960s café racer was the Triton, a blend of Triumph twin-cylinder engine and Norton Featherbed frame that gave the best of British motorcycling.

Right: BSA built the Rocket Gold Star both in this US export version, with raised handlebars and twin exhausts, and home market spec with low, clip-on bars and siamesed pipes. In either form it was one of the fastest bikes on the road.

BSA Rocket Gold Star (1962)

Engine:	Air-cooled ohv pushrod four-valve parallel twin
Capacity:	646cc (70 x 84mm)
Maximum power:	46bhp @ 6250rpm
Transmission:	Four-speed, chain final drive
Frame:	Steel twin downtube
Suspension:	Telescopic front; twin shocks rear
Brakes:	Drum front & rear
Weight:	418lb (190kg)
Top speed:	115mph (185km/h)

BSA's most memorable production twin of this period also owed much to a hybrid. The Rocket Gold Star was inspired by a one-off special that Oxfordshire dealer Eddie Dow had created by fitting a Gold Star single with a twin-cylinder engine. In 1962, BSA was set to replace its long-running 646cc A10 twin engine with a new A65 unit-construction powerplant (and similar 500cc version, the A50). The familiar 'pre-unit' motor was given a fitting finale by being bolted into a slightly modified Gold Star frame, to create the 'Rocket Goldie'.

The Rocket Gold Star motor was a tuned version of the existing Super Rocket unit, and used higher compression, hotter camshaft and racing style magneto ignition to produce 46bhp. The bike's look and specification generally mimicked that of the Gold Star, with silver-and-chromed petrol tank, low 'Ace' handlebars (for the UK market; higher for the US), big front drum brake and alloy wheel rims. With genuine 115mph (185km/h) performance plus handling to match, the Rocket Gold Star was a fine way to end the A10 line.

In a straight line, at least, the BSA had some worthy opposition from Royal Enfield, the small firm from Redditch, near Birmingham, that had long produced parallel twins of distinctive capacity and style. The Meteor, introduced in 1953, had a softly tuned 692cc engine because it was essentially two 346cc single-cylinder Bullet units. Three years later the Super Meteor increased peak output by 4bhp to 40bhp, but it was in 1958 with the launch of the Constellation that Enfield finally found some genuine performance.

Below: Royal Enfield's Constellation provided plenty of power from its big 692cc parallel twin engine, but the 'Connie' was too unreliable to become a big success.

The Constellation motor retained the 692cc capacity but was comprehensively overhauled and produced an impressive 51bhp, enough for a top speed of 115mph (185km/h). The big powerplant had plenty of low-rev torque too, but oil leaks and unreliability thwarted Enfield's hopes of success. Even fitting Ace bars and reworking the engine to make it more oil-tight didn't make the Constellation popular in the early '60s. Enfield then enlarged the motor again to create the 750cc Interceptor in 1962. Its extra size and pulling power were intended to appeal to the US market, but the Interceptor was not the hit that struggling Enfield desperately needed.

Since Indian had ceased production in 1953, Harley-Davidson had been the sole US manufacturer (although Enfield's Meteor had subsequently been given big fenders, and marketed as an Indian Chief). Harley's Sportster, designated the XL, had been popular since its launch in 1957, and reached new heights in following years with the high-performance XLCH. No official explanation was given for the extra initials, which some said stood for 'California' or 'Competition Hot'. The bike was developed from the stripped-down XLC that had been built in small numbers, mainly for Californian desert racers.

Whatever, the result was a lean, mean, hotted-up version of the 883cc pushrod V-twin; and one that fully lived up to the Sportster part of its name. With a tiny gas tank borrowed from Harley's single-cylinder Hummer (a 125cc two-stroke copied from the German DKW), single seat, relatively light weight and enough power for a top speed of well over 100mph (161km/h) in standard form, the XLCH was fast enough to compete with British 650cc twins.

Harley also updated its big twin range through the 1960s, and introduced the 'full-dressed' touring style complete with factory-supplied windscreen, panniers and other accessories. Early stages in the evolution had come in the late 1940s, with a new 1213cc (74ci), 55bhp V-twin engine whose smooth aluminium rocker covers prompted the nickname 'Panhead'. Hydraulically damped telescopic forks had replaced springers in 1949, resulting in the Hydra-Glide.

The Duo-Glide was created in 1958 with the introduction of twin-shock rear suspension. And in 1965, the addition of an electric starter resulted in the birth of the most famous big Harley of all, the Electra-Glide. It was huge, heavy, expensive, under-braked and not very fast. But the Electra-Glide was also comfortable, smooth and stylish enough to become not just a very successful tourer, but an icon whose name and character would survive several decades and numerous updates, albeit with its hyphen quietly dropped.

Harley struggled in the early 1960s, with a significant proportion of its business being police and other services, but there was plenty going on behind the scenes at Milwaukee. In 1960 the firm attempted to gain ground in the small-capacity markets by buying a 50 per cent stake in Aermacchi, a financially struggling Italian marque. Aermacchi's sporty 250cc single the Ala Verde was sold in the US as the Sprint, and was raced with some success.

During the 1960s, Harley began to acquire something of a cult status with a section of the American biking public, and to attract customisers who bolted longer forks, hard-tail frames and

Above: Early-'60s versions of Harley's Sportster were respectably quick machines that were a match for many British rivals, but the Milwaukee firm's 883cc V-twin became less competitive throughout the decade.

Below: Harley created the Electra-Glide in 1965 by adding an electric starter to the Duo-Glide, launching a long-running legend.

Left: Windshield, footboards and buddy seat gave the Electra-Glide a luxurious ride.

Above: The R69S was BMW's sportiest model for most of the 1960s, but the conservative German marque offered only white paintwork as an alternative to the standard black.

Below: Panther's traditional angled 'sloper' single-cylinder engine took the place of a frame downtube, doubling as a stressed member of the chassis. The Model 100 name came from the 598cc engine's long stroke of 100mm.

Right: The photo of this 1961 Model 100S is untypical, because the vast majority of Panther's big singles were fitted with sidecars.

custom-painted parts to bikes and also to the three-wheeled Servicar. The Servicar was far from the only non-two-wheeled Harley product, as the firm had diversified into the manufacture of golf carts and even boats, after taking over a boat-building firm called Tomahawk.

But sales and prospects were poor, and in 1965 Harley raised much needed capital by becoming a public company, with the Harley and Davidson families retaining a majority of shares. This allowed increased advertising but Harley failed to increase its feeble six per cent share of the US market. (Exports accounted for less than five per cent of production.) In 1969 the crippled company was bought by American Machine and Foundry (AMF), an industrial giant that was keen to expand its interests in the leisure market.

The situation was equally bleak in the European motorcycle industry. In Germany the downturn had begun in the late 1950s, resulting in Adler and Horex ceasing production, NSU turning from bikes to cars, and former giants DKW, Victoria and Express merging to form the Zweirad Union. In 1966, Hercules joined the Union, which was taken over by the large Fichtel & Sachs group three years later. Many small bikes and mopeds would follow, but Germany's days as a major motorcycling force were over.

BMW had also struggled in the late 1950s, with bike production down to little over 5000 units, and the company at one stage under threat of being taken over by Mercedes-Benz. But BMW survived, and in 1960 launched a new range of bikes with more powerful engines. The peaky and unreliable 500cc R50S lasted only two years, but the standard R50/2, and the 600cc R60/2 and sporty R69S were built throughout the decade. They gained numerous detail updates along the way but kept their conservative look with big fuel tanks, huge seats, Earles forks and black or white paintwork.

Many British bike builders were in far deeper financial trouble. After posting a profit in 1960, the Associated Motor Cycles group had begun losing money. In 1966 AMC was taken over by a firm called Manganeze Bronze Holdings, which had recently acquired Villiers, manufacturer of small engines. The new firm was named Norton Villiers, confirming that Norton was the prize asset among the AMC brands, and before long the other marques were discarded.

Left: This Royal Enfield Continental GT dates from 1967, so was one of the last to be built before the Redditch factory was closed. Despite a capacity of just 248cc, the single's café-racer look was backed by a fair turn of speed.

Below: Although Velocette's 1960-model Viceroy gave reasonable performance from its 250cc two-stroke engine, it lacked the style of rival Italian scooters and failed to sell.

Declining sales

James and Francis-Barnett, which had been building Villiers-engined lightweights of often similar design, were quickly closed down. AJS and Matchless were both famous old marques with much racing history. The Matchless G50, a 500cc single developed from AJS's famous 350cc racer the 7R or 'Boy Racer', had won races into the 1960s. But sales of the badge-engineered and often near-identical AJS and Matchless singles and twins had been slow for years, and by the end of 1967 Norton Villiers had axed the lot.

Panther was another old name to be put to sleep in 1967, after several years of ill-health. The Yorkshire firm had been building its 598cc Model 100, known as a 'sloper' due to its angled-forward single cylinder, from 1928 to 1963 with relatively few changes. Even the more recent 645cc Model 120 produced only a slow-revving 27bhp. In 1960 the firm had estimated that 90 per cent of Model 100s were attached to sidecars, so the rise of the Mini and its cohorts hit Panther particularly hard. There was a final attempt with a 250cc Villiers-engined twin, named the Red Panther after a model of that name whose success had rescued Panther in the 1930s. But when lightning failed to strike twice, the factory closed for good.

Royal Enfield survived to the end of the decade, but only just. Enfield made a brave fight, notably with its line of 250cc pushrod singles, which were repeatedly updated following the launch of the original Crusader model in 1956. That led to the tuned Crusader Sports, the Super 5 (named after its five-speed gearbox) and the Continental, which arrived in 1963 with a yet more powerful engine plus flyscreen and dropped handlebars.

The final fling was the following year's Continental GT, which was devised after Enfield contacted its dealers' young apprentices to ask what potential customers wanted. The result was an attractive bike that combined the flyscreen and low bars with a long red petrol tank, humped dual-seat and perforated dummy cooling rims for the front drum brake. The GT's light weight, 85mph (137km/h) top speed and good handling more than made up for its unreliable gearbox, and the bike was popular with British provisional licence holders who were limited to 250cc by the recent law change.

Below: Triumph's TR6 Trophy combined a powerful 650cc engine with stylish high-level pipe, and was very popular in the US.

That was not enough to save Royal Enfield, which had come under the control of financiers who decided that the motorcycle firm was worth less than its traditional factory site in Redditch,

Velocette Venom Thruxton (1965)

Engine:	Air-cooled ohv pushrod two-valve single
Capacity:	499cc (86 x 86mm)
Maximum power:	40bhp @ 6200rpm
Transmission:	Four-speed, chain final drive
Frame:	Steel single downtube
Suspension:	Telescopic front; twin shocks rear
Brakes:	Drum front & rear
Weight:	390lb (177kg)
Top speed:	105mph (169km/h)

Above right: Velocette's Venom Thruxton was the last and raciest of the firm's singles, with clip-on bars, tuned 499cc motor, big front brake, humped seat and firm suspension.

near Birmingham. Production of all singles was abandoned in 1967. The Interceptor 750 twin was built at Bradford-on-Avon in Wiltshire until 1970. After that, the only survivor was the humble Bullet single, which continued to be built in India where it had been produced under licence since the 1950s.

Another sad story was that of Velocette, whose problems had begun in 1960 with an attempt to move into the scooter market. The Viceroy, powered by a 248cc, two-stroke horizontally opposed twin, was a smooth and sophisticated device that handled well and was good for 70mph (113km/h). But its unusual styling failed to catch on with riders who preferred fashionable Vespas and Lambrettas, and by the early '60s the scooter boom was over. After all Velocette's expensive development and tooling, fewer than 1000 Viceroys were sold, and the glass-fibre-bodied LE Vogue was no more successful.

Velocette did at least have time to produce one last development of the singles for which the marque was famous. Since the late 1950s, Velocette's sporty pushrod singles had been the 500cc

Norton Commando (1968)

Engine:	Air-cooled ohv pushrod four-valve parallel twin
Capacity:	745cc (73 x 89mm)
Maximum power:	58bhp @ 6800rpm
Transmission:	Four-speed, chain final drive
Frame:	Steel spine with twin downtubes
Suspension:	Telescopic front; twin shock rear
Brakes:	Drum front & rear
Weight:	420lb (191kg)
Top speed:	115mph (185km/h)

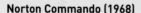

Left: BSA's standard 650cc parallel twin of the late '60s was the Thunderbolt, introduced in 1966 with single carb and 40bhp output.

Below: The Spitfire MkIV, released in 1968, was the fastest of BSA's 650 twins, and also featured a big front drum brake and new rear shocks. But like previous Spitfires its tuned 54bhp engine often gave problems when used hard.

Venom and 350cc Viper, both of which had become available in high-performance Clubman trim. After a Velo had won the prestigious Thruxton 500-mile (805km) race in 1964, the firm offered a race kit including big-valve cylinder head and Amal Grand Prix carburettor.

In 1965 these were incorporated into a new model, the Venom Thruxton, which also featured clip-on bars, rearset footrests, large petrol tank, humped seat, firm suspension and a big twin-leading-shoe front drum brake. Its 499cc engine produced 40bhp, good for genuine 90mph (145km/h) cruising and a top speed of about 105mph (169km/h). The Thruxton made a superb, if uncompromising, roadster, and a successful racer that won its class at the first Production TT in 1967. But by then Velocette's financial problems were deepening, and few bikes were built before production ended in 1970.

BSA was another victim of the scooter market in the early '60s, notably with a machine that was sold as both the BSA Sunbeam and the Triumph Tigress. Both were produced with 175cc two-stroke single (from the BSA Bantam) or new 250cc four-stroke twin engines. Like Velocette's Viceroy they lacked the style to attract the scooter crowd, and also suffered from overheating of the enclosed engines. This was by no means the only example of poor BSA engineering, as both Triumph's 200cc Tiger Cub and BSA's related C15 single had a string of problems.

BSA was nevertheless very profitable in the mid-'60s, largely due to the group's success in the United States. Exports accounted for 75 per cent of production by 1966, earning both BSA and Triumph the Queen's Award for Industry. At that point production had increased by 40 per cent in two years. New workers were employed, and BSA's Small Heath factory was modernized with an expensive, computer-controlled assembly system.

Lionel Jofeh, the former aircraft industry figure who took over as group motorcycle chief in 1967, based himself at a lavish, recently purchased new Research and Development centre at Umberslade Hall, a grand country house with peacocks on its lawn, situated south of Birmingham midway between the BSA, Triumph and Royal Enfield factories. It had a staff of 300 and cost an estimated £1.5 million per year to run, but would earn its nickname 'Slumberslade Hall' by producing little of value.

Opposite centre: With its raised bars and twin high-level pipes, Norton's Commando 750S had a stylish and distinctive look.

Opposite below: Norton's Commando 750, seen here in Fastback style with 1972-model front disc, was a fast and smooth-running roadster.

Right: Kawasaki's 1967-model W2TT Commander was the dual-purpose version of the Japanese firm's British-style 624cc parallel twin.

Below: Honda produced many dual-purpose models in the late '60s, mainly for the US market, including this CL450 parallel twin.

Bottom right: The CB450 parallel twin, known as the 'Black Bomber', arrived in 1965 to confirm that Honda was entering the big bike market.

There were still some great bikes to come from Britain, though, not least the Bonneville. By the late 1960s the T120 had arguably reached the peak of its development, thanks to improvements including a powerful twin-leading-shoe front brake, forks with two-way damping, a longer swingarm, and engine mods that improved reliability and oil retention. The Bonneville was lean and handsome, raced from zero to 100mph (161km/h) in the quarter mile, and handled better than ever.

'If you are a sporty rider and deem yourself a bit of a jockey, you know you are waiting for the day you can buy your Bonnie,' summed up an impressed tester from US magazine *Cycle World*. The Triumph backed up its performance on the track too, with four wins in the big 500-mile (805km) production race at Thruxton and Brands Hatch. John Hartle won the first Isle of Man Production TT in 1967, and two years later Malcolm Uphill set the first 100mph (161km/h) production lap of the island on the way to another victory.

Honda CB450 (1965)

Engine:	Air-cooled dohc four-valve parallel twin
Capacity:	445cc (70 x 57.8mm)
Maximum power:	43bhp @ 8500rpm
Transmission:	Four-speed, chain final drive
Frame:	Steel twin cradle
Suspension:	Telescopic front; twin shocks rear
Brakes:	Drum front & rear
Weight:	411lb (187kg)
Top speed:	102mph (164km/h)

The Bonneville gained a worthy rival in 1968 when Norton introduced the Commando 750. Its engine was the 745cc pushrod parallel twin from the Atlas, tuned slightly with increased compression to give 58bhp. The key Commando feature was its chassis, which incorporated the 'Isolastic' system of rubber mounting, designed to isolate the vibration that had traditionally plagued the Atlas and other larger-capacity twins. Provided its rubber bushes were well maintained, the Isolastic system, developed by a team headed by former Rolls-Royce engineer Dr Stefan Bauer, worked well.

There was plenty more that was good about the Commando. Its styling, complete with streamlined 'Fastback' tailpiece, was dramatic, and the beefy motor provided plenty of low-rev torque along with enough top-end for maximum speed of 115mph (185km/h). Equally importantly the new frame, in conjunction with Roadholder forks and Girling shocks, gave handling that was up to Norton's high standard. The Commando was fast, stable and comfortable, and became a big hit on both sides of the Atlantic.

BSA had great trouble convincing motorcyclists that its unit-construction 650cc A65 Star and 500cc A50 Star twins were an improvement on their A10 and A7 predecessors, following their launch in 1962. Interest picked up slightly in 1964 with the launch of the tuned A65 Rocket, whose good low-rev manners were matched by lively acceleration and a top speed of 105mph (169km/h). The following year's twin-carburettor A65 Lightning was faster still and, like its 500cc equivalent the A50 Cyclone, could also be ordered in Clubman trim with tuned and dyno-tested engine, clip-on bars, rearset footrests and humped seat.

In 1966 BSA replaced the Star model with the 40bhp single-carb Thunderbolt, which made a useful tourer, and introduced a new high-performance 650: the Spitfire MkII. This was a stylish flyer with a bright red petrol tank, new twin-downtube frame, and a Lightning Clubman spec engine that was further tuned with Amal GP carbs to give 54bhp. It looked great, raced to 120mph (193km/h) and handled well. But the tuned motor was horribly fragile, and often exploded in expensive fashion. Despite introducing Spitfire MkIII and IV versions in following years, BSA moved slowly to cure the problems.

Above: The XS-1, powered by a 654cc parallel twin engine, was Yamaha's first four-stroke roadster. Launched in the US market in 1969, it sold well and led to a string of successful twins including the XS-2 and various XS650 models.

Left: Suzuki's T500 two-stroke was called the Titan in the US and the Cobra in Britain. Launched in 1967, the 44bhp twin changed very little during eight years of production.

Honda challenges MV's reign

MV Agusta and Honda dominated grand prix racing in the 1960s, between them winning every 500cc and 350cc world title, plus six in the 250cc class. Honda's Jim Redman led the way with six 250 and 350cc titles, riding mainly four-stroke fours, before Yamaha's growing two-stroke challenge forced Honda to build one of its greatest ever bikes. The RC166, a compact and brilliantly engineered 247cc in-line six that produced 60bhp at 18,000rpm, took Mike Hailwood to the title in 1966 and '67. Hailwood also won both years' 350cc championships on a bored-out 297cc version.

MV were masters of the 500cc class, which the Gallarate firm dominated following the rival Italian marques' withdrawal from GP racing in 1957. John Surtees won his fourth title for MV in 1960, then Gary Hocking won one before Hailwood joined the Italian team to win four consecutive 500cc championships.

'Mike the Bike' then signed for Honda, to set up one of the great periods in motorcycle grand prix racing history.

Riding a powerful but ill-handling 500cc Honda four, Hailwood fought a series of epic battles with MV's new star Giacomo Agostini. In 1966, the Honda broke down in the final round at Monza, handing Ago and MV the title by just six points. In 1967 the championship race was even closer. In the penultimate round the British ace broke the lap record and was leading by half a lap when his Honda stuck in top gear. Hailwood won the last race but Ago retained the championship, not on

points or even race wins, which were equal, but on his greater number of second place finishes. Honda promptly quit GP racing, having made a huge impact but failed to lift the biggest prize.

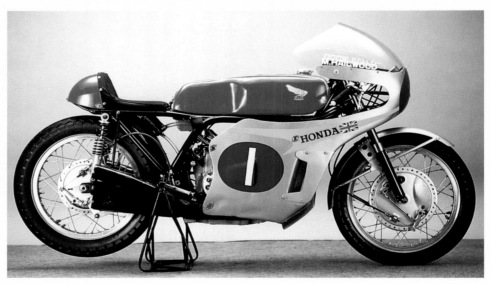

Above: The great Mike Hailwood won the 250 and 350cc double for Honda in 1966 and '67, but just missed the 500cc title in both seasons.

Above right: Honda's brilliant six-cylinder RC166 produced 60bhp at 18,000rpm, and took Hailwood to the world championship in 1966.

Top right: Short-circuit ace Dave Croxford leads world champion Giacomo Agostini (right).

By this time parallel twins were also being built in Japan by firms including Kawasaki, whose W2 Commander owed its design to BSA. In the 1950s Meguro, the firm taken over by Kawasaki, had copied the 500cc pre-unit A7 to create a model it called the M1. Kawasaki updated this, increased capacity to 624cc and renamed the bike the W1; then in 1967 released the tuned, twin-carburettor W2. This was built in both W2SS roadster and W2TT dual-purpose styles. It was good for 110mph (177km/h) and handled reasonably well, but suffered from typical parallel twin vibration. Although the W2 became the best-selling big bike in Japan, it made little impact abroad, where the Kawasaki name was still unfamiliar.

Honda introduced a more significant twin in 1965 with the CB450, which confirmed that the Japanese firm had set its sights on the big bike market. The 445cc Honda's style and layout echoed those of smaller models such as the 250cc CB72, but the CB450 differed by having twin overhead cams, and unusual torsion-bar valve springs. It had a humped petrol tank, twin-cradle frame and black paintwork that helped earn it the nickname 'Black Bomber' in Britain.

The CB450's 43bhp maximum gave an unexceptional top speed of just over 100mph (161km/h), but the motor was pleasantly smooth, flexible and reliable. Despite being slightly heavy at 411lb (187kg) the Honda handled well too, and made a comfortable tourer. It lacked the style or speed to challenge home-built 650cc twins in Britain, but was reasonably popular in the US. The British firms had been warned.

The Japanese twin that made the biggest impact, especially in the US, was Yamaha's XS-1. The engine of Yamaha's first ever four-stroke was similar to BSA's Lightning in its 654cc capacity and internal dimensions, but differed in using a single overhead camshaft instead of pushrods, and in having a left-foot gearchange with a five-speed box. The maximum output of 53bhp gave respectable acceleration with a top speed of 105mph (169km/h), and vibration was reasonable for a big parallel twin.

Chassis performance was less impressive, due to a combination of thin-tube frame and under-damped suspension. But with its high bars and lean lines the XS-1 was an attractive machine, and its reliability and competitive price also contributed towards making it a hit when launched in the US in 1969. In subsequent years the twin was updated with XS-2 and XS650 models that did much to establish Yamaha worldwide.

Suzuki's two-stroke attack

Suzuki was also gradually making a name for itself with a parallel twin, although unlike most of its Japanese contemporaries the T500 was a two-stroke. The lively T500 was based on the T20 Super Six, a quick and agile 250cc twin that was launched in 1966. The bigger model arrived a year later, powered by a heavily-finned, 492cc air-cooled motor whose 44bhp peak output gave a maximum speed of over 100mph (161km/h).

Above: Handling was not the Suzuki T500's strongest point, but the quick and well priced two-stroke cornered reasonably well.

Left: Suzuki's T20 was a quick and light 250cc two-stroke twin whose six-speed gearbox earned it the name 'Super Six'. It was capable of 95mph (153km/h), handled well, was raced successfully and did much to help make Suzuki popular following its launch in 1966.

Bridgestone 350 GTR (1966)	
Engine:	Air-cooled two-stroke parallel twin
Capacity:	345cc
Maximum power:	37bhp @ 7500rpm
Transmission:	Six-speed, chain final drive
Frame:	Steel twin cradle
Suspension:	Telescopic front; twin shocks rear
Brakes:	Drum front & rear
Weight:	330lb (150kg)
Top speed:	95mph (153km/h)

Right: The 350 GTR was stylish, fast and well built, but Bridgestone abandoned bike production in 1968 to concentrate on the tyres for which the Japanese firm is still well known.

Below: Moto Guzzi's V7 Special, launched in 1969, helped earn the Italian marque a reputation for fast and comfortable roadsters, powered by transverse V-twin engines.

Like many Japanese bikes of the time the T500 made fewer friends with its spindly frame and crude suspension, which gave marginal high-speed handling. But the Suzuki was quick, well priced and reliable, and it would remain in production until the mid-'70s, when it was updated with a disc brake and other modifications to create the GT500. The twin also formed the basis of the notoriously fast T500 racer, which was timed at over 150mph (241km/h) but earned the nickname 'Flexi-flyer' because of its scary handling.

The decade's other outstanding Japanese bike was another two-stroke parallel twin: the 350 GTR from Bridgestone, which built bikes as a sideline to its main business of tyre production. Unlike Suzuki's reed-valve roadsters, the GTR used disc-valve induction, which helped give a peak output of 37bhp from its 345cc engine. The GTR was agile, well built, and offered lively acceleration plus a top speed of 95mph (153km/h). Many who rode the Bridgestone following its US launch in 1966 were impressed. Two years later the GTR became available in Europe but shortly afterwards Bridgestone, under pressure from the rival Japanese manufacturers, quit bike production to concentrate on making tyres.

While most British and Japanese firms concentrated on singles or parallel twins during the '60s, Italian manufacturers found alternative ways of combining more than one cylinder. Moto Guzzi came upon its now famous transverse V-twin format by accident, as the layout was first used in a three-wheeled mountain vehicle called the 3x3, produced for the Italian military. Few were built but Guzzi revised the motor and used it to power a 703cc bike called the V7, which was released in 1967 and became popular, largely due to the simplicity and reliability of its softly tuned 40bhp engine.

Guzzi's real impact came with the V7 Special, introduced two years later with an engine enlarged to 757cc to give 45bhp. In other respects the pushrod-operated V-twin motor – with car-style dry clutch, four-speed gearbox and shaft final drive – was virtually unchanged. The Special was built for comfort and practicality, with high bars and a generous dual-seat. Nevertheless the

Easy Riders and Leather Boys

Two films highlighted the very different motorcycle cultures on opposite sides of the Atlantic in the 1960s. The decade's best and most influential movie was *Easy Rider*, the low-budget 1969 classic that portrayed Peter Fonda, Dennis Hopper and Jack Nicholson riding across the USA towards the Mardi Gras in New Orleans on a pair of chopped Harleys.

Easy Rider was built around writer/producer Fonda's take on the way his country's spirit of freedom – represented by his character, Captain America – was being challenged. As well as featuring great bikes, good acting, excellent photography and breathtaking scenery, *Easy Rider* pioneered the use of original recordings in a memorable soundtrack from artists including Steppenwolf and Jimi Hendrix.

By contrast, *The Leather Boys*, released in 1963, was a story of a young rocker in England. Many motorcyclists from London's Ace Café were used as extras, along with their Triumph and Norton bikes. While hardly a cinema classic, *The Leather Boys* had a better plot than 1968's psychedelic offering *Girl on a Motorcycle*, which starred Marianne Faithful and was also released with the title *Naked Under Leather*.

Best bike action in the movies came in *The Great Escape*, in which Steve McQueen memorably attempted to jump a barbed-wire fence on a bike that was supposed to be a captured German army BMW, and was in fact a lightly disguised Triumph Trophy 650. McQueen was a top rider who was picked to compete in America's International Six-Days Trial team. He did most of his own stunt riding

and also appears in the movie in a German uniform, chasing himself! But the big final jump was doubled by McQueen's friend and ISDT team-mate, Bud Ekins.

Guzzi handled well, was good for over 100mph (161km/h), and became highly regarded as an exotic grand tourer well suited to covering big distances in style.

Much of Ducati's production in the 1960s consisted of sohc singles, developed from the Gran Sport 100 of the mid-'50s. Among the best were the sporty models with low, clip-on handlebars, such as the 1962-model Diana 250 and its 1965 successor the Mach 1, which was capable of

Above: Clockwise from top right: The Leather Boys *starred rockers and their British twins; Peter Fonda and Dennis Hopper on their Harleys in* Easy Rider*; Steve McQueen prepares for fence-jumping action in* The Great Escape.

Right: Ducati's 350 Scrambler was launched in 1968 and was popular through the early '70s, especially in Italy and the US. The larger 450cc version of the Scrambler had a desmo engine, but many riders preferred the simpler 350.

Below: Ducati's Apollo prototype was good for over 120mph (193km/h), but the project was abandoned after the giant V4's excessive power and weight led to repeated tyre problems.

Below: MV Agusta enthusiasts were disappointed in 1967 when the Italian marque's first four-cylinder roadster was a curiously styled and poorly performing 600cc tourer.

105mph (169km/h) when tuned with Ducati's accessory hot cam and straight-through pipe. The Mark 3 Desmo, launched in 1969, brought desmodromic valvegear to the street in a quick and fine-handling sportster. One of Ducati's biggest hits was the Scrambler, a stylish dual-purpose single that was launched in 1962, and updated in 1968 with Ducati's new 'wide-case' engine design, in 250cc, 350cc and later 450cc capacities.

Ducati had suffered a very different outcome in 1964 when attempting to develop a 1257cc V4 cruiser, the Apollo. The giant bike was created at the request of the Italian firm's US importer, Berliner Corporation, which was very influential because it sold the majority of the factory's production in the early '60s. Fabio Taglioni's air-cooled sohc 90-degree V4 engine produced a phenomenal 100bhp in its original prototype form, but had to be detuned to 65bhp because no tyres then produced could cope with its power and weight. That meant the Apollo was not viable, so the project was scrapped after only two bikes had been built.

MV finally builds a four

One four-cylinder Italian bike that did reach production was MV Agusta's 600cc tourer, introduced in 1967. Like Ducati, MV built mainly singles, but the Gallarate firm had long considered producing a four developed from its all-conquering racebikes. MV chief Count Domenico Agusta did not want to build a production bike that could be raced, so the four was a shaft-drive touring machine whose modest 52bhp output gave a top speed of barely 100mph (161km/h). Inevitably, given its ugly, angular styling and high price, the four was a flop.

Britain's most notable multi-cylinder machines also had controversial looks. In 1969, BSA Triumph finally released the three-cylinder model whose development had begun four years earlier. Due to pressure from BSA Triumph's American importers, the triple was launched both as the Triumph T150 Trident and BSA Rocket Three. The two bikes shared unusual, angular styling and a 740cc ohv pushrod engine that produced 58bhp and was very much a development of previous twins.

Left: Triumph's T150 Trident was fast and handled well, but its angular styling was unpopular and the British bike's 740cc three-cylinder engine gave many problems.

Triumph T150 Trident (1969)

Engine:	Air-cooled ohv pushrod six-valve triple
Capacity:	740cc (67 x 70mm)
Maximum power:	58bhp @ 7250rpm
Transmission:	Four-speed, chain final drive
Frame:	Steel single downtube
Suspension:	Telescopic front; twin shocks rear
Brakes:	Drum front & rear
Weight:	468lb (212kg)
Top speed:	120mph (193km/h)

The triples scorched to 120mph (193km/h) with a tuneful exhaust howl and acceleration to match any bike on the road. They used different chassis, with the twin-cradle BSA frame angling its motor forward more than the single-downtube Triumph equivalent. Both bikes handled well despite being quite heavy. But the three-cylinder engine was unreliable, and the bikes' specification, including kick-starter, four-speed gearbox and drum brakes front and rear, confirmed they were very much machines of the 1960s. Few potential buyers liked either the slab-sided styling or the Trident's aquamarine colour, and sales were poor.

Unfortunately for BSA Triumph, the triples' limitations were soon highlighted by the arrival of the outstanding motorcycle not merely of the decade, but of the century: Honda's CB750. When it was unveiled in 1968, the world's first mass-produced four-cylinder bike was clearly a uniquely refined roadster. Its 736cc engine produced 67bhp, and incorporated a chain-driven overhead camshaft and an electric starter. By this time many motorcyclists had grown up on smaller Hondas, and were rightly confident that the four would be reliable and oil-tight.

The CB750's twin-cradle frame was competent rather than outstanding. Despite firm suspension the high-handlebarred four could not match the high-speed stability of the British triples. But the Honda was smooth and fast, with a top speed of 120mph (193km/h). It also came with an efficient disc front brake and a very competitive price. The CB750 was a huge success both when launched in the US in mid-1969, and when it became available in Europe the following year. The first 'superbike' had ushered in a thrilling new era of performance and sophistication.

Below: With its reliable four-cylinder engine, electric starter and disc front brake, Honda's CB750 revolutionized motorcycle design.

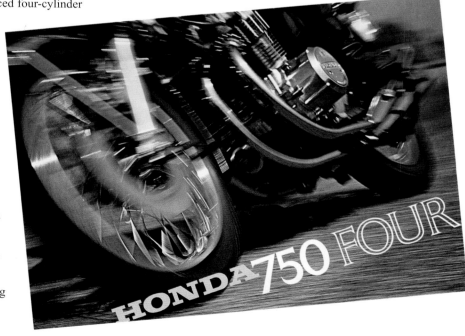

Superbikes
Roar In
1970s

Honda CB750 (1970)

Engine:	Air-cooled sohc eight-valve four
Capacity:	736cc (61 x 63mm)
Maximum power:	67bhp @ 8000rpm
Transmission:	Five-speed, chain final drive
Frame:	Steel twin downtube
Suspension:	Telescopic front; twin shocks rear
Brakes:	Single disc front; drum rear
Weight:	506lb (230kg) wet
Top speed:	123mph (198km/h)

Modern motorcycling began in the 1970s. Honda's spectacular CB750 heralded a decade that saw an explosion of performance, sophistication and mechanical variety, ending with the introduction of huge, six-cylinder machines that would have been unthinkable ten years earlier.

This revolution was led by the Japanese firms, especially Honda and Kawasaki, whose multi-cylinder 'superbikes' and high-performing smaller machines dramatically changed motorcyclists' expectations. The basic format of air-cooled engine, tubular steel frame, telescopic front forks and twin rear shocks remained. The Japanese introduced features such as more powerful engines, electric starters and disc brakes, plus much improved reliability and quality of construction.

Motorcycling was changing fast in more ways than just the machines and their country of origin. Outside the US many motorcyclists still did not own a car, and used bikes for everyday transport. But sidecars had almost disappeared, and the days of the motorcycle as a family vehicle were gone. In place of black leather jackets and waxed-cotton, the new breed of rider wore full-face helmets, colourful jackets, sometimes even racing-style one-piece leathers.

Although Japan quickly rose to become the dominant motorcycle manufacturing nation, by no means all the best bikes came from the East. Italian firms had long been leading producers of small-capacity machines, and turned to superbike manufacture with a variety of engine formats. The Italians could not match Japanese levels of reliability, but offered style plus superior chassis engineering that gave notably better high-speed handling.

Other countries' motorcycle industries struggled to compete. Harley-Davidson and BMW continued with their familiar twin-cylinder engine layouts, their erstwhile dominance by now a distant memory. The '70s would prove disastrous for the British motorcycle industry, recently the world's largest, as most of its remaining great names went out of business.

The bike that highlighted how far behind the British firms were, and did most to kill them off, was the CB750. On pure performance, Honda's four was not significantly ahead of the Trident and Rocket Three triples that Triumph and BSA had launched in 1969. The Japanese and British

Previous page: Honda's stunning six-cylinder CBX1000, launched in 1978, showed how far technology had advanced during the decade.

Below: Honda's CB500 shared much of the larger four's speed and sophistication along with less weight and more agile handling.

Right: The original CB750 was a fast and stylish bike producing a throaty roar from its four pipes, but later versions were slower and quieter.

bikes were closely matched on straight-line speed, and the triples generally handled better than the four, whose high bars revealed Honda's initial focus on the US market.

Where the CB750 scored was by backing up its smooth acceleration, throaty exhaust note and top speed of over 120mph (193km/h) with an unprecedented degree of user-friendliness. The 736cc four had only a single overhead camshaft and two valves per cylinder, unlike Honda's dohc, 16-valve racing fours that preceded it. But it revved reliably to 8000rpm and beyond, didn't leak oil and required far less maintenance than the British pushrod triples.

The CB750 was a huge success, not least in the US where it initially sold for more than the $1400 retail price, and where veteran racer Dick Mann gave Honda a further boost by winning the Daytona 200 on a modified four in 1970. The modern superbike had arrived, and motorcycling had taken a huge leap forward.

Yoshirou Harada, who headed the CB750 design team, had intended to uprate the model with a dohc engine after two or three years. That did not happen, and during the early '70s the four was detuned slightly to reduce emissions. Honda did, however, produce some excellent smaller-capacity fours, starting with the CB500, released in 1971, which combined 50bhp output with a lighter and more manoeuvrable chassis. The CB350, which followed two years later, was more compact and agile still. According to no less an authority than Soichiro Honda, it was the finest, smoothest Honda ever built.

Honda and his long-time business partner Takeo Fujisawa retired on the same day in 1973. The company they had built was by far the world's largest motorcycle firm and had also moved successfully into car production. Unusually, both men had prevented their sons from joining the company, and retained only honorary positions after retirement, rather than becoming directors as was normal in Japan.

Honda had plenty of competition when it came to building light, revvy roadsters, not least from Yamaha. Alongside its XS-2 and later XS650 four-stroke twins, developed from the XS-1, the firm built fast and popular two-strokes. The 350cc YR5, released in 1970, was the biggest of a

Top: Suzuki's T250 Hustler was an updated version of the T20 Super Six two-stroke twin, and was more stylish as well as more powerful.

Above: The CB350 four handled superbly and was reasonably successful in the US, but was too expensive to be sold in many European markets.

Left: Yamaha's YR5 provided plenty of performance thanks to its revvy 350cc twin-cylinder engine and light weight. It was the first in a long line of superb two-stroke middleweights.

Kawasaki H2 (Mach IV) (1972)

Engine:	Air-cooled two-stroke triple
Capacity:	748cc (71 x 63mm)
Maximum power:	74bhp @ 6800rpm
Transmission:	Five-speed, chain final drive
Frame:	Steel twin downtube
Suspension:	Telescopic front; twin shocks rear
Brakes:	Disc front; drum rear
Weight	454lb (206kg)
Top speed:	120mph (193km/h)

Above: Kawasaki's 500cc H1 triple had earned a fearsome reputation for high performance and evil handling by the time this disc-braked model was produced in the early 1970s.

Right: The 748cc H2 triple's raw power, high bars and relatively light weight combined to make the hydraulic steering damper, visible below the tank, a very useful accessory.

family of 250, 200 and 125cc parallel twins. The bigger model produced 36bhp, screamed to over 90mph (145km/h), and weighed just 330lb (150kg). The YR5 and its RD350 successors were fast, fun and brilliant value for money.

The firm that made an even bigger impression for fast and exciting two-strokes was Kawasaki. The line had started in the late 1960s with the H1, also known as the Mach III, a 498cc air-cooled triple that was very popular in the US. Three key figures ensured the Mach III's success there: it made 60bhp, weighed barely 400lb (182kg) and cost under $1000. It could beat almost anything away from the lights, and sold in huge numbers.

Owners soon found that the Mach III's highly tuned motor ran feebly until its power suddenly arrived at 5000rpm, when the bike often leapt forward with enough force to lift its front wheel or overwhelm its relatively simple and insubstantial chassis. Stories of the triple's scary performance earned it a fearsome reputation. In 1972 Kawasaki reacted in the spirit of the times – by launching a bigger, even more powerful follow-up, the 748cc H2, or Mach IV.

The H2 produced 74bhp at 6800rpm, 14bhp more than the smaller triple, and accelerated even harder to a top speed of 120mph (193km/h). Despite a slightly wider power band it was barely more practical than the Mach III. Few owners minded that, as they gripped the high handlebars tight while the H2 streaked to 100mph (161km/h) from a standstill in less than 13 seconds.

Kawasaki had done little to improve the original triple's chassis, and the H2 was also prone to wobbles. It did at least have not only a friction steering damper but also a frame lug for fitment of a hydraulic damper, a useful addition. Many owners were prepared to accept those chassis failings, because for generating speed and excitement, few bikes could even approach the H2.

Suzuki also made an impact with a 750cc two-stroke triple, but the GT750 was a much bigger, softer all-rounder, with bulbous styling and a liquid-cooled engine that produced 67bhp at 6500rpm. The GT750's initials stood for Grand Tourer, and the bike lived up to its name. It was built more for flexibility and comfort than outright performance, and despite a respectable 110mph (177km/h) top speed was best suited to cruising in leisurely fashion as its weight, chassis design and upright riding position did not reward aggressive riding.

Left: Suzuki's original 1972-model GT750J was admired for its water-cooled two-stroke triple engine's smoothness and flexibility, rather than its outright performance. Pink paintwork and drum front brake were quickly revised.

Below: The final GT750B of 1977 was slightly more powerful than the original model, and had a twin disc front brake. The triple earned a loyal following, being known as the 'Water Buffalo' in the US and the 'Kettle' in Britain.

Decline of the two-strokes

Suzuki developed the triple over the years before eventually it became a victim, like other two-strokes including the firm's own quick and capable air-cooled GT550 triple, of tightening emissions regulations, especially in the US. Last in the line was the GT750B of 1977. By then Suzuki had all but abandoned its alternative attempt at a luxury bike, the RE-5, powered by a 497cc liquid-cooled Wankel rotary engine. The 62bhp RE-5, launched in 1975, was smooth and sophisticated; but also far too heavy, complex and expensive.

A rival rotary, Sachs-DKW's air-cooled 294cc W2000, was simpler and lighter – but slower, barely cheaper and equally unsuccessful. By contrast, fellow German firm BMW stuck to its simpler air-cooled boxers, production of which was moved from Munich to Berlin. BMW had introduced its 745cc R75/5 back in 1969, along with smaller R60/5 and R50/5 siblings. These retained the familiar pushrod-operated flat twin engine layout, but abandoned the Earles fork front suspension system used during the 1960s.

The German firm even made an attempt to liven up the appearance of its traditionally black or white roadsters. Other colours were introduced, and in 1972 the R75/5 came in 'toaster tank' form with a smaller, chrome-sided fuel tank. That option did not last long but the shaft-drive twin's smooth cruising ability, stable handling, refinement and reliability made it popular in some markets, despite a high price.

Those attributes also applied to the striking flagship that BMW introduced in 1973. The R90S was the sports version of the standard R90/6 boxer, launched at the same time, and used a tuned, 67bhp version of the new 898cc motor. It featured a steering damper, larger fuel tank, and second front brake disc. The R90S also incorporated the novelty of a headlamp fairing which, along with a striking smoked paint scheme, gave a unique look.

More importantly, the fairing allowed the BMW's rider to make full use of the impressive performance. The German bike's blend of 125mph (201km/h) top speed, relaxed cruising ability, excellent handling, reliability and high-quality finish put it in a league of its own in 1973. The BMW was very expensive, costing twice as much a Honda's CB750 in many markets, and was

BMW R90S (1973)

Engine:	Air-cooled ohv pushrod four-valve flat twin
Capacity:	898cc (90 x 70.6mm)
Maximum power:	67bhp @ 7000rpm
Transmission:	Five-speed, shaft final drive
Frame:	Steel twin downtube
Suspension:	Telescopic front; twin shocks rear
Brakes:	Twin discs front; single disc rear
Weight:	474lb (215kg) wet
Top speed:	125mph (201km/h)

Top right: BMW attempted to give its 1972-model R75/5 more style with a chrome-sided fuel tank, but the 'toaster tank' was not popular with the marque's generally conservative customers.

Above: With its headlamp fairing, smoked paint scheme and blend of high cruising speed and fine handling, the R90S was one of the outstanding superbikes of the 1970s.

outsold by the cheaper R90/6. But as well as being an outstanding bike, it showed the way forward for motorcycle design. The boxer even made a useful racer, as Reg Pridmore's victory in the 1976 US Superbike championship proved.

The era's other most memorable German bike was more expensive still, and very different. Friedel Münch had begun developing his Mammut (Mammoth) back in the mid-'60s, around a 1085cc NSU car engine. During the '70s he built small numbers, refining the design along the way. The fuel-injected version of the Mammut produced over 100bhp, and had unbeatable straight-line performance despite its vast weight. Production would continue until the early 1980s, with capacities of up to 1500cc.

By contrast, Spain's bike manufacturers had concentrated on small-capacity machines since the country's motorcycle industry had been established after the war. While Sanglas stuck to four-stroke singles, Montesa, Derbi, Bultaco and Ossa produced a wide variety of on- and off-road machinery, mostly with two-stroke engines of less than 250cc. The Spanish firms were successful in road-racing, with Ossa's Santiago Herrero and Derbi's Angel Nieto prominent.

The best known Spanish roadster was Bultaco's Metralla, a two-stroke single that was repeatedly updated through the 1960s and 1970s. But the Spanish firms, whose home market had been protected by import restrictions, struggled in the more competitive climate that followed General Franco's death in 1975. By the end of the decade, they would be crippled by falling sales and workers' disputes. That would leave them vulnerable to take-over by the Japanese giants, especially Honda and Yamaha, which were increasingly adopting a policy of 'globalization' by establishing factories all over the world.

Kawasaki continued to concentrate mainly on large capacity motorcycles, but the other three Japanese firms built a huge variety of small bikes and scooters. Most were forgettable but one that stood out was Yamaha's popular FS1-E, a 49cc moped that was introduced in Britain in 1973, after 16-year-olds had been restricted to machines with 'pedal assistance'. Once its pedals were locked in place, the 'Fizzy' provided its teenage rider with a top speed of over 40mph (64km/h) and excitement out of all proportion to the bike's capacity. Rival 'Sixteener Specials' included Honda's SS50, Suzuki's AP50 and Italian flyers from Garelli and Fantic.

Trail bike heritage

Yamaha's success with small-capacity dual-purpose bikes dated back to the '60s, and included the early-'70s DT175 two-stroke on which many people had experienced trail riding for the first time. The 1977-model XT500, whose 30bhp sohc four-stroke single engine gave generous amounts of low-rev torque, initiated a new era of larger dual-purpose motorcycles. Two years later it faced new competition from Honda's XL500S, developed from the XR500 enduro single.

Meanwhile the British industry, which had turned from the single to the parallel twin, had been struggling to modernize that engine layout. BSA Triumph had been in deep financial trouble from the start of the decade, and had needed its redesigned 1971 twins to be a big success. But the BSA Lightning 650 and Triumph Bonneville 650 were a disaster. Developed at the expensive Umberslade Hall research and development facility, they had new frames that gave a much higher seat, and were so unpopular that the chassis had to be hastily redesigned.

The firm hit further problems with another twin, the Edward Turner-designed dohc 350 that was due to be sold as the BSA Fury and Triumph Bandit. Turner's prototype ran so poorly that it was abandoned. The racing triples campaigned successfully in Formula 750 races at Daytona and elsewhere showed that British bikes could still be competitive, but their days were numbered. At the end of 1971, BSA announced that the group had lost £8 million during the year. Chairman Eric Turner resigned, and the competition department was closed.

After a further big loss the following year, the BSA/Triumph group was merged with Norton Villiers to form Norton Villiers Triumph. The aim was to create a stronger company backed by government finance, but NVT ran into problems almost immediately when attempting to rationalize by moving Triumph production from its traditional Meriden factory to BSA's old Birmingham plant, which built Trident engines. The Triumph workers objected and occupied the Meriden factory for 18 months, delaying Trident production because components were kept there.

Triumph did at least manage to produce one more outstanding bike in the X-75 Hurricane, an eye-catching version of the 750cc triple that was conceived by the firm's US agent and designed

Above left: This 1978-model Bultaco Metralla 250 GTS was the last of the Spanish firm's simple but effective Metralla two-stroke singles.

Above: Future world champion Barry Sheene discusses a Bultaco TSS350 with his father Frank and the marque's boss, Don Paco Bulto.

Below: This BSA 650 Lightning was built in 1971, the first year of the controversial 'oil-in-frame' twins with their much taller seats.

Kawasaki Z1 (1973)

Engine:	Air-cooled dohc eight-valve four
Capacity:	903cc (66 x 66mm)
Maximum power:	82bhp @ 8500rpm
Transmission:	Five-speed, chain final drive
Frame:	Steel twin downtube
Suspension:	Telescopic front; twin shocks rear
Brakes:	Single disc front; drum rear
Weight:	542lb (246kg) wet
Top speed:	132mph (212km/h)

Above and top right: Triumph's X-75 Hurricane was a uniquely stylish version of the triple.

Below: As well as a powerful four-cylinder engine, the Z1 boasted very attractive looks.

in the States by Craig Vetter, a custom bike builder and fairing manufacturer. With its wasp-waisted tank-seat unit, kicked-out front forks and a trio of silencers on its right side, the Hurricane looked stunning. As arguably the first 'factory custom' it made a lasting impression, although fewer than 1200 were built.

There was only one multi-cylinder machine at the top of most motorcycle enthusiast's wish list in 1973, however. Kawasaki's Z1 blasted onto the scene, its 903cc dohc four-cylinder engine producing 82bhp – fully 15bhp more than Honda's CB750. That was enough to give the Kawasaki a top speed of over 130mph (209km/h), making it a clear 10mph (16km/h) faster than any other bike on the road. The eight-valve motor was also smooth, flexible and outstandingly reliable, and earned a reputation for being bulletproof even when tuned.

The Z1 was also very good-looking, with rounded lines and a compact rear duck-tail that neatly offset the muscular air-cooled engine. But the Kawasaki's combination of power and 542lb (246kg) of weight was at times too much for its relatively ordinary chassis. To combat high-speed instability many owners fitted steering dampers and aftermarket rear shock units, built by specialists such as Marzocchi of Italy.

Such was the Z1's performance lead that Kawasaki did little to change it, merely altering cosmetic and minor details before adding a second front brake disc in 1976, when the bike was renamed the Z900. By that time it had become known as the King, and had earned Kawasaki a lasting reputation for power and strength.

Harley-Davidson was also laying the foundations of a dynasty of its own, in a very different way. In 1971, the US firm's styling chief, Willie G. Davidson, had created the Super Glide, using a collection of styling cues including a large 'boat-tail' rear end. The Super Glide was not a particularly strong seller, but it earned Harley plenty of attention, and provided a platform for future models.

Meanwhile, Milwaukee's V-twins were attracting a new breed of custom builders, led by Arlen Ness. The 'Bay Area' style (Ness and others were based around San Francisco) was longer and lower than the traditional chopper look. Radical customs such as Ness's Accel Bike and Strictly Business inspired many Harley owners to modify their own bikes, using components from both Milwaukee and aftermarket specialists.

Meanwhile Italian manufacturers were establishing their own distinctive styles and engine formats. Laverda, based at Breganze in north-eastern Italy, had begun producing parallel twins in the late 1960s, in 654cc and then 744cc capacities. The most famous twin was the SFC, introduced in 1971. Designed primarily for endurance racing and painted orange, it featured a half-fairing, clip-on bars, rearset footrests and single seat. The SFC's tuned, sohc engine produced 70bhp, enough for a top speed of 125mph (201km/h). The SFC was produced in small numbers until 1976, gaining power and an uprated chassis along the way.

Laverda also launched the format for which it would become best known when in 1973 an additional cylinder was added, creating the 981cc triple that was initially called simply the 3C. The bigger dohc motor produced a claimed 80bhp, and the 3C combined simple but attractive styling with a competent chassis. Relatively few were exported but the 135mph (217km/h) triple was already making an impression.

Italy's most famous racing marque remained MV Agusta, which had dominated 500cc grand prix racing for more than a decade, without releasing a roadgoing replica. Finally MV's autocratic boss Count Domenico Agusta relented, and in 1972 the firm introduced the 750 Sport, a stylish roadburner with a 743cc dohc four-cylinder engine and high quality chassis.

Like the racebikes, the Sport used gears to drive its overhead camshafts, though it also retained the tourer's shaft final drive, reportedly because Count Agusta did not want owners to race it. The tuned motor produced 65bhp, enough for a top speed of 115mph (185km/h) plus impressive acceleration. 'In a straight drag with a Kawasaki Z1 it lost only a few yards up to 100mph [161km/h],' reported British magazine *Bike*.

Handling was generally good, too, although the MV's heavy drive shaft gave the rear suspension a difficult time. Early models had a Grimeca front drum brake, which was replaced by twin discs in 1973. The exotic Sport could be ordered with a full- or half-fairing, or a flyscreen. But despite its high price the bike cost so much to make that it was not profitable for MV, which was also making little money on its small-capacity singles.

Above: The Z1's handling did not match the performance of its magnificent 82bhp engine, leading to much work for aftermarket frame specialists and shock absorber manufacturers.

Above: Harley's Super Glide featured an unusual 'boat-tail' rear end that was removed by many dealers, but the eye-catching V-twin played an important part in the firm's revival.

Left: Laverda's raw and single-minded 750 SFC parallel twin was a street-legal production racer, and was painted orange to help factory lap-scorers spot it during an endurance race.

MV Agusta 750 Sport (1973)	
Engine:	Air-cooled dohc eight-valve four
Capacity:	743cc (65 x 56mm)
Maximum power:	65bhp at 7900rpm
Transmission:	Five-speed, shaft final drive
Frame:	Steel twin downtube
Suspension:	Telescopic front; twin shocks rear
Brakes:	Twin discs front; drum rear
Weight:	506lb (230kg) dry
Top speed:	115mph (185km/h)

Above right: MV Agusta's 750 Sport was the race-replica four the Italian firm's fans had hoped for, although very few could afford one.

Below: Ducati's Desmo 250 produced only 30bhp but had styling and handling in abundance.

Opposite below left: The 900SS provided storming performance and superb handling.

Opposite below right: British ace Paul Smart's victory in the prestigious Imola 200 race in 1972 gave the Bologna factory a huge boost.

Ducati also progressed from building singles to superbikes, starting when chief engineer Fabio Taglioni combined a pair of cylinders at 90 degrees to form a V-twin. The basic single-pot engine design had been uprated over the years, notably when being given desmodromic valvegear in 1969. In 1973 the Desmo range of 250, 350 and 450cc singles was restyled and given a distinctive yellow finish by Leopoldo Tartarini, the former Ducati works racer who would later found Italjet.

Taglioni's first V-twin was the 750GT, launched in 1971. Its 748cc sohc engine used conventional valve springs, produced 50bhp, and was a softly tuned all-rounder. Two years later came the 750 Sport, which provided extra performance from a hotted-up, 56bhp motor. The Sport was slim, light and racy, with clip-on handlebars, rearset footrests, single seat and bright yellow paintwork. With a top speed of 125mph (201km/h) it was fast enough to show a clean pair of Conti pipes to most rival roadsters.

Ducati's most significant event was its victory in the prestigious 1972 Imola 200-mile (322km) race. Factory riders Paul Smart and Bruno Spagiarri finished first and second on rapid 750cc V-twins fitted with desmo valvegear. Ducati then produced a roadgoing replica, which was popular so more were built, named the 750 Super Sport instead of Imola Replica as before. The sleek half-faired roadster was silver, like the fully-faired racer, and featured a tuned 748cc desmo motor. It provided a unique blend of raw performance, stable handling and minimalist style.

Ducati built only about 200 units of the 750SS, but in 1975 used it as the basis of the bike for which the firm would become best known: the 900SS. This was powered by an enlarged 864cc version of the bevel-drive desmo V-twin, which produced 79bhp. Like the smaller model the 900SS was a single-minded street racer, with unfiltered 40mm Dell'Orto carbs, booming Conti pipes, half-fairing, clip-on bars, rearsets, single seat, firm suspension and twin Brembo front discs. In many respects it was the quintessential Italian superbike.

The uncompromising 900SS had no electric starter or anything else that was not needed for pure performance. It thundered to a top speed of 135mph (217km/h), and handled superbly thanks to a combination of rigid chassis, relatively light weight, long wheelbase and taut suspension. Although expensive, demanding of maintenance and too extreme for many riders, it had few rivals as a pure-bred sporting superbike for road or production racing use.

Ducati's softer V-twin

Ducati introduced another significant model in 1975 with the more versatile 860GT. Angular styling by car designer Giorgetto Giugiario was matched with a softly tuned motor that produced 70bhp. High handlebars did little to boost handling or high-speed comfort. But the following year's 860GTS, featuring lower bars, an electric starter and second front brake disc, was a capable sports-tourer with plenty of character.

Ducati was not the only Bologna-based firm producing V-twins. Alfonso Morini had begun making bikes under the name MM in the 1920s, and had ridden one to a class win in the 1927 Italian Grand Prix. After the war he built single-cylinder roadsters and some successful racers under his own name. In 1974, Moto Morini introduced a pair of roadsters, the 3¹/₂ Strada and 3¹/₂ Sport, powered by an air-cooled, 72-degree pushrod V-twin engine.

The standard Strada model's raised handlebars and dual-seat made for a practical all-rounder. But it was the stylish Sport, with its low bars and humped seat, that attracted more attention. Higher compression and a hotter camshaft provided extra power, and little V-twin's 39bhp output gave a top speed of just over 100mph (161km/h). With firm suspension and just 337lb (153kg) of weight the Morini handled superbly, too. Although impractical and too expensive to sell in large numbers, it earned a loyal following.

The Italian firm best known for long-distance bikes was Moto Guzzi, which found a profitable niche in 1971 with a US export version of its 757cc V7 Special. The California featured higher bars plus the screen and panniers with which the Special was commonly fitted, and was well received. For 1972 Guzzi enlarged its pushrod V-twin engine to 844cc, added a five-speed gearbox and made the shaft-driven California more freely available, confirming the arrival of a tourer that would be a mainstay of the range for decades to come.

In 1971 Guzzi had also introduced an important high-performance model, the V7 Sport. This used a more compact and powerful version of the firm's transverse V-twin engine, with capacity reduced slightly to 748cc to allow entry in 750cc races. Peak output was rated at 52bhp, roughly

Above: *Ducati's 1973-model 750 Sport did not have desmodromic valvegear, but the V-twin's performance and racy look made it popular.*

Ducati 900SS (1975)

Engine:	Air-cooled sohc four-valve 90-degree V-twin
Capacity:	864cc (86 x 74.4mm)
Maximum power:	79bhp at 7000rpm
Transmission:	Five-speed, chain final drive
Frame:	Steel ladder
Suspension:	Telescopic front; twin shocks rear
Brakes:	Twin discs front; single disc rear
Weight:	414lb (188kg) wet
Top speed:	135mph (217km/h)

Right: Ducati launched its sports-touring V-twin
line in 1975 with the GT860. Its softly tuned 864cc
engine was impressively flexible, but the angular
GT's performance was marred by its exposed
riding position, marginal high-speed stability and
lack of an electric starter – though one could be
ordered as an accessory.

Below: A racy riding position, bold styling and
superb handling helped earn Moto Morini's 3¹/₂
Sport many admirers, even though the little 344cc
V-twin produced a mere 39bhp.

Opposite below: Moto Guzzi's original Le Mans
850 offered a unique blend of styling, V-twin
performance and stable handling.

70bhp at the crankshaft. An alternator on the front of the crank allowed engineer Lino Tonti to design a lower frame with top rails between the cylinders, where the old dynamo had been.

The V7 Sport was an elegant bike, with lime-green paintwork plus, on the first 150 units, a red frame. Its motor required revving hard, and responded with smooth cruising and 125mph (201km/h) top speed. The Sport was stable, and cornered well despite the heavy shaft-drive system. For 1974 it was replaced by the 750S, featuring twin front discs instead of the Sport's twin-leading-shoe drum. Then came the 750S3 which, like the 850cc T3 tourer introduced at the same time, also featured a rear disc. Guzzi's linked system used the handlebar lever to work one front disc, with the foot pedal operating the other front plus the rear disc, and was highly rated by most riders who tried it.

Guzzi's most famous model followed in 1976, when the 750S3 was enlarged to 844cc and revamped to create the 850 Le Mans. With its small headlamp fairing, distinctive lipped seat and its transverse V-twin engine's cylinders on display, the Le Mans was arguably the most beautiful of the great Italian superbikes of the 1970s. Increased compression ratio, unfiltered 36mm Dell'Orto carbs and a free-breathing exhaust gave a peak output of 80bhp, 8bhp up on the 750S, plus stronger midrange.

Top speed was 130mph (209km/h), and the Le Mans' fairing and racy riding position meant the performance was very usable. Firm suspension helped give stable handling, and ensured the Le Mans' status as one of the most desirable machines on the road. But Alejandro de Tomaso, the Argentinean car baron who had bought both Guzzi and Benelli in the early '70s, was reluctant to invest in the firm, and the Le Mans' appeal gradually faded.

The most powerful and fastest of the era's great Italian superbikes was Laverda's Jota. This was a tuned version of the 3CL triple, created by Slater Brothers, the firm's British importer. Laverda had produced the 3CL in 1976 by modifying the 3C with cast wheels, triple discs and a tail fairing. Brothers Roger and Richard Slater tuned its 981cc dohc engine with high-compression pistons, factory endurance race cams and a free-breathing exhaust. They also added rearset footrests and a humped seat.

Laverda's snarling triple

The result was the Jota: a snarling, 90bhp brute that ran roughly below 4000rpm, then came alive with vicious acceleration and a soulful exhaust bellow as it charged towards a 140mph (225km/h) top speed that made it the world's fastest roadster in 1976. Handling was good provided the rider was prepared to manhandle the big, heavy triple. One who did was Slaters' racer Pete Davies, who dominated the British production series. Although the tuned triple was officially a UK-only model, it was sold elsewhere. When Laverda enlarged the motor to 1116cc to create the 1200 model in 1978, Slaters again produced a tuned version, the Mirage. The name was later used by Laverda for the standard 1200.

Like Laverda, Benelli entered the big-bike market with a parallel twin, the Tornado 650, before moving on to multi-cylinder superbikes. The Tornado, which entered production in 1971, was a torquey but unexceptional roadster. It was followed three years later by the more glamorous 750 Sei, powered by motorcycling's first transverse six-cylinder engine.

Ironically, the Sei (Italian for Six) was not particularly fast, as its softly-tuned, 71bhp sohc engine meant the broad Benelli ran out of speed at 115mph (185km/h). The 748cc engine, which resembled one-and-a-half Honda CB500 units, was flexible and smooth, if not particularly reliable. For a bike that weighed 484lb (220kg) the Sei handled well, and made a pleasant all-rounder. But that wasn't enough to make it popular given the inevitably high price. The same was true of Benelli's four-cylinder models, the 500 Quattro and the diminutive 254, whose capacity was just 231cc.

Another glamorous superbike whose performance didn't live up to its price was Harley-Davidson's 1977-model XLCR1000 Café Racer, a big, black V-twin with a headlamp fairing and plenty of aggressive attitude. Such a sporty-looking V-twin was a departure for Harley, although the American firm had a road-racing pedigree of sorts. Following parent group AMF's purchase of Aermacchi, Italian ace Walter Villa had won four 250 and 350cc world titles on Harley-badged two-stroke twins from the former Aermacchi factory at Varese in northern Italy. Harley's roadgoing range also included small-capacity two-strokes from the same source.

Top: The first high-performance Guzzi was the 750 Sport, launched in 1971 with adjustable bars, 70bhp output and big front drum brake.

Above: Guzzi's 1975-model 750 S3 was notable for its striking paintwork and the linked triple disc brake system that gave the bike its name.

Moto Guzzi Le Mans 850 (1976)

Engine:	Air-cooled ohv pushrod four-valve 90-degree transverse V-twin
Capacity:	844cc (83 x 78mm)
Maximum power:	80bhp @ 7300rpm
Transmission:	Five-speed, shaft final drive
Frame:	Steel spine
Suspension:	Telescopic front; twin shocks rear
Brakes:	Twin discs front; single disc rear (linked system)
Weight:	476lb (216kg) wet
Top speed:	130mph (209km/h)

Laverda Jota (1976)

Engine:	Air-cooled dohc six-valve triple
Capacity:	981cc (75 x 74mm)
Maximum power:	90bhp at 8000rpm
Transmission:	Five-speed, chain final drive
Frame:	Steel twin downtube
Suspension:	Telescopic front; twin shocks rear
Brakes:	Twin discs front; single disc rear
Weight:	521lb (236kg) wet
Top speed:	140mph (225km/h)

Above: Laverda's most famous models, the 1200cc Mirage (left) and 1000cc Jota, began their existence as standard triples that were tuned by the Italian firm's British importer.

Right: Benelli's 650 Tornado parallel twin was launched in 1971, with this 750S following two years later, featuring a new front brake. Many parts were rubber-mounted against vibration.

The XLCR was built in Milwaukee and was powered by the 998cc pushrod-operated V-twin engine from the Sportster, unchanged except for black finish and a siamesed exhaust that maintained its 61bhp peak output. A new frame, box-section swingarm, alloy wheels and triple discs gave a sporty specification. The Café Racer's fairing and flat bars made it a useful bike for highway cruising, but its high-rev vibration, 115mph (185km/h) top speed and four-speed gearbox confirmed that this was no sports bike, and sales were poor.

Harley had proved it could build a rapid V-twin with the XR750 dirt-track racer. Introduced unsuccessfully in 1970, the XR was revamped with a new aluminium engine two years later, and took Mark Brelsford to the first of the bike's many championships, which included a hat-trick for Jay Springsteen from 1976-78. Another XR750-mounted star was Evel Knievel, the stunt rider

who became a legend for the number of cars and buses he jumped over, and for the number of bones he broke.

Harley's most significant roadster was the laid-back Low Rider, launched in 1977. Developed relatively inexpensively using parts from several other models, the Low Rider derived a new look from its short suspension, long wheelbase and low, stepped seat. The bike was harshly suspended, but it had plenty of character and appealed to many Harley enthusiasts, for whom style was far more important than performance.

Harley was still struggling financially but the situation was even worse in Britain, where the recently formed Norton Villiers Triumph group, handicapped by the Meriden workers' sit-in, had lost several million pounds in 1974. There was one final fling for Triumph, in the following year's T160 Trident, which combined handsome new styling with significant improvements over the T150 triple. The 740cc motor's peak output was unchanged, but it finally gained an electric starter and left-foot gearchange.

The motor was angled forward in a new frame that improved handling and ground clearance, in conjunction with new forks and a longer swingarm. The Trident was heavy, at over 500lb (227kg), but cornered well. It was also fast, with a 125mph (201km/h) top speed plus stirring top-end acceleration. Despite a high price and some unreliability, it was popular, with roughly 7000 being sold in 1975.

NVT advertised the Trident alongside Norton's Commando, highlighting the 'Power Choice' between three or two cylinders. In 1973 the Commando motor had been enlarged to 830cc, adding to its already strong mid-range. But although both bikes had their supporters, the end was approaching for NVT. By late 1975 the group was in receivership, the Small Heath factory was about to be closed, and NVT had turned its attention to the humble Easy Rider moped, assembled using parts bought from abroad.

Ironically the only NVT factory still building big bikes was the Triumph plant at Meriden, where the much publicized workers' sit-in had led in 1975 to the creation of the Meriden Co-operative, backed by government subsidies. Triumph had enlarged its 649cc parallel twin engine to 744cc, creating the T140 Bonneville, which had more mid-range torque, albeit with more

Above: The Benelli 750 Sei's six shiny exhaust pipes emphasized its unique engine layout, but the softly tuned Italian multi lacked the power and speed to justify its inevitably high price.

Below left and right: Harley's XLCR Café Racer had the long, low look of a racy V-twin sports machine, but its modest 61bhp output and heavy handling told a different story.

Racing's Two-stroke Takeover

In the early '70s, MV Agusta's domination of 500cc grand prix racing came under increasing threat from two-strokes, led by Yamaha. The Italian factory's most successful rider was Giacomo Agostini, who won seven consecutive 500cc titles on the roaring red 'Gallarate fire engines' before Britain's Phil Read took over, retaining the championship for MV in 1973 and '74. Ironically it was Italian idol Agostini who became the first two-stroke

500cc champion, when he won on a straight-four Yamaha in 1975.

MV, its 17-year winning streak ended, had no answer to the more powerful two-strokes, and Barry Sheene won the next two championships on a square-four RG500 Suzuki. Yamaha's Kenny Roberts then began a US takeover of grand prix racing when he arrived in 1978 to win the first of three consecutive titles, pioneering a power-sliding riding style adapted from dirt-track racing.

Roberts also won many races on arguably the most famous two-stroke of all, Yamaha's TZ750. The straight-four TZ, whose engine was essentially a pair of TZ350 twins side-by-side, won many big races including the Daytona 200, and in 1977 it was ridden to the first Formula 750 world championship by Canadian Steve Baker.

Ironically the TZ's most memorable victory was not a road-race, but Roberts' dirt-track

triumph at the Indianapolis Mile in 1975. Yamaha's four-stroke twin was uncompetitive against Harley-Davidson's XR750, so 'King Kenny' rode a bike built around the 120bhp two-stroke four, fitted with a button to kill the power from one cylinder in turns. Roberts mastered the vicious bike to score a remarkable last lap win, after which the TZ dirt-tracker was promptly banned for being too fast and dangerous. Even the iron-hard Roberts didn't complain.

Above: Giacomo Agostini won 13 world titles for MV, then two more on two-stroke Yamahas.

Top right: Kenny Roberts rode the fearsome TZ750 to a famous victory before it was banned.

Below: Harley's XR750 V-twin dominated US dirt-track racing for much of the 1970s.

vibration too. The Co-op began building the Bonneville and its single-carb derivative the TR7 Tiger, both of which already traded on retro appeal.

This was emphasized by the success of the 1977-model Silver Jubilee Bonneville, built to celebrate Queen Elizabeth II's 25 years on the throne. The Jubilee combined an unchanged 52bhp motor and near-standard chassis with silver paintwork, extra chrome and a blue seat. Like the standard Bonnie it vibrated at high revs and was less sophisticated and reliable than Japanese rivals. It was also light, handled well and had lively performance, best used well short of the 110mph (177km/h) top speed. The Co-op sold more than the planned 2000 units before the weakening US dollar caused a slump in that vital market. Debts rose, and more workers were laid off.

Low-volume production

By this time the rest of the British industry's output was limited to machines built by hand in small numbers, such as the Silk 700S, a 653cc two-stroke parallel twin. The bike's creator, Derbyshire-based George Silk, was a Scott enthusiast, and his 47bhp liquid-cooled 700S engine was a development of the Scott unit. The Silk handled well, thanks to a rigid Spondon Engineering frame and good suspension, but was expensive and ran poorly at low speed. More than 100 were built but the 700S would not survive the decade.

An even more ambitious British project was the Quasar, the futuristic roofed machine intended to provide its rider with the weather protection and comfort of a car. Designer Malcolm Newell's wedge-shaped glass-fibre bodywork enclosed a tubular steel frame. The Quasar's 848cc

liquid-cooled four-cylinder engine came from a Reliant three-wheeler. Although it produced only 40bhp, the excellent aerodynamics allowed 90mph (144km/h) cruising. But at £3500 in 1976 the Quasar cost twice as much as a Japanese superbike, and fewer than 20 were built.

The design of more conventional touring bikes had by this time taken a step forward with the launch in 1977 of BMW's R100RS, which combined a new 980cc flat twin engine with a full fairing that provided unprecedented weather protection. The pushrod boxer motor's 70bhp output gave a top speed of over 120mph (193km/h), but the BMW's key asset was its rider's ability to use that performance for long distances with minimal fatigue. Stable handling, optional panniers and shaft final drive added to the R100RS's long-distance ability. A year later BMW followed it with the R100RT, whose taller fairing, more upright riding position and larger dual-seat made for an even more relaxed and comfortable ride.

Ironically a model that would eventually have far more impact on the motorcycle touring world had arrived in 1975 to a very mixed reception. Honda's GL1000 Gold Wing was not specifically a tourer; it was a giant, unfaired bike powered by a liquid-cooled, 999cc sohc flat four

Above: The futuristic and streamlined Quasar, built in England's West Country, offered effortless cruising and a reclined, fully enclosed riding position. But it was too unusual and expensive to be a commercial success.

Left: By 1977 Triumph's T140 Bonneville was notable more for its character than for the performance of its 744cc parallel twin engine. That year's Silver Jubilee special edition was a success for the Meriden factory co-operative.

Right: BMW's R100RS brought a new dimension to long-distance riding in 1977 with its efficient and streamlined full fairing, which allowed the 980cc boxer engine's performance to be used in unprecedented comfort.

Above: Honda's CX500 was built for the US market with high bars, but in Europe the efficient shaft-drive V-twin was regarded as a long-distance workhorse, and was the most popular choice of city dispatch riders.

Right: The R100RT tourer featured higher handlebars and a taller, less streamlined fairing than its BMW stablemate the R100RS, giving a more upright riding position. Many owners also fitted accessory hard panniers.

engine that made 80bhp. The Wing had bulbous styling, a dummy fuel tank (fuel lived under the seat), and weighed a massive 639lb (290kg) with fuel. It was smooth, flexible, and softly sprung. Its specification included shaft final drive and Japan's first triple disc brake system.

Some motorcyclists in Europe, especially, disliked the Gold Wing, notably the tester at *Bike* magazine, which slated the bike under the headline: 'Two Wheeled Motor Car'. The GL1000 certainly had faults, as its upright, exposed riding position prevented the engine performance from being exploited, and the bike's weight inevitably gave soggy handling. As a long-distance machine the Wing was compromised by its hard seat and small fuel tank.

But the response was positive in the US, where many older riders appreciated the Gold Wing's assets: power, flexibility, smoothness, and effortless cruising ability when heavily loaded. This it

Honda GL1000 Gold Wing (1975)	
Engine:	Liquid-cooled sohc eight-valve flat four
Capacity:	999cc (72 x 61.4mm)
Maximum power:	80bhp at 7500rpm
Transmission:	Five-speed, shaft final drive
Frame:	Steel twin cradle
Suspension:	Telescopic front; twin shocks rear
Brakes:	Twin discs front; single disc rear
Weight:	639lb (290kg) wet
Top speed:	125mph (201km/h)

often was, because many owners added accessories, from fairings and luggage to extra chrome and lights. Honda was slow to produce a fully equipped Wing, so the accessory makers also loved the model. By the end of the decade, more than 200,000 had been sold and the cult of the Gold Wing was firmly established.

Another of Honda's most popular bikes was the contrastingly compact CB400F, whose lean good looks and sweet-running four-cylinder engine made an attractive combination on its introduction in 1975. The 408cc sohc four's flat handlebars and rearset footrests gave a sporty riding position, and the four-into-one exhaust system's four downpipes swept across the engine in eye-catching fashion.

The four's maximum output of 37bhp made it competitive with rival two-strokes such as Suzuki's GT380 triple and Yamaha's RD400 twin, giving a top speed of 100mph (161km/h) provided the rider crouched down low. Good fuel economy, reliability, agile handling and a keen price made the CB400F popular in Europe, though less so in the US. Many riders were disappointed when in 1977 Honda replaced it with the CB400T, a twin that was slightly faster and cheaper, but lacked the four's character and style.

Honda developed its range of fours fairly successfully during the '70s, without reproducing the excitement or all-conquering performance of the original CB750. That model was taken in two directions, the sporty CB750F and a bulkier, four-piped touring model, the CB750K. Honda's best effort came in the 1977 with the CB750F2. This was a revamped version of the previous year's 750F1, featuring tuned, 73bhp engine, strengthened frame, new suspension, innovative alloy-rimmed 'Comstar' wheels, flat bars and a four-into-one pipe. It was good for 120mph (193km/h) and handled well, but Honda's sohc 750cc line had been allowed to continue for too long, and had lost its performance lead.

That was clear from the simultaneous arrival of hot new rivals from each of the other Japanese manufacturers. Kawasaki's Z650 gave away almost 100cc to the F2, but the dohc four produced 64bhp and was good-looking and robust. Kawasaki's US advertising screamed that 'Right out of the crate it will out-perform any 750 in the world!' It wasn't quite true, but the Z650 still sold well.

Above left: The original GL1000 Gold Wing was a large but relatively normal looking unfaired roadster. Its bulbous dummy tank contained electrical components, a kickstart lever and some storage space; fuel lived under the seat.

Below: Honda's CB400F combined a revvy, reliable four-cylinder engine with fine handling and a competitive price. But arguably its best feature was the unique exhaust system, with four downpipes curving across the motor.

Yamaha's troubled triple

Yamaha's three-cylinder XS750 was the firm's first four-stroke superbike, and looked impressive with its 747cc dohc engine, featuring 64bhp output and shaft final drive. Initial reports were favourable. The Yamaha was smooth, flexible and powerful, with a top speed of 120mph (193km/h) and effortless cruising ability. It also handled well and was comfortable. But the promise turned to disappointment when the engine proved unreliable, and sales did not recover despite numerous modifications and the arrival of the more powerful XS850 in 1980.

Suzuki had no such problems with the GS750 four that was launched in 1977, and which shared the reliability of the Kawasaki Z900 from which its dohc engine design was clearly derived. The 748cc Suzuki unit produced 68bhp, making it the most powerful 750 on the market, and the GS had a chassis to match, with a strong twin-downtube frame and excellent suspension. Top speed was over 120mph (193km/h); handling was precise and stable. The GS750 was an outstanding machine that instantly established Suzuki's four-stroke credentials, as did the capable GS550 four that was introduced at the same time.

Suzuki scored again a year later with the GS1000. Like the smaller GS models, the 997cc newcomer was an air-cooled dohc four with pleasant but unimaginative styling. The difference this time was that the GS1000's maximum output of 87bhp was 4bhp up on Kawasaki's rival Z1000, making the GS the world's most powerful four-cylinder superbike.

The GS1000's frame was a stronger version of the GS750's, and the bigger bike also featured air-assisted forks, damping-adjustable shocks and a second front brake disc. The Suzuki stormed to a top speed of 135mph (217km/h), and was reasonably smooth and very reliable. Equally importantly the GS's handling was notably superior to that of its rivals. Here at last was an open-class Japanese superbike that could be ridden hard without weaving or wobbling. Suzuki followed it with the attractive, bikini-faired GS1000S, plus a pair of shaft-drive touring models, the GS850 and GS1000G.

Yamaha's first four-cylinder superbike, the XS1100, also came with shaft final drive. The 'Excess Eleven', introduced in 1978, was a huge machine whose 1101cc dohc engine produced an

Above: Kawasaki's Z650 four resembled the Z1000 in styling and engine layout. The smaller model's 110mph (177km/h) performance and competitive price made it a hit.

Right: Yamaha's XS750 triple promised much with its powerful and smooth-running three-cylinder engine, but was hit by unreliability of parts including its ignition and primary chain.

Suzuki GS1000 (1978)	
Engine:	Air-cooled dohc eight-valve four
Capacity:	997cc (70 x 64.8mm)
Maximum power:	87bhp @ 8000rpm
Transmission:	Five-speed, chain final drive
Frame:	Steel twin downtube
Suspension:	Telescopic front; twin shocks rear
Brakes:	Twin discs front; disc rear
Weight:	533lb (242kg) wet
Top speed:	135mph (217km/h)

impressive 95bhp, and which weighed more than 600lb (272kg) when its big fuel tank was full. The Yamaha had unbeatable low-rev acceleration and a top speed of over 130mph (209km/h), but it was built for distance rather than speed, with soft suspension and a big seat.

Attempts to make full use of the XS's engine performance inevitably ended in disappointment, as the big four's power and weight overwhelmed its chassis, producing wobbles. Predictably the Yamaha flopped in Europe, but it was more popular in the US, where its standard-fitment fairing mounts were utilized by many touring riders. Yamaha even produced a fully-faired Martini version with an innovative full fairing whose top section turned with the handlebars.

Kawasaki's Z1000, which had succeeded the Z900 and featured a bored-out, 1015cc engine, was joined in 1978 by the sportier Z1-R. This featured angular styling, silver-blue paintwork and a matching bikini fairing. Bigger carbs and a four-into-one exhaust system increased maximum output to a claimed 90bhp, and the chassis was modified with a strengthened frame and new suspension. The Z1-R was stylish and good for 130mph (209km/h) but its handlebar-mounted fairing hindered high-speed stability, and firm shocks gave an uncomfortable ride. Even so, this was the fastest and best big Kawasaki so far.

Honda's most successful newcomer of 1978 was a very different bike: the CX500, a plump, liquid-cooled transverse V-twin with shaft final drive. Its 50bhp pushrod engine allowed comfortable 80mph (129km/h) cruising and was very robust once some early mechanical problems had been cured. That plus good brakes and fuel economy made the 'plastic maggot' popular with dispatch riders, who tolerated its curious styling and heavy handling.

The Japanese twin that made the biggest impact in the US was Yamaha's XS650 Special, a revamped version of the familiar parallel twin featuring high bars, small tank and short mufflers. By 1979 the Special was on sale in Europe alongside a restyled, high-barred Z650SR version of

Above left: With its rigid steel frame and firm, damping-adjustable suspension, Suzuki's GS1000 was the best-handling open-class superbike yet from a Japanese manufacturer.

Above: Suzuki's GS750 became the firm's first four-stroke superbike when it was launched in 1977, and its brilliant all-round performance made the 68bhp four an instant success.

Action Movies

Some of the best motorcycling movies of the 1970s feature racing of one sort or another. *On Any Sunday*, the most famous bike sport film of all, covers US dirt-track, motocross, desert racing and the notoriously steep Widowmaker hillclimb. Stars including Mert Lawwill, Malcolm Smith and Steve McQueen help make director Bruce

Brown's 1971 documentary very watchable. Ten years later, Don Shoemaker and Ed Forsyth co-directed a competent sequel, *On Any Sunday 2*.

Robert Redford stars in *Little Fauss and Big Halsy*, a 1970 movie centred on a pair of motocross racers. The decade's other biggest bike-sport film is 1979's *Silver Dream Racer*, based on the road-racing exploits of actor/pop

star David Essex. Although not totally convincing, it includes some neat bikes and genuine racing action along with the story of a privateer racer's struggle to the top. The decade's other best-known biking movie, the 1973 release *Electra Glide in Blue*, is a less spectacular story of a US cop with a Harley and an attitude problem.

Above: The dirt-track action in On Any Sunday *included plenty of spectacular crashes.*

Top centre: Silver Dream Racer *included action sequences shot at British race circuits.*

Above right: The star of Electra Glide in Blue *poses with chief actor Richard Blake.*

Right: This Yamaha XS1100 is the US spec model with high bars and short pipes. The huge shaft-drive four was a successful touring model in the US, but sold poorly in most other countries.

Kawasaki's four. The Japanese factory custom had arrived, and future years would see similarly adapted versions of many other models.

Honda finally introduced a twin-camshaft four in 1979, ten years after the CB750. The CB900F and similarly styled CB750FZ owed much to Honda's mighty RCB four-cylinder endurance racers, and differed from their rivals by containing 16 valves. They also shared an angular 'Eurostyle' shape that was similar to that of Honda's humble 400 and 250cc Super Dream

Left: The 1978-model Kawasaki Z1-R's angular styling incorporated a handlebar-mounted fairing that gave the rider useful wind protection, but hindered high-speed stability.

twins. The larger 901cc unit produced an impressive 94bhp, and the CB900F also had a sophisticated chassis, with air-adjustable forks and damping-adjustable shocks. With strong mid-range performance, top speed of over 130mph (209km/h) and handling to match, the CB900F was Honda's best big four yet.

Japanese bikes' chassis performance was finally starting to match their engines. But the old failings had inspired numerous specialists, who had built bikes around Japanese engines, most commonly Kawasaki's fours. Nico Bakker in Holland, Georges Martin in France, Fritz Egli in Switzerland, and various British specialists including the Rickman brothers, Colin Seeley, Spondon Engineering and Harris Performance, had created fast, exotic specials that were generally much lighter and handled far better than mass-produced superbikes.

The outstanding chassis specialist was Bimota. Inspired by co-founder and design genius Massimo Tamburini, Bimota had already created advanced chassis with which Yamaha and

Below: Honda's CB900F was a significant because it was designed mainly for the European market, with a notably sportier nature than previous US market-led machines.

Left: Honda's factory RCB fours dominated endurance events including the Le Mans 24 Hours and Bol d'Or during the late 1970s.

Above: Bimota's SB2 was in a different league to mass-produced superbikes in 1977, from its streamlined full fairing, via its supremely rigid chassis to its self-supporting aluminium seat.

Right: The Magni MV Agusta, built in small numbers by former race team boss Arturo, resembled the factory racers with its full fairing, twin-cradle frame and curved pipes.

Opposite top left: Honda's stunning CBX1000 made do without frame front downtubes to make its 24-valve engine more visible. For a big, heavy bike it handled very well.

Opposite centre right: Kawasaki's liquid-cooled Z1300 required a large radiator that hid the front of its engine, but the huge, slab-sided six still looked like nothing else on two wheels.

Harley-Davidson had won road-race world championships. The first Bimota streetbike, the HB1, had been built in small numbers around a Honda CB750 engine in the mid-'70s. But it was with the Suzuki GS750-powered SB2 that the firm from Rimini made its mark.

The SB2 was a stunningly advanced machine, with a curvaceous tank-seat unit that was made from glass-fibre lined with aluminium, so required no rear subframe. The sophisticated tubular steel frame was hugely rigid, and held a vertically mounted rear shock unit, operated via a rising-rate mechanism. Other features included lightweight alloy wheels, triple Brembo discs and numerous machined alloy parts. The streamlined Bimota was good for over 130mph (209km/h), weighed 60lb (27kg) less than the GS750 and handled far better than any mass-produced superbike. Only 70 were built, mainly because the SB2 cost three times as much as a standard GS750, but it had provided a glimpse of motorcycling's future.

Another Italian specialist was former MV Agusta race team manager Arturo Magni. MV had updated its four-cylinder 750S to produce the 790cc America, and in 1977 enlarged the dohc engine to 837cc to create the Monza. Prepared by Magni, who had set up a tuning business near the factory, the Monza produced 85bhp and thundered to a top speed of 140mph (225km/h). Few of these sublime but unprofitable bikes were built before, in 1978, MV abandoned bikes to concentrate on its main business of producing helicopters. Magni also built a small number of an even more exotic MV, featuring a chain-drive conversion plus his own frame, based on the stronger, twin-loop design of the works racebikes. Finally MV's four had a chassis worthy of the marque's racing heritage.

Benelli provided a late flourish when the Pesaro firm enlarged its 750 Sei's six-cylinder engine to 906cc, creating the 900 Sei. But even this produced only 80bhp and the Sei was outshone by another six: Honda's CBX1000. The 1047cc, dohc engine contained 24 valves and produced 105bhp, making the Honda the world's most powerful production bike when it was launched in 1978. The CBX looked superb, too, with the view of its wide, air-cooled engine unhindered by frame downtubes.

Honda CBX1000 (1978)	
Engine:	Air-cooled dohc 24-valve six
Capacity:	1047cc (64.5 x 53.4mm)
Maximum power:	105bhp @ 9000rpm
Transmission:	Five-speed, chain final drive
Frame:	Tubular steel
Suspension:	Telescopic front; twin shocks rear
Brakes:	Twin discs front; disc rear
Weight:	573lb (260kg) wet
Top speed:	135mph (217km/h)

The sporty CBX was shaped by Honda's former multi-cylinder racebike designer Shoichiro Irimajiri. It provided ferocious and smooth acceleration towards a top speed of 135mph (217km/h), with a stirring exhaust howl. Despite Honda's innovative use of magnesium and plastic the CBX was heavy, at 573lb (260kg), but it handled and braked very well. Most who rode the CBX loved it, and the six boosted Honda's staid image. But it was far more expensive than fours of equivalent performance, and was not a sales success.

The CBX was one of the first models to be built at Honda's new US factory in Maryville, Ohio, which began producing bikes in 1979. By this time the Japanese giant had been using foreign production for almost two decades, after establishing a Belgian base to assemble mopeds back in 1962. Honda plants in Asian countries including Thailand began production in the mid-'60s, followed by factories in countries including Mexico, Brazil and Nigeria in the '70s.

Motorcycling's final act of the decade was another six-cylinder machine, Kawasaki's Z1300, which was even bigger, heavier and more powerful than the CBX. The slab-sided Kawasaki's 1286cc dohc liquid-cooled engine produced 120bhp, fully 15bhp more than the Honda, and the Kawasaki weighed more than 660lb (300kg) with fuel. With its upright riding position, sheer size and shaft final drive, the Z1300 was intended as a grand tourer.

Although its exposed riding position limited its practical cruising speed, the big Kawasaki was stunningly fast, whirring smoothly to 135mph (217km/h). It also handled and braked very well for such a big machine. Despite that it failed to sell in large numbers, partly because, like the CBX, it was more expensive than rival fours. The big, thirsty six also arrived in the wake of an oil crisis, just as the West German government had introduced a 100bhp power limit. Some reports suggested that the Z1300 would lead to bikes being banned. As the 1970s drew to a close, the giant Kawasaki seemed to some people to be a warning that after a decade of many highlights and much progress, motorcycling was spiralling out of control.

Kawasaki Z1300 (1979)	
Engine:	Liquid-cooled dohc 12-valve transverse six
Capacity:	1286cc (62 x 71mm)
Maximum power:	120bhp @ 8000rpm
Transmission:	Five-speed, shaft final drive
Frame:	Steel twin cradle
Suspension:	Telescopic front; twin shocks rear
Brakes:	Twin discs front; disc rear
Weight:	672lb (305kg)
Top speed:	135mph (217km/h)

Fire and Water
1980s

If motorcycling as most current riders know it began in the 1970s, then it was the following decade that did most to shape the modern bike. The race towards ever-larger and more powerful unfaired machines ended in 1979 with Kawasaki's Z1300 six. From then on, development continued in more diverse and generally more practical directions. By the end of the decade, most of the key features of today's bikes would be in place.

At the start of the '80s, even the most sophisticated bikes were generally unfaired and had air-cooled engines, tubular steel frames and twin rear shock absorbers, just like their predecessors of ten years earlier. All that quickly changed. By the second half of the decade, many large and even some smaller bikes had fairings, liquid-cooled engines, aluminium frames and single rear shock units with rising-rate linkages.

They also incorporated some less visible developments, including engines with four or even five valves per cylinder. Wider, smaller-diameter wheels increasingly wore tubeless radial tyres. Most tyres and disc brakes worked as well as could be expected in wet weather, unlike many of their dangerously rain-affected predecessors. Not all the decade's technical developments were positive, however. Poorly designed bodywork and needlessly complex features, such as Honda's enclosed brake discs, increased the cost of parts and servicing.

Japan's grip on the worldwide motorcycle market was stronger than ever, but even the big four suffered when sales in many key markets fell dramatically in the early '80s. Yamaha had grown quickly until that point, and was firmly established as the second largest manufacturer, but the firm's attempt to close the gap with Honda proved ill-timed. The sales slump resulted in huge over-production and a price war that was damaging to both companies. By autumn 1982, it was estimated that well over a million unsold Japanese bikes were being stored in the US and Canada, stacked in crates inside huge warehouses.

Yamaha survived, after making heavy losses and producing some notably mediocre and under-developed bikes, especially V-twins such as the XV550 and 981cc TR1. Honda reduced its range and emerged with status reinforced but with problems of its own. Mechanical failures suffered by

Above: The top superbike at the start of the 1980s was Suzuki's GSX1100, an old-style naked machine with air-cooled four-cylinder engine, twin rear shocks plus lots of bulk and weight.

Right: Kawasaki's GPz1100 arrived in 1981 with a traditional twin-shock chassis format and even a two-valves-per-cylinder engine, but its fuel-injection system added a futuristic touch.

Previous page: The VFR750F did much to restore Honda's reputation for top quality engineering.

Left: *Yamaha's RD350LC was one of the great bikes of the early '80s, and became a cult machine thanks to its unbeatable blend of outrageous performance and value for money.*

Yamaha RD350LC (1981)

Engine:	Liquid-cooled two-stroke parallel twin
Capacity:	347cc (64 x 54mm)
Maximum power:	47bhp @ 8500rpm
Transmission:	Six-speed, chain final drive
Frame:	Steel twin downtube
Suspension:	Telescopic front; single shock rear
Brakes:	Twin discs front; drum rear
Weight:	331lb (150kg)
Top speed:	110mph (177km/h)

models including the VF750F were an embarrassment to the firm that had introduced reliable motorcycling to the world.

Manufacturers in other countries were even more vulnerable. The British industry finally faded away almost completely, and Italian firms including Ducati, Moto Guzzi and Laverda suffered from low production levels and lack of finance for investment. Harley-Davidson survived, with the help of a controversial US government tariff on large-capacity imported bikes.

Demand for motorcycles had fallen partly because in the major markets bikes were by now regarded mainly as 'luxury' items, so might be dispensed with in a financial downturn. Once the economies recovered, so did bike sales. Meanwhile the riding experience was getting better as riders benefited from improvements in clothing and accessories, as well as machinery. The best 'waterproof' clothing really did keep out the rain; full-face helmets gained anti-scratch visors that dramatically improved night-time visibility. Sports bike riders increasingly wore colour-matched leathers, though only racers got to ride on a track.

Bikes became increasingly specialized during the 1980s, epitomized by the arrival of fully equipped luxury tourers, and at the other extreme by Suzuki's light and racy GSX-R750, which began the race-replica revolution in 1985. But there were also plenty of capable machines of various capacities for riders who needed versatility or economy. For those who found the technology race too much, the growing interest in classic bikes provided a welcome alternative.

The top superbike of 1980 would be the last of the old-style unfaired, air-cooled fours to hold that position. Suzuki's GSX1100 looked ungainly but was a fine example of the type. Its 1075cc engine, enlarged from that of the GS1000, incorporated Suzuki's first 16-valve cylinder head. The GSX combined a peak output of 100bhp with storming mid-range delivery, and could run at over 135mph (217km/h) for as long as its rider could hang on to the bars. Its traditional twin-shock chassis gave excellent handling, too, despite 551lb (250kg) of weight.

Honda finally responded to demands for weather protection when in 1980 it upgraded the Gold Wing. The basic model became the GL1100, with a more powerful, 1085cc flat four engine plus a new chassis incorporating air suspension. But the year's more important arrival was the

Below: *Yamaha's 1982-model XS650 Heritage Classic was a typical 'factory custom', built for the US market with high bars, stubby exhaust pipes, plus fat dual-seat and rear tyre.*

Honda CB1100R (1981)

Engine:	Air-cooled dohc 16-valve four
Capacity:	1062cc (70 x 69mm)
Maximum power:	115bhp @ 9000rpm
Transmission:	Five-speed, chain final drive
Frame:	Steel twin downtube
Suspension:	Telescopic front; twin shocks rear
Brakes:	Twin discs front; disc rear
Weight:	518lb (235kg) dry
Top speed:	142mph (229km/h)

Above: *Honda's CB1100R outclassed all comers.*

Right: *Suzuki's Katana 1100 combined high performance with sharp and original styling.*

Suzuki GSX1100S Katana (1982)

Engine:	Air-cooled dohc 16-valve four
Capacity:	1075cc (72 x 66mm)
Maximum power:	111bhp @ 8500rpm
Transmission:	Five-speed, chain final drive
Frame:	Steel twin downtube
Suspension:	Telescopic front; twin shocks rear
Brakes:	Twin discs front; disc rear
Weight:	545lb (247kg) wet
Top speed:	140mph (225km/h)

fully-dressed GL, called the Interstate in the US and the De Luxe in Europe, which featured a large fairing, hard luggage and crash-bars as standard.

The big machine was immediately popular, and two years later was followed by the Aspencade, which added a sound system, passenger backrest and an on-board compressor to adjust its suspension. The Aspencade, named after a US rally popular with Gold Wing riders, weighed a massive 766lb (347kg) with fuel, but was fast, smooth and supremely comfortable. The age of the luxury tourer had arrived, as Yamaha confirmed in 1983 with its XVZ1200 Venture, a smooth-running V4 with under-seat fuel tank and similarly lavish level of equipment.

At the other end of the scale, the most popular arrival was Yamaha's RD350LC two-stroke, which screamed onto the scene in 1981, except in the US where it failed to meet emissions regulations. The LC initials stood for Liquid Cooled, and the parallel twin was descended from the lively air-cooled RD400 roadster and Yamaha's all-conquering liquid-cooled TZ250 and 350 racebikes. Its 347cc engine produced 47bhp (a near-identical RD250LC made 35bhp), enough to send the rev-happy 'Elsie' to a top speed of 110mph (177km/h).

The LC's race-developed chassis featured a cantilever rear suspension system, with a single shock unit mounted diagonally under the seat. At just 331lb (150kg) with fuel the Yam was light, and despite slightly soft forks it handled superbly. It was also reliable, well braked and reasonably priced. In Britain its sales were boosted still further by the televised RD350 Pro-Am race series, which pitted professional riders against top amateurs on identical standard bikes, and produced memorably close and spectacular racing.

Kawasaki's GPz1100 arrived in 1981 to challenge for the title of best naked, air-cooled superbike. Unlike Suzuki's GSX1100 the GPz's new 1089cc engine used two valves per cylinder, and a fuel-injection system that helped give a maximum of 108bhp – enough for fearsome acceleration and a top speed of 140mph (225km/h). The Kawasaki's twin-shock chassis featured air-assisted forks and gave reasonable handling, despite the bike's weight. The GPz was very much a superbike of the old school, but it restored Kawasaki's reputation for high performance. Similarly styled GPz750 and GPz550 fours added style and speed in their respective classes.

Left: The last of Ducati's long line of bevel-drive V-twins was the 973cc Mille Replica that was produced only in 1985, the year in which the Bologna firm was taken over by Cagiva.

Below: Ducati's 1981 star was the Pantah 600. Like the original Pantah 500 of two years earlier, the 583cc V-twin used belts instead of bevel shafts to drive its overhead cams.

But the unfaired fours were blown away by the sophisticated star of 1981, Honda's CB1100R. This was not a mass-produced superbike, it was Honda's first 'homologation special' – a purpose-built production racer of which only 1000 units would be built. The 1100R sold for twice as much as the CB900FZ from which it was developed, and was created to win big production events in Australia (especially the famous Castrol Six Hour) and South Africa.

Honda enlarged the 901cc 16-valve engine to 1062cc, and tuned it with increased compression ratio to give 115bhp, also adding numerous strengthening modifications. The chassis featured a more rigid frame and the most sophisticated cycle parts yet seen, including air-assisted, damping adjustable forks, and twin-piston front brake calipers. The 1100R looked racy, with a half-fairing and single seat, and it delivered on the track, winning numerous endurance events and dominating the UK Superstock championship.

The CB1100R also made a superb road bike. Its big motor was flexible and smooth, and the fairing allowed effortless high-speed cruising towards a 142mph (229km/h) top speed. Suspension control, braking and ground clearance were all outstanding, although the fairing triggered a slight high-speed weave. Honda cured that with the following year's fully-faired CB1100R-C, which was further ahead of the pack than ever.

Suzuki sharpens its attack

The most significant new superbike of 1982, however, was a machine that would be built in much greater numbers than Honda's flagship – and which was even more visually striking. Suzuki's Katana 1100, named after a Samurai warrior's sword, was a single-minded sportster with a pointed nose, small flyscreen, low clip-on bars and a swooping tank-seat section. Based on the GSX1100, it was styled by German firm Target Design, which had previously shaped BMW's R90S.

Suzuki tuned the 1075cc 16-valve motor with new carburettors, airbox, camshafts and alternator, adding 11bhp to give a maximum of 111bhp. The unchanged frame held new suspension parts including forks equipped with a hydraulic anti-dive system borrowed from

Suzuki's grand prix racers. The result was a memorable bike that provided style, 140mph (225km/h) performance and stable handling at a sensible price. It was also firm and uncomfortable at slow speed, but few owners minded that and the Katana became a long-running success. Suzuki followed the original model with a 1000cc Katana for production racing, watered-down middleweight Katanas, and even tiny 250 and 400cc replicas for the Japanese market.

While Suzuki was bringing aggression and flair to the so-called 'Universal Japanese Motorcycle' four-cylinder format, most Italian manufacturers were having a difficult time. Ducati's most notable bikes of the early '80s had both been launched in 1979. The 900SS Hailwood Replica was built to commemorate 'Mike the Bike' Hailwood's heroic comeback victory, aged 38, in the previous year's Isle of Man Formula One TT. The green, white and red painted, fully-faired V-twin was even less practical than the standard 900SS, but it looked great, sold well and would remain in the range, through several updates, until 1985. Tragically Hailwood, arguably the greatest motorcycle racer of all, was killed in a car crash in 1981.

Ducati's other newcomer was more significant because the 499cc air-cooled V-twin engine of the Pantah 500, with belt drive to single desmodromic camshafts, would form the basis of the marque's engines for several decades to come. The Pantah's two-valves-per-cylinder motor produced 52bhp, had no kick-starter and was notably quieter and more sophisticated than its predecessor. The bike was good for 120mph (193km/h), and handled and braked very well. With its tall fairing and efficient exhaust system the Pantah lacked the style and raw appeal of the old V-twins, and it was expensive. But it showed the way forward for Ducati, and in 1981 its engine was enlarged to 583cc to create the Pantah 600, with an extra 6bhp and reshaped bodywork.

While Ducati was developing a new generation of engines in its familiar V-twin format, BMW was planning a move away from its traditional flat twins. The K100 arrived in 1984, powered by a completely new longitudinal four-cylinder, shaft-drive engine designed to take the German firm into the 21st century. The 987cc liquid-cooled engine's cylinders were arranged horizontally, with the crankshaft on the right. Peak output was 90bhp, with the emphasis on low-rev torque.

That helped make the K100 easy to ride, but the bike disappointed in other areas. Top speed was close to 130mph (209km/h) but the high bars and hard seat meant its performance could not

Above: With its 987cc in-line four-cylinder engine with cylinders arranged horizontally, the K100 was a radical departure for BMW, which was planning to abandon its flat twins.

Right: In typical BMW fashion the K100 was soon followed by a K100RS sports-tourer with a streamlined fairing. Equally predictably, a more relaxed K100RT tourer was not far behind.

The Turbo Craze

The most vivid examples of Japanese manufacturers' obsession with complex engineering in the early 1980s were the turbocharged bikes released by each of the 'Big Four'. Honda began in 1982 with the CX500 Turbo, a striking, fully-faired machine powered by a turbocharged version of the firm's transverse V-twin engine. Turbos are best suited to large, multi-cylinder engines that give a smooth exhaust flow, so the 497cc CX unit made Honda's job especially difficult.

Nevertheless the CX500 Turbo produced 82bhp, well up on the standard CX500's 50bhp, and proved reliable. The rest of the bike was almost as high-tech, with fuel-injection, anti-dive forks, Pro-Link rear suspension and twin-pot brake calipers. As well as suffering from turbo lag, the delay between throttle opening and acceleration, the Honda was far too complex, heavy and expensive to sell in serious numbers. The CX650 Turbo, launched a year later, had less lag plus more power and a top speed of 135mph (217km/h).

Honda's rivals opted for the more obvious in-line four engine layout. Yamaha was first to respond. Its XJ650 Turbo featured a stylish and efficient full fairing but the bike's 125mph (201km/h) performance was disappointing. The same was true of Suzuki's XN-85, whose 673cc engine produced 85bhp and gave performance no better than that of a normally aspirated 750cc four.

Fastest and best of the bunch was the last, Kawasaki's Z750 Turbo, which arrived in 1984 with scorching acceleration and a top speed of almost 140mph (225km/h). But the Turbo was competing with Kawasaki's own GPZ900R, which offered similar performance and price, plus no turbo lag and less chance of expensive mechanical problems. While the 900R became a lasting hit, the turbo bikes were quietly abandoned by all four manufacturers.

be used for long. The K100 was also a big, heavy machine whose soft front suspension did not encourage hard riding. BMW had more success with the K100RS, whose full fairing gave good weather protection. Combined with the relaxed riding position, the result was a competent sports-tourer. Touring-oriented K100RT and 'luxury' LT models further broadened the four's appeal, although many riders still preferred the boxers.

While BMW was preparing to abandon flat-twin engines, the layout was still being enthusiastically utilized elsewhere, notably in the Soviet Union. After the war, several Soviet factories had begun producing bikes based on captured BMW twins, and had carried on doing so with few modifications. Four decades later the crude but cheap boxers were being imported to the West, to be sold with added chromework and sometimes with sidecars attached. Similarly outdated BMW replicas were also being built in China, alongside the huge numbers of smaller two-strokes that were emerging from that nation's growing motorcycle industry.

Like BMW, Honda made a dramatic move to a new engine layout: the V4. When it was introduced in 1982, the V4 seemed so well suited to motorcycle use that some thought it would lead bikes away from in-line fours for ever. Honda's 748cc 90-degree, 16-valve motor produced

Above: Honda's CX500 Turbo was too complex and expensive to be a commercial success, but the V-twin was stylish, fast and comfortable.

Below: Many people were surprised when Honda debuted its 748cc V4 engine in the heavy and strangely styled VF750S, or Sabre in the US.

Above: Honda's VF750F, known as the Interceptor in the US market, was fast, handled well, looked good and was set for huge success – until its engine proved unreliable.

an impressive 79bhp, was compact, and had perfect primary balance plus space in the Vee for carburettors. Liquid-cooling prevented traditional problems of overheating rear cylinders. Surely the V4's time had finally come?

Honda's first mistake was to debut the V4 in 1982 both in a cruiser variant, the US-market V45 Magna, and a sportier machine called the VF750S, or Sabre in the US. The Sabre included TRAC anti-dive and Pro-Link single-shock rear suspension, as well as shaft final drive. The motor was smooth and powerful, though the VF's high handlebars meant its 120mph (193km/h) performance could not be used for long. More importantly the bike weighed over 500lb (227kg) with fuel, and had curious styling and vague handling.

Honda answered most of the criticisms a year later with the VF750F, called the Interceptor in the US. This was a much more stylish and sporty machine with a half-fairing, belly-pan, and a new chassis that combined a frame of square-section steel with 1983's racing-inspired fashion item, a 16-inch front wheel. Power was up to 90bhp, pushing top speed to 130mph (209km/h), and the V4 had looks and handling to match. It quickly became very popular, only for Honda's delight to turn to embarrassment when the engine suffered a series of mechanical problems. In some markets Honda responded by doubling its engine warranty to 24 months, but the firm's reputation would take years to recover.

Alternative V-twin layout

Fortunately for Honda there were fewer problems with its new V-twin, the VT500, which unlike the popular CX500 and later CX650 had its cylinders arranged in line with the bike. The softly tuned VT produced 50bhp and echoed the CX in its use of liquid-cooling and shaft drive, but had a narrower, 52-degree cylinder angle. The VT was a slimmer and more stylish bike that was also comfortable, reliable and handled well. It took over from the CX as a dispatch riders' favourite.

Most of Honda's efforts remained concentrated on its V4 range, which grew quickly with a string of models. The VF400F, also launched in 1983, was rev-happy, quick, agile and reliable, albeit also complex and expensive. The following year saw the VF500F, complete with stylish full

Right: The 1984-model VF1000R was a homologation special, with exotic chassis parts and tuned V4 engine, but was surprisingly uncompetitive in production racing.

fairing and 120mph (193km/h) performance, plus two 998cc V4s. The VF1000F looked like the 750F and combined fine handling with a flexible and reliable 116bhp powerplant.

Top of Honda's 1984 range was the VF1000R, a fully-faired super-sports machine which, like the CB1100R before it, was a street-legal production racer built in small numbers. Its engine held gear-driven cams and was tuned to give 122bhp, its fairing was reinforced with lightweight carbon-fibre, and its chassis featured fully adjustable suspension and four-piston front brake calipers. The 1000R was comfortable, stable and good for 150mph (241km/h). But it was too heavy and slow-steering to be outstanding on the track, and as a roadster it was far too expensive.

Kawasaki created contrasting superbikes in 1984, by refining the in-line four-cylinder layout for which it had been best known since the Z1 of 11 years earlier. At the end of that line of high-performance air-cooled fours came the Z1100R. With its bikini fairing, green paintwork, high bars and gold remote-reservoir shocks, the 1100R was a replica of the factory racer on which Eddie Lawson had won the US Superbike championship in 1981 and '82. The 1089cc four produced 114bhp and the Z1000R was stylish, fast and flexible, if rather crude and not particularly stable at high speed.

Kawasaki's more important and successful newcomer began a new generation of liquid-cooled, 16-valve fours. The GPZ900R was a sophisticated machine whose 908cc engine also featured a balancer shaft and six-speed gearbox. Its peak output of 113bhp was slightly below that of the old GPz1100 and the Z1100R, but the 'Ninja' had an aerodynamic full fairing that helped increase its top speed to over 150mph (241km/h). The bike also had a sturdy steel frame that used the motor as a stressed member, plus firm suspension that helped give excellent handling.

The GPZ900R was a stunningly fast bike that was also compact, reliable, smooth and comfortable, thanks to its flat bars and efficient fairing. At over 500lb (227kg) it was no lightweight but it was raced very successfully in production events as well as becoming a hugely popular roadster. It was later updated with a 17- instead of 16-inch front wheel, and remained in Kawasaki's range into the 1990s in a sports-touring role, outlasting its intended replacements the GPZ1000RX and ZX-10.

Kawasaki GPZ900R (1984)

Engine:	Liquid-cooled dohc 16-valve four
Capacity:	908cc (72.5 x 55mm)
Maximum power:	113bhp @ 9500rpm
Transmission:	Six-speed, chain final drive
Frame:	Steel spine
Suspension:	Telescopic front; single shock rear
Brakes:	Twin discs front; disc rear
Weight:	502lb (228kg) dry
Top speed:	155mph (249km/h)

Above: Kawasaki's Z1100R copied Eddie Lawson's US Superbike championship-winning racer in its headlamp fairing, lime green paintwork and 'sit-up-and-beg' riding position.

Left: The modern era began for Kawasaki with the brilliant GPZ900R, which hid a powerful 908cc liquid-cooled 16-valve four-cylinder engine behind its streamlined full fairing.

Above: Yamaha's FJ1100 was intended as an out-and-out sports bike but was outperformed by the GPZ900R on its launch in 1984, and made its mark as a fast and comfortable sports-tourer.

The other outstanding large-capacity sports machine of 1984 found itself relegated to the role of sports-tourer almost immediately because it could not compete with the GPZ on pure performance. But Yamaha's FJ1100 became such a success as a long-distance roadburner that, following a capacity increase that produced the FJ1200 in 1986, it too would remain in production with few changes well into the following decade.

The FJ's appeal was built on its relatively simple air-cooled four-cylinder engine, which differed from the old XS1100 unit by having 16 valves, and final drive by chain rather than shaft. The original 1097cc motor produced 125bhp and was more notable for its storming low-rev performance, which was further boosted by the increase to 1188cc that resulted in the FJ1200. The chassis, based on a square-section steel tube frame, gave sound handling with the emphasis on stability. A half-fairing, large fuel tank and broad dual-seat were other features that helped make the FJ popular for long-distance travel.

The other outstanding Yamaha of 1984 was far less successful than the FJ, ironically because it was too focused a sports machine. In fact the RD500LC was as close as any recent bike to a grand-prix-winning racer, as its look and 499cc liquid-cooled two-stroke V4 engine were inspired by the factory YZR500 that Eddie Lawson was riding to victory in that year's world championship. With a peak output of 90bhp, a top speed of almost 140mph (225km/h) and a dry weight of just 392lb (178kg), the V4 had the figures to back up its racy appearance.

The RD500LC also handled brilliantly, thanks to a high quality chassis that combined a square-section tubular steel frame with a single rear shock located under the engine. Along with the rev-happy engine, which came alive at 6000rpm with a fierce burst of acceleration and a high-pitched scream from the exhaust, it made the Yamaha superbly entertaining on the right road, as well as very fast on a racetrack. But drawbacks including excessive vibration, poor fuel consumption and a high price prevented the two-stroke from selling in big numbers.

Much the same was true of the rival that the RD faced in 1985, when Suzuki launched its RG500 Gamma, a follow-up to the previous year's superbly agile RG250 Gamma twin. Like the

Above and right: In 1986 Yamaha enlarged the FJ's air-cooled 16-valve engine to 1188cc to create the FJ1200, which remained a popular long-distance roadburner well into the '90s.

bikes on which Barry Sheene, Marco Lucchinelli and Franco Uncini had recently won world titles, the RG500 was a square four two-stroke. At just 433lb (196kg) it was even lighter than the RD, thanks to a frame which, like that of the works RG500 racebike, was made from aluminium. The fully-faired, 95bhp Gamma was every bit as stylish, fast, agile and impractical as its Yamaha rival. Unfortunately for Suzuki, it was more successful.

Honda's two-stroke challenger, the NS400R, was subtly different. Its 387cc two-stroke motor was a V-triple, like that of the NS500 on which the outrageously talented young Louisiana star 'Fast Freddie' Spencer had won Honda's first 500cc world title two years earlier. With a claimed 72bhp the NS couldn't match the straight-line speed of its 500cc rivals, despite weighing just 365lb (169kg) wet. But the compact triple handled brilliantly, thanks partly to the first aluminium frame that Honda had used on a streetbike. Despite that, the NS was no more commercially successful than the RD and RG, and the two-stroke race-replica revolution faded.

Instead, motorcycle design took a giant leap forward in a different direction, due to an even faster and equally purposeful Suzuki released at the same time: the GSX-R750. With the exception of Honda's CB750, the original GSX-R was arguably the most influential machine of recent decades, as it introduced the concept of the ultra lightweight, aluminium-framed four-cylinder race-replica, and so is the bike to which most modern sports machines owe their design. The Suzuki was also hugely popular in its own right, and started a GSX-R dynasty that grew to include smaller models plus the larger GSX-R1100 and, later, the GSX-R1000.

The original GSX-R750 was based on Suzuki's 998cc endurance race bikes of the previous year, with its twin-headlamp fairing and use of 18-inch wheels instead of the fashionable 16-inchers. Its 749cc dohc 16-valve engine was cooled by oil rather than either water or the air of its GSX750 predecessor, and produced a competitive 100bhp. The motor was compact and very light, with its cam-cover cast in magnesium instead of aluminium.

The GSX-R's chassis was even more radically light, based on an aluminium frame which at 18lb (8kg) weighed half as much as the GSX's steel equivalent. That helped give stunning

Above: Honda's NS400R was a dead ringer for Freddie Spencer's 500cc world-championship-winning triple, but produced only 72bhp and was no more successful than its two-stroke race-replica rivals from Yamaha and Suzuki.

Below right: Suzuki's GSX-R750 rocked the motorcycle world on its introduction in 1985, with a combination of high-revving power, light weight and aggressive attitude that led to a new breed of super-sports machines.

Suzuki GSX-R750 (1985)	
Engine:	Oil-cooled dohc 16-valve four
Capacity:	749cc (70 x 48.7mm)
Maximum power:	100bhp @ 10,500rpm
Transmission:	Six-speed, chain final drive
Frame:	Aluminium twin downtube
Suspension:	Telescopic front; single shock rear
Brakes:	Twin discs front; disc rear
Weight:	388lb (176kg) dry
Top speed:	145mph (233km/h)

acceleration to a top speed of 145mph (233km/h), provided the peaky motor was kept between 7000rpm and its 11,000rpm limit. The lack of weight was just as beneficial under braking and in corners, where the racy Suzuki was equally outstanding. The GSX-R was also uncomfortable, impractical and sometimes unstable, until calmed with a longer swingarm a year later. Its success proved that plenty of riders were happy to ignore such details when the performance and image were so right.

Suzuki waited only a year before unleashing an even more complete superbike in the near-identical shape of the GSX-R1100, which added blistering mid-range power to the original model's many attributes. At 433lb (196kg) dry the 1100 was 45lb (20kg) heavier than the 750, due to many apparently identical parts being slightly larger and stronger. But not only was the GSX-R1100 faster still and easier to ride, it also handled and braked superbly and was by some distance the world's fastest and most exciting sports bike.

Yamaha's poor timing

It was Yamaha's misfortune that its impressive FZ750 had been released in 1985 to compete with the GSX-R750. In most other years the spotlight would have been on the FZ, whose 749cc liquid-cooled four-cylinder engine introduced the angled-forward cylinders and five-valves-per-cylinder layout that would form the basis of Yamaha's big-bike range for years to come.

The FZ was a less focused and more practical bike than the GSX-R, and its engine was as notable for mid-range output as for its 105bhp maximum. Top speed equalled the Suzuki's 145mph (233km/h), and although the Yamaha couldn't quite match the lighter bike for acceleration, it was easier to ride. It also handled very well, thanks to a strong frame of square-section steel tubes. But the half-faired FZ750 was not the sales success that its performance and innovative design deserved.

Yamaha did, however, have an unlikely hit in 1985 with the V-Max, the unique and supremely powerful V4 that would become a long-lived legend. The V-Max, designed in the US, was the two-wheeled equivalent of a V8 muscle car, and featured fake alloy air-scoops jutting out of the

Left: The GSX-R1100, which followed the 750cc model in 1986, had similar twin-headlamp styling. Its storming mid-range performance and stronger five-speed gearbox helped make an even faster and more accomplished bike.

Below: Although Yamaha's FZ750 four handled superbly and had a powerful and flexible four-cylinder engine, its sales were disappointing. But the FZ's 20-valve cylinder head layout would be used by Yamaha's for years to come.

side of its dummy fuel tank. The Max's performance was real enough, however. Its 1198cc liquid-cooled motor was a highly tuned version of the V4 from the Venture tourer, and incorporated a system called V-boost that linked the four carburettors, providing extra power at high revs.

The result was a snarling, aggressively styled 143bhp beast that stormed away from the line faster than anything else on wheels. The Yamaha's poor aerodynamics limited top speed to 140mph (225km/h) but the heavy, crudely suspended chassis meant that was quite exciting enough for most riders. The V-Max's performance and brutal image earned it a cult following, though it was initially detuned in markets including Britain. The bike would barely be updated while remaining in production well into the 21st century.

By coincidence 1985, the centenary of the first ever motorcycle journey by Daimler's Einspur, was an outstanding year for new bikes. Kawasaki provided another with the GPZ600R. The fully-faired, liquid-cooled Kawasaki was based on the GPz550, one of several popular air-cooled 550s. The GPZ was the first 600cc four, and its aggressive style and specification set the standard for the class that would become motorcycling's most popular and competitive.

The Kawasaki's 592cc dohc 16-valve engine produced a maximum of 75bhp and needed revving towards its 11,000rpm redline to give of its best. Compact dimensions, a rigid steel perimeter frame and 16-inch wheels gave agile handling. Ridden hard, the GPZ delivered 130mph (209km/h) top speed and thrilling all-round performance that inspired the rival Japanese firms to develop rival fours of their own.

Harley-Davidson would also come to regard 1985 as very important. The company narrowly avoided having to file for Chapter 11 (bankruptcy) protection in December of that year, when vital extra finance was agreed within hours of a deadline set by its banks. In 1981 Harley had been bought from parent company AMF by a group of 13 managers, headed by Vaughan Beals and including design ace Willie G. Davidson and future Chairman Jeff Bleustein. After losing $30

Yamaha V-Max (1985)

Engine:	Liquid-cooled dohc 16-valve 72-degree V4
Capacity:	1198cc (76 x 66mm)
Maximum power:	143bhp @ 8000rpm
Transmission:	Five-speed, shaft final drive
Frame:	Steel twin downtube
Suspension:	Telescopic front; twin shocks rear
Brakes:	Twin discs front; disc rear
Weight:	560lb (254kg) dry
Top speed:	140mph (225km/h)

Above: The V-Max's brutal styling, enhanced by fake air-scoops on each side of the dummy tank, helped make the V4 a long-running sales success despite – or perhaps partly because of – its mediocre handling and scary reputation.

Right: Harley-Davidson took a big step forward in the mid-'80s when it fitted its Softails with the new generation Evolution V-twin engine. Many owners added extras such as tassels and custom pipes, adding to Harley's profit.

million that year, the revitalized firm had broken even in 1983, and was set to benefit from President Ronald Reagan's five-year protection scheme, which initially put a tariff of 49.4 per cent on imported bikes of over 700cc capacity.

The Japanese manufacturers responded by increasing production in their US factories, and by introducing 699cc versions of their most popular 750cc models. But the tariff helped Harley to survive, and to continue production of models powered by the recently introduced, new-generation 1340cc V-twin engine known as the Evolution. This retained the familiar air-cooled, 45-degree layout but was a notably more powerful, sophisticated, reliable and cool-running unit.

Introduced in seven models including the much improved Electra Glide giant tourer, the Evo motor set Harley on course for a period of sustained success that few people would have believed possible. The 1985-model Heritage Softail, with its hidden rear suspension giving a 'hard-tail' look, emphasized the focus on traditional styling. In 1986 Harley became a public company once again, and made a profit on sales of 36,000 bikes. The firm would increase sales, turnover and profit every year consistently into the 21st century.

A comeback was also under way in Italy, where in 1985 Cagiva took over struggling Ducati, then state-owned and building only a few thousand bikes annually. Cagiva, based at the former Aermacchi Harley-Davidson factory on the banks of Lake Varese, had been founded in 1978 by brothers Claudio and Gianfranco Castiglioni (whose father, CAstiglioni GIanni of VArese, gave his name to the firm). It had quickly become successful in the Italian 125cc market. After reaching an agreement to build Ducati-engined bikes in 1983, Cagiva bought the Bologna firm two years later, and began its recovery with a stylish 750cc V-twin called the F1 Replica whose full fairing bore the names of both Ducati and Cagiva. During the next two years Cagiva also bought Husqvarna, the Swedish off-road specialist, and Moto Morini, whose ageing 350cc V-twin engine found a new home in the striking, fully-faired Dart.

Other struggling Italian marques were less fortunate. Moto Guzzi had suffered from lack of investment for years, and reached a low point in 1985 with an updated version of its Spada II, a sports-tourer powered by the Mandello firm's 949cc transverse V-twin engine. Guzzis had long

Racing's V4 Revolution

The world's fastest bikes during the 1980s were the 500cc two-stroke V4s that dominated grand prix racing from 1984. Until then, the winning layout changed repeatedly. Yamaha's Kenny Roberts won on a straight four in 1980, followed by victories for Suzuki's RG500 square four, ridden by Italians

Marco Lucchinelli and Franco Uncini, in 1981 and '82; and Honda's NS500 V-triple, by Freddie Spencer, in 1983.

Once Eddie Lawson had won the 1984 championship on Yamaha's 140bhp YZR500, there was no doubting the powerful and compact V4 two-stroke layout's superiority. Yamaha's design used twin crankshafts, geared together and spinning in opposite directions. Honda's NSR500, introduced the same year with an unsuccessful chassis layout that put its fuel tank under the engine, had a single crank that reduced friction at the expense of extra width.

Spencer proved the redesigned, more conventional NSR500's speed in 1985 when he rode it to half of his 500 and 250cc world championship double. From then on the 500cc

title was swapped between factories: Yamaha's Lawson, Honda's Wayne Gardner, then Lawson again. When 'Steady Eddie' joined Honda in 1989, the aluminium-framed NSR produced over 160bhp but handled horribly. The Californian tamed it to win his fourth and last 500cc crown.

been famed for stable handling but when fitted with the current fashion item of a 16-inch front wheel, without geometry changes to compensate, the Spada was prone to frightening wobbles. Meanwhile Benelli, also owned by Argentinean Alejandro de Tomaso, had built small numbers of the six-cylinder 900 Sei, and four-cylinder 654, 504 and 304 models. But the unprofitable firm was producing mainly small-capacity bikes when in 1989 it was bought by the Biesse industrial group, which planned a range of bikes all with capacities of just 50cc.

Above left: Californian Eddie Lawson retained his yellow 500cc champion's No.1 plate on a Honda NSR500 in 1989, becoming one of only a handful of riders to have won the 500cc world title for two different manufacturers.

Above: Honda's single-crankshaft NSR500 went through several major revisions following its introduction in 1984. The NSR was generally the most powerful of the factory V4s, but its chassis performance was often less impressive.

Left: Bimota's 1982-model HB2, powered by the 16-valve motor from Honda's CB900F, proved that small specialist firms could still provide cutting-edge chassis design. But mass-produced Japanese superbikes were closing the gap.

Right: The success of the stylish DB1, designed by Federico Martini, rescued Bimota from financial problems in 1986. Beneath the all-enveloping glass-fibre were a 750cc Ducati V-twin engine and steel ladder frame.

Below: Laverda's long line of air-cooled triples came to an end with the SFC1000, a characterful sports-tourer that produced 90bhp and handled well, but which struggled to compete with more modern and cheaper machines.

Above: The Meriden factory workers' co-operative continued producing Triumph twins into the 1980s, and introduced many updates while lacking the finance for a major redesign. This 1981-model TR7 Tiger 750 features electronic ignition, left-foot gearchange and smoother-running crankshaft, but not the electric starter that was an optional extra.

Bimota, too, had hit financial problems despite starting the decade with some fine bikes including the HB2, powered by the four-cylinder engine from Honda's CB900F. Japanese advances in chassis technology had reduced the demand for the Rimini firm's expensive, hand-built bikes. In 1986 Bimota bounced back with an all-Italian creation, the DB1, which combined a 750cc Ducati V-twin engine with a steel ladder frame and a striking, all-enveloping fairing/tank/seat unit. The 76bhp Bimota's 130mph (209km/h) top speed was modest for such an expensive bike. But its style, light weight and agility made the DB1 a sales success that put Bimota back in the black, at least for a while.

Laverda in decline

Laverda, another famous old Italian marque, was in deeper trouble. The Breganze firm had tried hard to modernize its famous air-cooled triple, with some success. The Jota 120 of 1982, with a smoother, 120-degree firing order instead of the old 180-degree arrangement, was a fine superbike of the old school. In the same year Laverda introduced the RGS1000, which combined more modern styling with a softer, more flexible three-cylinder engine whose more restrictive exhaust system enabled the bike to pass stricter noise regulations. But the RGS lacked the raw appeal and competitive speed of the old triples.

In 1984 Laverda created the RGS1000 Corsa by tuning the 981cc engine to give 90bhp, and the following year used this motor to power a new model, the SFC1000. This had reshaped bodywork and many new chassis parts, and was a stylish and charismatic sports-tourer with a top speed of 140mph (225km/h) and good handling. But the SFC was far too expensive to sell in big numbers, and Laverda lacked the finance to develop its planned range of three-cylinder middleweights. The final batch of SFC1000s left the Breganze factory in 1987, and Laverda production came to an end.

By this time the British motorcycle industry, too, had all but disappeared. There had been glimmers of hope during the decade, not least with the high-profile unveiling in 1980 of the Hesketh V1000, a V-twin sports-tourer developed by Northamptonshire-based aristocrat Lord

Alexander Hesketh, who had previously owned a successful Formula One car racing team. The 992cc 90-degree dohc engine, designed and built by speedway specialists Weslake, used four valves per cylinder and produced 86bhp. The high-quality chassis combined a tubular steel frame with Marzocchi suspension and Brembo brakes from Italy.

The exotic Hesketh was billed as a 'two-wheeled Aston Martin'. Its engine was smooth and flexible, and the small fairing allowed leisurely cruising plus a top speed of 120mph (193km/h). Despite weighing over 500lb (227kg), the V1000 handled and braked well, too. But its gearbox was poor and the expensive, hand-built Hesketh was horribly unreliable. Only 149 bikes had been built when the firm went bust in 1982. Lord Hesketh formed a new company and began production of a fully-faired touring model, the Vampire, but few had been built when Hesketh abandoned bikes for good.

Triumph's final fling

Of the great old British marques, only Triumph had started the decade still producing bikes. The Meriden workers' co-operative continued to build 744cc parallel twins in fairly small numbers, and in 1980 introduced an optional electric starter to the Bonneville and its single-carb sibling the

Above and below: The Hesketh V1000 promised much when launched in 1980, but its 992cc V-twin engine proved unreliable. Although the firm soon folded, a handful of updated V1000s would be built on the same premises years later.

Right: The VFR750F was one of the most important bikes that Honda had ever introduced. By the time this V4 was built in 1989, the VFR had been updated with a 17-inch front wheel plus an adjustable screen, and had done much to restore Honda's reputation for high-quality engineering.

Honda VFR750F (1986)

Engine:	Liquid-cooled dohc 16-valve 90-degree V4
Capacity:	748cc (70 x 48.6mm)
Maximum power:	105bhp @ 10,500rpm
Transmission:	Six-speed, chain final drive
Frame:	Aluminium twin spar
Suspension:	Telescopic front; single shock rear
Brakes:	Twin discs front; disc rear
Weight:	436lb (198kg)
Top speed:	145mph (233km/h)

Below: The gigantic GL1500 Gold Wing brought a new dimension to long-distance motorcycling, with its smooth 1520cc flat-six engine and unprecedented level of luxury.

TR7 Tiger. Both were pleasant enough machines that handled well and had a certain nostalgic appeal, but their build quality and reliability, as well as performance, were far behind Japanese levels, and demand was limited.

Production of the Tiger ended in 1981, when it was replaced by a short-lived dual-purpose model, the Tiger Trail 750, which performed poorly both on- and off-road. In 1982 Triumph introduced the TSS, whose eight-valve cylinder head increased peak output by 7bhp to 57bhp, and top speed to 120mph (193km/h). But without the finance to develop more modern alternatives to the old pushrod twin the co-operative was doomed. Production was halted at the end of 1982, and Triumph went into liquidation shortly afterwards.

The Triumph name was bought from the liquidator by a Midlands builder named John Bloor, who kept a very low profile. Bloor allowed Les Harris, the boss of Devon-based Triumph parts specialist Racing Spares, to restart production of the Bonneville under licence. Harris had built about 1200 bikes when in 1988 he was told that the licence would not be renewed, and that production of the pushrod twin was over for good. Harris instead tried to revive the Matchless name with a model called the G80, powered by a 494cc sohc single engine from Rotax of Austria, but few were built.

Mighty Honda had meanwhile faced difficulties of its own in the mid-'80s, as rushed development had resulted in engine problems for models including the VF750F and the CBX550, a lively in-line four that had been plagued by camchain trouble. Several other Honda models had suffered with less serious ailments such as poor gearshifting and weak clutches, and the marque's reputation for quality and reliability had suffered. When in 1986 Honda unveiled a new generation V4, the VFR750F, it arrived to an unprecedented level of scrutiny.

Thankfully for Honda, the VFR proved a magnificent bike that would earn a lasting reputation for exceptionally high build quality. Its 748cc engine retained not only the VF's 90-degree, 16-valve V4 layout but also its compression ratio and internal dimensions. Lighter components, gear-driven cams and larger carbs helped boost peak output by 15bhp to 105bhp. The new aluminium frame held air-adjustable forks and a rear shock whose preload could be set using a remote knob behind a sidepanel.

Fully faired and subtly finished in single colour paintwork, the VFR was a classy sports-tourer whose blend of performance and comfort won praise from almost everyone who rode it. Its flexible and smooth V4 motor gave a top speed of over 140mph (225km/h). The VFR handled very well and was comfortable, well equipped and – most importantly of all, in the circumstances – supremely reliable. By the time the VFR was updated with a reshaped fairing and a 17-inch front wheel in 1988, the model had become known for unmatched versatility and refinement, and had done much to restore faith in Honda's engineering.

Honda had found its Gold Wing tourer simpler to develop than its V4 line, notably when enlarging the flat-four engine to 1182cc, to create the GL1200. But the extra weight of the fully-dressed Wing had taken its toll on performance, and the 1987-model Gold Wing was slightly slower than the original GL1000 of 12 years earlier. Finally Honda abandoned the four-cylinder motor altogether, and created the GL1500 Gold Wing around a new flat-six powerplant with a capacity of 1520cc.

The huge, liquid-cooled sohc six produced a maximum of 100bhp at 5200rpm, along with vast reserves of smooth torque at almost any revs. The GL1500 was gigantic, with a wide fairing, long wheelbase, plus luggage and sound systems that contributed to a dry weight of almost 800lb (363kg). Its starter motor even doubled as a reverse gear to help when parking. The Wing was fast, comfortable and handled well considering its size. It was also very expensive, but as a motorbike for stress-free long-distance travel, it was in a class of its own.

Top and above: Honda's CBR600F, known as the Hurricane in the US, represented a significant change of direction for the world's largest motorcycle firm: away from V4s to a new line of liquid-cooled 16-valve straight fours. The fast, fine-handling and competitively priced CBR was an immediate worldwide success.

Left: Yamaha entered the open-class super-sports battleground with the FZR1000, whose blend of powerful 20-valve four-cylinder engine and aluminium 'Deltabox' frame would remain popular for many years to come. This 1989 model incorporated Yamaha's EXUP exhaust valve to boost mid-range performance.

Above: Bimota's exotic YB6 EXUP, also known as the YB8, housed a Yamaha FZR1000 engine in an aluminium beam frame of the Italian firm's own manufacture. The roadster was closely based on Virginio Ferrari's 1987 Formula One world-championship-winning YB4 racer.

Below right: The sublime RC30, or VFR750R to give the V4 its full name, was the spitting image of Honda's all-conquering RVF factory racebike. Fast, agile and rewarding to ride, the RC30 was a hit despite its high price, and was almost unbeatable in production-based racing.

The GL1500's high specification and price contrasted with the more prosaic design of an important pair of 1987 Hondas: the CBR600F and CBR1000F. The CBRs represented a move away from V4s, back to the in-line layout that Honda had popularized with the CB750. The new Hondas shared rounded, all-enveloping styling that hid their liquid-cooled four-cylinder engines from sight. The motors themselves were more conventional, incorporating chain-driven twin camshafts, 16 valves and six-speed gearboxes.

Only the Honda engines' liquid cooling, compact size, light weight and impressive power outputs revealed their modernity. The CBR1000F produced 133bhp, shot smoothly to 160mph (257km/h), handled well for a 488lb (221kg) motorbike, and was a capable and comfortable sports-tourer. And the CBR600F was a real star. Its 85bhp motor was smooth, revvy, reliable and capable of powering the compact four to 140mph (225km/h). The 600F's fine handling, versatility and competitive price added to its appeal, and soon the Honda was the best-selling bike in many markets. Numerous updates would help the CBR remain at or near the top of the competitive middleweight sports bike sector for years to come.

The other most significant arrival in 1987 was Yamaha's FZR1000, an eagerly anticipated sportster that introduced the twin-spar aluminium Deltabox frame, based on that of Yamaha's 'Genesis' factory racebike. The FZR's 989cc engine was an enlarged version of the liquid-cooled, 20-valve unit that had been introduced two years earlier in the FZ750. It produced generous mid-range delivery and a maximum of 125bhp, which matched the output of Suzuki's GSX-R1100, the Yamaha's main rival.

The FZR was an aggressive super-sports machine, and proved more popular than the versatile FZ. Its motor delivered smooth power from as low as 2000rpm, and kicked hard at the top end to send the Yamaha to a top speed of almost 160mph (257km/h). The chassis gave a brilliant blend of stability and agility. On performance, style and price the FZR was very competitive, and it brought Yamaha to the forefront of superbike design. Two years later the motor was enlarged to 1002cc, increasing peak output to 140bhp. The FZR also gained an electronically operated exhaust valve whose acronym led to the model often being known as the 'EXUP'.

Spanish engineer Antonio Cobas had designed the first twin-spar aluminium frame for a 250cc, Rotax-engined racing machine in 1982, leading a revolution in chassis design. Bimota

Honda RC30 (1988)

Engine:	Liquid-cooled dohc 16-valve 90-degree V4
Capacity:	748cc (70 x 48.6mm)
Maximum power:	112bhp @ 11,000rpm
Transmission:	Six-speed, chain final drive
Frame:	Aluminium twin spar
Suspension:	Telescopic front; single shock rear
Brakes:	Twin discs front; disc rear
Weight:	407lb (185kg) dry
Top speed:	155mph (249km/h)

Trail Bike Twins

BMW discovered a successful new format in 1980 with a dual-purpose version of its boxer twin, the R80G/S. With a torquey, 37bhp engine, striking looks and a rugged, versatile chassis, it was an entertaining bike that surprised many riders with its ability both on- and off-road. Three victories in the gruelling Paris-Dakar Rally in the early '80s, by Frenchman Hubert Auriol and Belgian's Gaston Rahier, enhanced the boxer's appeal. When the updated, 980cc R100GS was launched in 1987 it became the best-selling bike in Germany. By the end of the decade, more than 50,000 units of the GS had been sold.

The Japanese manufacturers joined in with a variety of dual-purpose twins. Honda's Transalp, developed from the VT500 roadster in 1987, combined a 587cc in-line V-twin engine with an integrated fairing/tank unit. That in turn led to the XRV650 Africa Twin, with Paris-Dakar style twin-headlamp fairing, big tank, tall seat and rugged image. By 1989 the Africa Twin had gained a more powerful,

742cc V-twin engine to compete against Yamaha's equally large and rally-influenced XTZ750 Super Ténéré, whose parallel twin motor was developed from that of the quirky but versatile TDM850 roadster.

Above left: Gaston Rahier won the Paris-Dakar Rally on this much modified BMW R80G/S.

Top centre: Yamaha's XTZ750 Super Ténéré twin was better off-road than many owners realized.

Top right: BMW's R80G/S inaugurated the twin-cylinder dual-purpose bike's rise in 1980.

Above: Honda revised their versatile Africa Twin several times during the decade.

Left: Californian Fred Merkel, pictured riding with a misted screen at Donington Park in 1989, won the first two World Superbike titles for Honda on a factory-supported RC30.

Ducati 851 (1988)

Engine:	Liquid-cooled dohc eight-valve 90-degree V-twin
Capacity:	851cc (92 x 64mm)
Maximum power:	100bhp @ 8250rpm
Transmission:	Six-speed, chain final drive
Frame:	Tubular steel ladder
Suspension:	Telescopic front; single shock rear
Brakes:	Twin discs front; disc rear
Weight:	396lb (180kg)
Top speed:	140mph (225km/h)

Above right: In 1989 Ducati introduced the relatively simple air-/oil-cooled four-valve 900SS (left), as well as comprehensively revamping the liquid-cooled eight-valve 851.

Below: Buell's RS1200 emphasized its Harley engine by leaving the V-twin unit on display. It handled well, thanks to an innovative frame with rear shock located under the motor.

adopted the twin-spar format for its YB4 racer, with which Virginio Ferrari won the Formula One world title in 1987. Ferrari's factory YB4 was powered by Yamaha's FZ750 engine, as was the YB4 IE roadgoing replica launched a year later. Bimota quickly followed this with a similar YB6 model using the engine from the FZR1000.

Both the YB6 and its successor the YB8, which used Yamaha's exhaust-valve equipped 1002cc engine, were fast and fine-handling bikes. The YB8 was more compact and 50lb (23kg) lighter than the standard FZR. Bimota also claimed extra power from its less restrictive silencer, taking peak output to 147bhp. The YB8 was a success for Bimota, which built more than 650 of the exotic machines over the next few years.

Honda's race-replica V4

By contrast Honda's annual production was about three million bikes, but the outstanding machine of 1988 was the similarly exclusive RC30. Like its CB1100R and VF1000R predecessors, the bike also known as the VFR750R was a homologation special; created as a basis for competition success with little regard for cost. It was closely based on Honda's mighty RVF, the V4 factory racer that had dominated world championship endurance and Formula One racing in the mid-'80s. The compact RC30 was almost a carbon copy, with its twin-headlamp fairing, single seat and a rigid twin-spar aluminium frame that was rumoured to be cast using the same dies as the RVF's. It had a single-sided swingarm, as used on Honda's endurance racers to speed wheel changes.

Power came from a tuned and lightened version of the VFR750F sports-tourer's 748cc liquid-cooled 90-degree V4 engine, modified with an RVF-style 360-degree crankshaft, instead of the 750F's 180-degree set-up. Bigger carbs, titanium conrods and a complex single-muffler exhaust system combined to give 112bhp output with impressive reliability. The RC30 was uncomfortable and impractical in town, with its racy riding position and tall first gear. But on the open road or racetrack it stormed towards a top speed of 155mph (249km/h) at a thrilling rate.

The RC30 was equally brilliant in the bends, where its light weight, lavishly equipped chassis and compact dimensions helped give outstanding handling and braking. Honda's exotic race-replica cost almost twice as much as rival 750s, but it made a fine road bike as well as a hugely successful racer. Britain's Carl Fogarty rode a race-kitted RC30 to the Formula One world championship in 1988 and '89, and America's Fred Merkel achieved a similar double victory in the new World Superbike class, which quickly displaced F1 to become the leading four-stroke race series.

Ducati would eventually rise to dominate World Superbikes in the 1990s, basing its success on the ground-breaking 851 that was launched in 1988. With its powerful dohc eight-valve V-twin engine the 851, named after its capacity, was the bike that brought Ducati thundering into the modern era under Cagiva control. Chief engineer Massimo Bordi retained the Bologna firm's trademark 90-degree V-twin layout and desmodromic system of positive valve closure, and added four-valve heads, liquid cooling and fuel-injection to create a powerplant that produced 100bhp with greatly increased refinement and tuning potential.

The 851 retained Ducati's familiar steel ladder frame construction, and featured high quality suspension and brakes. But ironically the original 'tricolore' model, finished in patriotic red, white and green, was fitted with 16-inch wheels and handled poorly. Revamped a year later with restyled red paintwork, an extra 4bhp and most importantly with the 17-inch wheels it should have worn all along, the 851 was transformed into a fast and fine-handling sportster.

In 1989 Ducati also introduced another important model, a 904cc air-cooled V-twin that was named the 900 Super Sport after its famous forebear of the '70s. Its softly tuned, sohc two-valves-

Above: British road racing enjoyed an upsurge of spectator interest in 1989 when Norton team-mates Steve Spray and Trevor Nation (pictured) rode to numerous victories on the powerful, flame-spitting rotary racer.

Below: Norton had begun work on a Wankel rotary-engined bike in the mid-'70s, and developed the 588cc machine in conjunction with several UK police forces before releasing the limited-edition Classic roadster in late 1987.

Right: In 1989 Norton updated the rotary engine with liquid cooling to power the Commander tourer, featuring big fairing and built-in panniers. This bike is being used by a motorcycling paramedic in central London.

Below: Kawasaki's ZXR750 produced a relatively modest 105bhp and was heavy by super-sports standards. But striking styling and a competitive price, plus some enthusiastic brochure copy, made the ZXR a big success.

per-cylinder desmo motor produced a modest 83bhp, and the 900SS also had a simple chassis with no rising-rate rear suspension system. But it combined a 135mph (217km/h) top speed and strong mid-range performance with stable handling and plenty of V-twin charm. A competitive price also helped to make the 900SS a success, founding a Super Sport dynasty that would grow to include 750, 600 and 400cc models.

The year's other new air-cooled V-twin sportster came from the small town of Mukwonago, Wisconsin. Erik Buell was a former racer and Harley-Davidson engineer who had started a firm building sports bikes powered by the V-twin motors from nearby Milwaukee. His RR1000 and RR1200 Battletwin models featured all-enveloping bodywork that was good for aerodynamics but disguised the Harley connection. So Buell created a half-faired model, the RS1200, that left its 1203cc Sportster V-twin motor in view.

Buell's key feature was his Uniplanar engine mounting system, which used rods and joints to restrict engine vibration to the vertical plane. This allowed the engine to be rubber-mounted while also adding rigidity to the tubular steel ladder frame. Other innovative touches included a horizontal rear shock, located under the engine and working in tension rather than compression. Buell also designed the brake calipers, anti-dive system and bodywork. Inevitably the hand-built RS1200 was expensive, and with its 60bhp Sportster engine it was not particularly fast. But it rumbled up to 120mph (193km/h), handled well and put Erik Buell's innovative, American-built bikes on the map.

Norton's Classic was an equally unusual bike that provided an unlikely success story. The Classic, an unfaired roadster with a 588cc 79bhp rotary engine, was the result of more than a decade of low-budget development work by the small firm, now based at Shenstone in Staffordshire. Norton sold a limited run of 100 Classics, and also developed a faired touring version, the Commander. Interest snowballed when a handful of employees, led by engineer Brian Crighton, built an aluminium-framed rotary racer. In 1989 Steve Spray rode the fire-spitting, 135bhp Norton to two major UK championships, to the delight of huge crowds.

Style, speed and value for money

Kawasaki's ZXR750 scored a more predictable sales success in 1989. With its race-team-inspired paint scheme and a big pair of air ducts leading from its fairing nose towards a powerful in-line four-cylinder engine, the ZXR750 looked as though it belonged on a world championship race grid. Its 748cc engine was a tuned version of the rather bland GPX750 roadster's liquid-cooled 16-valve unit, and its chassis was based on that of Kawasaki's aluminium-framed ZXR-7 racer.

But the ZXR was no limited-edition race-replica like Honda's RC30 and Yamaha's similarly exotic but less successful rival, the 749cc OW01 in-line four. The ZXR was a mass-produced machine whose competitive price was as important a figure as its 105bhp peak power output. The Kawasaki screamed towards a top speed of 150mph (241km/h) at a thrilling rate, feeling suitably racy thanks to its stretched-out riding position and firm suspension. The ZXR750 won few races but was a worthy rival to Suzuki's GSX-R750, which had been comprehensively redesigned with more rounded styling, a new chassis and a reworked engine.

Even the ZXR750 looked ordinary alongside 1989's most striking new bike, BMW's K1. With its brightly coloured, all-enveloping bodywork, the 987cc longitudinal four was a striking machine by any manufacturer's standards, let alone those of the German firm that was known for efficient but unexciting tourers. In conjunction with the huge front mudguard, the K1's fairing and large rear section gave a wind-cheating shape unmatched even by Japanese race-replicas.

BMW had shaped the K1 that way both to highlight the firm's new, more adventurous approach, and to improve performance because the engine's peak output was being kept to 100bhp, the voluntary German limit. The bike's unmatched aerodynamics meant that it managed a top speed of 145mph (233km/h), and the softly tuned motor was also impressively flexible. Despite its racy looks the K1 was no sports bike. Its shaft drive system contributed to a weight of no less than 570lb (259kg), and the conservative steering geometry and long wheelbase added to the bike's slow-steering, ultra-stable feel.

Flaws included annoying vibration above 5000rpm, and the rear bodywork's broad storage pockets, which held little and made panniers impossible to fit. But in other respects the K1 was a capable sports-tourer that rivalled Yamaha's FJ1200 for fast and comfortable long-distance travel, and it signified the start of a new era at BMW. As the 1980s came to a close it was clear that, with motorcycles regarded by many buyers as leisure purchases rather than mere transport, all manufacturers were under pressure to develop innovative and exciting machines.

BMW K1 (1989)	
Engine:	Liquid-cooled dohc 16-valve in-line four
Capacity:	987cc (67 x 70mm)
Maximum power:	100bhp @ 8000rpm
Transmission:	Five-speed, shaft final drive
Frame:	Tubular steel space frame
Suspension:	Telescopic front; monoshock rear
Brakes:	Twin discs front; disc rear
Weight:	570lb (259kg)
Top speed:	145mph (233km/h)

Below: Aerodynamic, all-enveloping bodywork, which incorporated the large front mudguard, helped give BMW's K1 high cruising and top speeds, even though its 987cc engine's maximum output had been limited to 100bhp.

Weekend
Warriors
1990s

Above: A mildly customized Harley was the ideal bike for the new breed of American enthusiast.

Previous page: The updated 1998-model 900SS was one of many new models from rejuvenated Ducati towards the end of the decade.

Below: Kawasaki's 750cc Zephyr was the middle of three naked retro fours of the same name.

Below right: Honda's CB750, known as the Nighthawk in some markets, was a budget 'standard' built initially for the US market.

Motorcycling came of age in the 1990s. The days when a motorbike was a poor man's alternative to a car seemed long ago, as increasingly bikes were the toys of affluent middle-aged men – ironically, often the same people who had fuelled a biking boom as impecunious youths two decades earlier. The new breed of motorcyclist often rode not to go anywhere in particular, but simply for fun on a sunny Sunday morning.

If there was one firm riding on top of the new wave, it was Harley-Davidson. The dark days of the company's fight for survival in the '80s seemed far away as Harley's sales and share price soared to new heights every year. Newspapers and general interest magazines ran features on Rich Urban Bikers (or 'RUBs' as they were known), each noting that beneath the mean-looking black leather most riders were well-educated professionals, in their 40s or above.

Harley's growth was concentrated in the US, where the Milwaukee firm had captured half of the market for large-capacity machines. Success came from targeting rising middle-class disposable income, with bikes that combined traditional American styling, large-capacity V-twin engines, non-threatening performance and much improved build quality and finish. Equally important was the clever marketing that emphasized Harley's cool image, and the fostering of the Harley Owners Group, which strengthened brand loyalty and provided owners with places to ride.

Elsewhere, especially in Europe, Japanese manufacturers continued to dominate, and the focus was much more on performance. On summer weekends, twisty roads from England's Peak District to the Alpine foothills echoed with the exhaust notes of bikes of a wide variety of capacities and styles. Riders of many of the sportier machines wore one-piece leathers containing body-armour, and with removable knee-pads whose scuff marks confirmed the dramatic cornering angles possible on sticky radial tyres.

Transverse four-cylinder engines remained the normal choice for large-capacity bikes of most types, but other layouts, notably the V-twin, would continue to be successful. Engine performance had increased to the point where the fastest bikes' top speeds were more than double most

Kawasaki ZZ-R1100 (ZX-11) (1990)	
Engine:	Liquid-cooled dohc 16-valve four
Capacity:	1052cc (76 x 58mm)
Maximum power:	145bhp @ 9500rpm
Transmission:	Six-speed, chain final drive
Frame:	Aluminium twin spar
Suspension:	Telescopic front; single shock rear
Brakes:	Twin discs front; disc rear
Weight:	502lb (228kg) dry
Top speed:	175mph (282km/h)

countries' national limits. That created political problems, not least the early-'90s threat of a Europe-wide 100bhp limit. After determined opposition from increasingly well organized and co-ordinated riders' pressure groups, the 100bhp limit would be defeated in most countries, France being a notable exception.

Such had been the advance in chassis engineering during the 1980s that despite their unprecedented straight-line speed, most bikes had handling, brakes and tyres to match. Frames were generally very rigid, whether made from steel or the increasingly popular aluminium. Suspension on many bikes, especially sports machines, was adjustable for hydraulic damping. This gave potential for better handling but demanded correct setting-up, and a higher level of rider skill.

In many countries, that increased knowledge and experience was available via high-speed riding, both on 'track days' and through more formal, circuit-based riding or racing schools. The track school format, pioneered in the US in the '80s by former racer Keith Code's California Superbike School, was widely copied and adapted. With motorcycles' performance becoming increasingly at odds with roadgoing speed limits and traffic density, and speed cameras becoming an added threat in some countries, track days were welcomed by riders and the motorcycle industry alike.

While sports bikes' performance raced ahead, manufacturers also strove to find lucrative niches that could be filled with a purpose-designed model and a slick marketing campaign. Japanese firms began to acknowledge their heritage, with 'retro-bikes' such as Honda's CB750 Nighthawk and Kawasaki's Zephyr range of naked fours in 1100, 750 and 550cc sizes. All were designed to tempt 'born-again bikers', returning to two wheels after a break for kids or careers, with memories of the 1970s.

But there was only one four-cylinder Kawasaki dominating the headlines in 1990. The ZZ-R1100 (ZX-11 in the US) ripped onto the superbike scene with a stunning 1052cc 16-valve four-cylinder engine whose 'ram-air' system of forced induction, developed from Formula One car racing, helped give a peak output of 145bhp. Combined with bulbous but aerodynamically efficient bodywork, that sent the ZZ-R screaming to a 175mph (282km/h) top speed that made it by some distance the world's fastest streetbike.

Above left: Kawasaki's mighty ZZ-R1100, called the ZX-11 in the US, was a searingly fast 16-valve four whose 145bhp output was delivered with the help of motorcycling's first 'ram-air' induction system, as used in F1 car racing.

Below: For crossing continents in high-speed comfort few bikes came close to matching Honda's ST1100. The transverse V4's peak output was limited to 100bhp, but the 'Pan European' was fast, smooth and civilized.

Above: Suzuki's RGV250 was far from the world's most practical bike, but on the right road the little V-twin was brilliant fun.

Above right: Honda successfully revamped the CBR600F every couple of years through the '90s, improving performance and retaining the versatility on which its popularity was based.

Below: Honda's ultra-racy, Japanese-market NSR250R was one of the most advanced bikes of the early '90s.

There was much more to the Kawasaki than straight-line performance. The ZZ-R was big and quite heavy but its rigid twin-spar aluminium frame, which like the engine was based on that of the previous ZX-10, held firm suspension that gave excellent stability even at high speed. The full fairing made that phenomenal performance very usable, as did a comfortable seat and such details as good mirrors and a strong pillion grab-rail. The ZZ-R1100 was refined, handled well, and proved superbly reliable. Most important of all, it was blindingly fast.

Honda produced a sports-tourer of contrasting style and focus in 1990 with the ST1100, whose emphasis was on distance rather than speed. Its 1084cc liquid-cooled engine was a V4, but unlike previous Honda layouts this one placed its cylinders across the frame, facilitating the shaft final drive. The Pan European, as the ST was also known, was developed by Honda's German subsidiary, and its engine's 100bhp output remained within that country's voluntary power limit.

The big, softly-tuned V4 motor was very smooth and flexible, giving the Honda effortless performance to a top speed of 135mph (217km/h). Along with its large fairing, huge fuel tank, broad seat and built-in panniers, that made the ST an excellent long-haul machine, albeit one whose conservative steering geometry and 614lb (279kg) of weight produced ponderous handling. The Pan European was more efficient than fun but hit its intended target, and would become a lasting success.

Kawasaki had also introduced a four-cylinder ZZ-R600 alongside the larger 1100, to compete in the popular middleweight sports division against Yamaha's FZR600 and Honda's CBR600F. The Kawasaki's revamped 599cc liquid-cooled 16-valve engine produced a class-leading 95bhp, good for over 140mph (225km/h), and was held by a frame made from aluminium, rather than steel like that of its GPZ and GPX600 predecessors.

The ZZ-R's closest rivals also had steel frames, but both were sportier than the large and roomy Kawasaki. Yamaha's FZR600, which had been launched in 1989, was a rev-happy and rapid 90bhp machine with crude suspension. It provided little practicality or comfort, but lots of high-revving entertainment. Honda's versatile and hugely successful CBR600F got better still in 1991 when it was revamped with fresh styling and a more powerful, 100bhp engine.

Small bikes, big thrills

While many European riders regarded 600cc as the perfect compromise between performance and cost, in Japan the hot class for high-tech sports machines was 400cc. Honda's CBR400RR and Suzuki's GSX-R400R, both in-line fours, and their V4 rival the VFR400R were tiny, high-revving bikes that handled superbly thanks to ultra-light chassis, but were too expensive to be sold outside Japan. Super-sports 250cc two-strokes were also popular in Japan. Some, notably Kawasaki's KR-1 and Suzuki's RGV250, were sold in Europe.

Honda's 1994 NSR250R race-replica was notably high-tech, as it featured a 'smart-card' that slotted into the steering head. Alternative cards could be used to alter the two-stroke V-twin's engine management system, giving instant tuning. The NSR and other exotica reached Europe in

Below: Harley revitalized its Sportster 1200 in 1991 with a mildly tuned V-twin engine, five-speed box and belt final drive. It was slow, vibrated and had mediocre handling. But it also looked great and sold well – as did the similarly styled, budget-priced Sportster 883, whose capacity echoed that of the original 1957 model.

Above: Suzuki updated the GSX-R750 with a liquid-cooled engine in 1992, by which time the 16-valve four's storming performance and aggressive, wheelie-happy personality had earned it a cult following around the world.

Below: For British bike enthusiasts the decade's best surprise was the rebirth of Triumph, with a range of modular three- and four-cylinder superbikes. This prototype 900 Trophy was painted in contrasting colours for evaluation.

Below right: Norton's expensive rotary-engined F1 sportster, left, was inspired by Steve Spray's championship-winning racebike.

small numbers when enterprising dealers began trading in 'grey' models ignored by official importers. More worrying for some countries' importers were 'parallel imports', familiar models sourced independently from abroad and sold cheaply. Some importers were forced into big price reductions to overcome the problem.

Honda had suffered a more serious setback when in 1990 it had attempted to reverse falling US sales and market share with a bold new machine, the PC800 Pacific Coast. This was a large, rounded device, designed by Honda's car division to entice a new generation of non-motorcyclists onto two wheels. Beneath its expanse of plastic the Pacific Coast held an 800cc, in-line V-twin engine from the VT800 Shadow cruiser. It produced 50bhp and gave quiet running with a top speed approaching 120mph (193km/h). The Coast was lighter than it looked, and handled reasonably well. But few people bought one, despite an expensive TV advertising campaign.

Honda's US slump contrasted with the rise of Harley-Davidson, whose Sportster was the top-selling bike of 1990. That year saw the introduction of the Fat Boy, whose blend of 1950s-inspired styling and disc wheels would prove a hit. In 1991 the Sportster 1200 was updated with a more powerful, 50bhp engine, five-speed gearbox and final drive by belt, as already used by the firm's 1340cc 'Big Twins'. The Sportster was still crude and not very fast, but it looked as cute as ever and continued the success story.

While cruisers dominated the US market, elsewhere attention was focused on the open-class super-sports battle between Suzuki and Yamaha. Suzuki had blundered in 1989 by updating its original GSX-R1100 with the ill-handling GSX-R1100K. That model was followed a year later by the 1100L, which replaced the K model's stiff front forks with a new pair whose 'upside-down' design, derived from road-racing, was claimed to give increased rigidity.

The GSX-R1100L shared its predecessor's uprated 1127cc 141bhp four-cylinder engine, and combined searing straight-line speed with much improved handling. In 1991 it faced fresh opposition from Yamaha's FZR1000RU, an uprated version of the old favourite with sharper styling, unchanged 140bhp 20-valve 1102cc powerplant and a pair of upside-down forks of its own. The two rivals were good for about 165mph (266km/h) and were closely matched in every way. Suzuki also revised its popular GSX-R750 to good effect.

Triumph Trophy 1200 (1991)	
Engine:	Liquid-cooled dohc 16-valve four
Capacity:	1180cc (76 x 65mm)
Maximum power:	125bhp @ 9000rpm
Transmission:	Six-speed, chain final drive
Frame:	Steel spine
Suspension:	Telescopic front; single shock rear
Brakes:	Twin disc front; disc rear
Weight:	529lb (240kg)
Top speed:	153mph (246km/h)

At the opposite end of the scale to the mass-produced fours was Norton's F1, a compact rotary sportster derived from the marque's British championship-winning racer. The F1's 588cc liquid-cooled engine produced 95bhp, and was held by a high-quality aluminium frame, based on the racer's and built by local specialists Spondon Engineering. The F1's power and 422lb (191kg) weight figures matched those of a typical Japanese 600, as did its 145mph (233km/h) top speed.

The rotary felt very different, thanks to its smooth mid-range power surge and unique exhaust howl. But the expensive F1 had rough edges including snatchy low-rev response, poor fuel economy and a tendency to overheat. In 1991 Norton introduced the cheaper F1 Sport, featuring simpler bodywork and less expensive cycle parts. Few were sold, despite another burst of Norton glory when Steve Hislop rode the rotary racer to victory in the 1992 Senior TT.

By this time the British motorcycle industry was celebrating the sensational rebirth of Triumph, which in 1991 had appeared with a range of three- and four-cylinder superbikes. When the old Triumph firm had gone into liquidation in 1983, the name had been bought by John Bloor, owner of a Midlands-based building firm. Bloor was worth over £100 million but was unknown in the bike world, and most people assumed Triumph had died.

But Bloor and his small team spent the next eight years developing a range of modern bikes amid great secrecy at a purpose-built plant at Hinckley in Leicestershire, not far from Triumph's old Meriden works. The dohc, liquid-cooled engine layout owed much to Japanese practice (notably Kawasaki's GPZ900R) but incorporated a unique modular concept that echoed plans that BSA-Triumph's Bert Hopwood had produced back in 1973, but which had been abandoned after the company's financial collapse.

Bloor's Triumphs used either three or four cylinders, plus a choice of short- or long-stroke crankshafts, to create four engines that powered six models. All combined the same steel frame with Japanese-made suspension parts of varying specification. The basic roadster was the Trident, a naked triple of 749 or 885cc capacity. It was stylish and handled well, and the larger model combined generous mid-range torque with a 130mph (209km/h) top speed.

Top left: *Top of reborn Triumph's initial six-model range was the Trophy 1200. The fast and fine-handling sports-tourer was remarkably competitive with its Japanese rivals.*

Above: *Triumph's modular system meant that the larger-engined naked roadster, the Trident 900, shared its 885cc engine, plus its frame, tank, seat and many other parts, with the fully-faired Trophy 900 sports-tourer.*

Above: The NR750 was beautiful, and crammed with technology that only Honda could have developed. But the V4 was very heavy, and its oval pistons were of little benefit on a roadster.

Honda CBR900RR (1992)	
Engine:	Liquid-cooled dohc 16-valve four
Capacity:	893cc (70 x 58mm)
Maximum power:	123bhp @ 10,500rpm
Transmission:	Six-speed, chain final drive
Frame:	Aluminium twin spar
Suspension:	Telescopic front; single shock rear
Brakes:	Twin discs front; disc rear
Weight:	407lb (185kg) dry
Top speed:	160mph (257km/h)

Above right: The initial 1992-model CBR900RR, called the FireBlade in most markets, took super-sports performance to a new level thanks to its unprecedented blend of powerful 893cc engine and light, compact chassis.

Impressive sports tourer

Triumph's two Daytona sports bikes, handicapped by the modular concept, were less impressive. But the four-cylinder Trophy 1200 was a fine sports-tourer that matched its Japanese rivals in almost every area. Its 1180cc 16-valve motor produced 125bhp, giving smooth acceleration to a top speed of over 150mph (241km/h). The Trophy also handled and braked well, and was comfortable and competitively priced. Equally importantly, all the new Triumphs proved oil-tight and very reliable. The firm soon became established in the UK market, and began exporting a growing number of bikes, initially to France and Germany, as Triumph's 200-strong workforce aimed for an annual target of 10,000 units.

In the year that one reluctant new industry hero emerged, motorcycling's greatest figure of all passed away. Soichiro Honda died in August 1991, aged 84. The motorcycle firm that he had started in a Tokyo shed in 1948 now had over 80,000 employees, and factories in more than 40 countries. With bike production growing steadily towards a 1996 peak of over five million units, Honda remained by far the industry's largest and most influential force.

Honda launched one of its fastest and best ever bikes in 1992, in defiance of the lingering threat of a 100bhp limit in Europe, the new bike's intended main market. The CBR900RR, known as the FireBlade in most countries, was relatively conventional in its liquid-cooled, four-cylinder engine layout and its twin-spar aluminium frame. But this was a gloriously sharp-edged machine whose unprecedented performance resulted from a combination of big-bike horsepower and light weight. The contrast with its heavier super-sports rivals was striking.

The FireBlade's 893cc 16-valve engine produced a maximum of 123bhp, and equally importantly was barely bigger or heavier than Honda's CBR600F powerplant. The frame held thick 45mm diameter forks that were not the fashionable upside-down design, and which held a 16-inch front wheel instead of the 17-inch norm. The CBR's steering geometry was racy, and it weighed just 407lb (185kg), comparable with a middleweight four rather than its open-class rivals.

Performance was addictively thrilling. The Honda couldn't match its larger-engined GSX-R and FZR rivals for mid-range torque, but delivered fierce, high-revving acceleration towards a top

Forkless Failures

In the early '90s, many people were convinced that telescopic forks were an inherent weakness in a motorcycle chassis. The previous decade's Elf project, backed by Honda, had been abandoned after failing to make a 'forkless' factory NSR500 GP racer competitive. But some engineers continued to experiment, notably Pierluigi Marconi of Bimota. Marconi had written a thesis on alternative suspension design as a student, and at Bimota he put it into production with the Tesi ('*thesis*' in Italian).

The Tesi 1D, released in 1991, featured a twin-sided front swingarm, working a single

shock unit. Its handlebars were linked by rods to the front wheel, which pivoted on a bearing inside its hub in order to steer. The Tesi was fast, thanks to its 904cc dohc V-twin Ducati engine, and the forkless front end gave outstanding stability under braking. But the complex system of rods reduced the rider's feedback from the front wheel, and was prone to bearing wear. Equally importantly, the Tesi's exotic construction resulted in a very high price. Few were sold, and the Tesi was a commercial disaster for Bimota.

Yamaha fared little better with its 1993 forkless sports-tourer, the GTS1000. The GTS

suspension system, designed a decade earlier by New Mexico-based engineer James Parker, featured a horizontal aluminium beam running from the wheel hub to a pivot on the frame. Steering was via a telescoping vertical strut linking the hub and handlebars. The system gave excellent stability but the GTS1000, powered by a four-cylinder FZR1000 engine detuned to 100bhp, had flaws including poor fuel range, excess weight and a high price. The Yamaha's showroom failure ensured that most bikes would continue to use telescopic forks for years to come.

speed of 160mph (257km/h). Its light, racy chassis gave wonderful agility, plus an occasional flap of the handlebars to keep the rider's attention focused at all times. The Blade would lose a little of its raw excitement as chief engineer Tadao Baba refined it through the decade, but its emphasis on performance through light weight would have a lasting influence on super-sports design.

Above left: Bimota's forkless Tesi, more than a decade in development, was a costly failure that almost bankrupted the small Italian firm.

Top centre: The sales failure of Yamaha's GTS1000 was blamed on its front suspension system, but the sports-tourer had other flaws.

Above: Soichiro Honda had long since retired, but his old firm backed research into alternative front suspension systems through its support for the Elf racer project.

Left: After getting into financial trouble with the Tesi, Bimota was once again saved by the success of a conventional bike – this time the stylish Ducati 900SS-engined DB2 of 1993.

143

Right: Guzzi's Daytona 1000, fashioned by American engineer 'Dr John' Wittner, combined a new 95bhp, eight-valve V-twin engine with fresh styling and a chassis inspired by that of Wittner's racebikes.

Opposite top: Ducati's aggressively styled M900 Monster was such a hit following its launch in 1993 that it generated a new class of naked roadster, as well as prompting Ducati to create a family of Monsters in various capacities.

Opposite centre right: Having once announced that its traditional flat twins would be dropped, BMW revived the boxer with the R1100RS, whose torquey eight-valve engine was matched by an innovative and fine-handling chassis.

Opposite below right: BMW's entry-level F650 was a bold step for the German marque, as the single was built in Italy around a motor from Rotax of Austria. The 'Funduro' performed well and earned BMW many new customers.

By contrast, Honda's other 1992 sports bike, the exotic, oval-pistoned NR750, occupied a technological cul-de-sac that no other manufacturer would have considered entering. The NR owed its existence to the NR500 four-stroke racebike with which Honda had attempted to take on the rival two-strokes on its return to grand prix racing in 1979. Limited to four cylinders, Honda had attempted to mimic a V8 by creating a V4 with pistons shaped like a running track, each with eight valves and two conrods.

Honda had never managed to make the NR500 competitive, and had abandoned the project in 1981 without a rostrum finish. But development of the engine continued, and the NR750 was launched 11 years later, incorporating high-tech features including a titanium-coated windscreen, and twin silencers set into a carbon-fibre reinforced tailpiece. The NR750 was a wonderfully stylish machine, as well as a hugely expensive one of which just 1000 units were planned.

Right: Ducati's Supermono racer combined sleek styling with brilliant engineering, as its 550cc 75bhp single-cylinder engine's dummy conrod dramatically reduced vibration. Sadly, hopes of a roadgoing version came to nothing.

Ducati M900 Monster (1993)	
Engine:	Air/oil-cooled sohc four-valve 90-degree V-twin
Capacity:	904cc (92 x 68mm)
Maximum power:	73bhp @ 7250rpm
Transmission:	Six-speed, chain final drive
Frame:	Tubular steel ladder
Suspension:	Telescopic front; single shock rear
Brakes:	Twin discs front; disc rear
Weight:	406lb (184kg)
Top speed:	130mph (209km/h)

The engine's maximum output of 125bhp at 14,000rpm made the NR the world's most powerful 750, and gave a top speed of almost 160mph (257km/h). But despite much use of lightweight materials, the NR weighed an excessive 488lb (221kg). Although its polished aluminium frame, single-sided swingarm and high quality suspension gave good handling, the NR's flat power delivery meant it was not particularly exciting to ride, and no quicker than rival 750s costing a fraction of its price.

Bimota was not used to producing bikes in bigger numbers and for a lower price than a Honda, but that's what happened in 1993. Not with the long-awaited forkless Tesi, which had been a commercial flop on its release two years earlier, but with the more conventional DB2 that rescued the Italian firm's fortunes. Powered by the air/oil-cooled 904cc V-twin from Ducati's 900SS, the DB2 was a stylish, compact sportster that gained in agility what it lacked in straight-line speed. By Bimota standards the 140mph (225km/h) DB2 was inexpensive, and its sales success helped the firm recover from the disappointment of the Tesi.

Meanwhile Moto Guzzi had begun a fightback in 1992 with the Daytona 1000, a new generation V-twin with transverse, shaft-drive layout in the oldest Italian marque's own style. The American name was no coincidence, because the Daytona was inspired and created by 'Dr John' Wittner, a Philadelphia dentist-turned-tuner whose rapid self-built Guzzis had been very successful in twins racing in the late '80s. Guzzi boss Alejandro de Tomaso brought Wittner to the factory to develop a roadgoing version, and the Daytona was the result.

The sleek, half-faired Daytona was powered by a 992cc air-cooled V-twin with a new 'high-cam' valve design and four valves per cylinder. Fuel-injection helped increase output to 95bhp. The Daytona's chassis was based on that of Wittner's racebikes. It combined a steel spine frame with Marzocchi forks, and a rear suspension layout that counteracted the drive-shaft's effect on handling. The Daytona rumbled towards its 150mph (241km/h) top speed with a typically long-legged feel. Stable handling, good brakes and plenty of character contributed to an enjoyable bike that belatedly brought Moto Guzzi into the 1990s.

Ducati had also uprated its V-twin line-up in 1992, with the 900 Superlight, a sportier, single-seat version of the 900SS. The Bologna firm was fighting back under Cagiva control. Its eight-

Above: Reborn former East German marque MuZ's Skorpion Sport was a stylish and innovative machine. Its prototype used a Rotax engine, but production versions were powered by a 660cc five-valve single unit from Yamaha.

Above: After beating Honda to win the 250cc world title, Aprilia launched a fitting replica with the RS250. It combined the Italian firm's own bodywork and aluminium frame with a two-stroke V-twin engine from Suzuki's RG250.

Right: Cagiva's effort in the 500cc grand prix class was rewarded when Eddie Lawson won the firm's first victory in 1992. But despite further success in 1993, financial pressures forced boss Claudio Castiglioni to quit racing.

valve flagship the 851, uprated to 888cc in 1991, won three consecutive World Superbike championships, ridden by Frenchman Raymond Roche and America's Doug Polen. In 1993 Ducati unveiled the stunning Supermono 550 racer, designed by South African Pierre Terblanche, and powered by a dohc single-cylinder desmo engine, designed by chief engineer Massimo Bordi, that used a dummy conrod to reduce vibration. The Supermono was raced successfully but plans for a roadgoing model would repeatedly be postponed.

Ducati's success continued in 1993 with the M900 Monster, a naked all-rounder whose aggressive style would inspire a new generation of unfaired bikes. The Monster was created by Miguel Angel Galluzzi, Cagiva's Argentinean designer, who sketched a naked V-twin in his spare time, then persuaded factory bosses to put it into production. Its air-cooled sohc 904cc V-twin engine, from the 900SS, was housed in a frame from the super-sports 888, complete with rising-rate rear suspension.

The Monster's high-quality cycle parts gave excellent handling and braking by naked bike standards. The torquey V-twin engine and lack of weight ensured plenty of straight-line performance too, along with a liking for wheelies. This was a bike that was huge fun to ride at a slower pace, yet which had plenty of street cred. Despite a high price the Monster immediately generated so much demand that Ducati increased production to a quarter of the factory's 1993 total of 20,000 bikes. Soon the M900 was joined by M750 and M600 Monsters, and a naked-bike revolution was under way.

The other outstanding European twin of 1993 was BMW's R1100RS, a boxer whose appearance confirmed a remarkable change of heart. When BMW had introduced its new range of liquid-cooled fours and triples in the mid-'80s, word from Munich was that the traditional flat twins were heading for extinction. But public resistance was so strong that BMW not only introduced updated twins but developed a new boxer motor: a 1085cc fuel-injected air-/oil-cooled unit whose high-cam, four-valves-per-cylinder layout gave a maximum of 90bhp.

The R1100RS was equally notable for its chassis, which incorporated a clever new 'Telelever' front suspension system. This resembled telescopic forks, but the legs were hollow and joined to a horizontal arm that pivoted on the engine and operated a single shock unit. With stable handling allied to its flexible engine, reasonable wind protection, generous fuel range and powerful anti-

Left: Ducati's 916 backed up its gorgeous looks with thundering performance from its eight-valve desmo V-twin engine, and superb handling from its tubular steel-framed chassis.

Ducati 916 (1994)	
Engine:	Liquid-cooled dohc eight-valve 90-degree V-twin
Capacity:	916cc (94 x 66mm)
Maximum power:	114bhp @ 9000rpm
Transmission:	Six-speed, chain final drive
Frame:	Tubular steel ladder
Suspension:	Telescopic front; single shock rear
Brakes:	Twin discs front; disc rear
Weight:	429lb (195kg) dry
Top speed:	160mph (257km/h)

lock brakes, the RS represented a fine comeback for the sports-touring boxer. Within two years it would be joined by a naked R1100R and R850R roadsters, plus an R1100RT tourer with bigger fairing and more upright riding position.

BMW's radical single

BMW had lacked an entry-level model since abandoning singles production in the late '60s. That changed in 1994 with the F650 Funduro. This was evidence of a radically different approach because it was built in Italy, by Aprilia, around a liquid-cooled 652cc single-cylinder engine from Austrian firm Rotax. The F650 was also the first chain-drive model in BMW's 70-year history. With striking looks, 100mph (161km/h) performance and good handling, the Funduro was indeed fun to ride. It was competitively priced, and quickly became a success.

The F650 was not the year's only new German single. The former East German firm MZ, known for efficient but ugly commuter bikes, had been reborn after German reunification as MuZ. The firm's boss Petr-Karel Korous commissioned British consultants Seymour Powell to design a roadster around the 48bhp engine from Yamaha's XTZ660. The result was the striking Skorpion, available as a bikini-faired sportster and a naked roadster. With 100mph (161km/h) performance and agile handling from an innovative frame of large-diameter steel tube, it was a promising start for MuZ.

Meanwhile Aprilia was going from strength to strength. Ivano Beggio, who had begun motorcycle production in 1973 after taking over the family bicycle business, had found rapid success by assembling bikes using components sourced almost exclusively from outside, rather than manufactured in-house. Beggio had concentrated on small two-stroke sports machines and trail bikes, investing heavily in research and development via racing. In 1994 Aprilia produced 100,000 bikes, double the total of three years earlier, and beat mighty Honda to win both 250cc and 125cc world championships.

The following year the firm from Noale in north-eastern Italy celebrated rider Max Biaggi's 250cc title with a race-replica, the RS250. Its sleek bodywork echoed that of the factory racebike, and the RS featured a similar specification: liquid-cooled, two-stroke V-twin engine, strong

Below: Few small-capacity bikes have matched the style of Gilera's CX125, with its swoopy bodywork and mono-arm suspension at front and rear. But the two-stroke was not a success.

Above: Cagiva's Cucciolo, named after subsidiary Ducati's first ever bike, was one of scores of scooters from Italian manufacturers.

Below: Italjet's Formula 125 was very unusual for a scooter in having a twin-cylinder engine, but in most markets it was restricted to 12bhp.

aluminium twin-spar frame, and high-quality cycle parts. The 249cc motor, from Suzuki's RGV250, was modified with new cylinder heads that boosted power to 70bhp. The lightweight Aprilia screamed to 130mph (209km/h) and handled brilliantly. The final touch was a GP-style lap-timer in the cockpit, activated by a switch on the handlebars.

Cagiva had spent years battling against the Japanese factories in the even more competitive 500cc grand prix class, and had finally achieved notable success. Americans Eddie Lawson and John Kocinski won GPs on the Italian firm's V4 in 1992 and '93 respectively, and Kocinski briefly led the championship in the following season. Then Cagiva quit grand prix racing amid rumours of financial trouble.

Those problems would cause the delayed arrival of the bike that was the undoubted star of 1994. Ducati's 916 combined style, speed and poise to stunning effect. Designed by former Bimota co-founder Massimo Tamburini and his small team at the Cagiva Research Centre in San Marino, the 916 was a uniquely beautiful motorbike, from its sharp nose to the exhaust tailpipes poking from beneath its seat.

The 916cc eight-valve V-twin desmo engine was based on Ducati's previous 888cc unit, and used a revised fuel-injection system and new exhaust to produce 114bhp. Ducati had considered an aluminium frame before sticking with its traditional steel ladder, and added an aluminium single-sided swingarm that gave a dramatic look, in conjunction with a widest-yet 190-section rear tyre. Details included adjustable steering geometry and a transverse-mounted hydraulic damper above the steering head.

With its compact dimensions, firm suspension and aggressive riding position, the 916 was an uncompromising super-sports bike. Its powerful, smooth and soulful motor sent the bike thundering to a top speed of well over 150mph (241km/h) and produced plenty of mid-range torque. Handling was a sublime blend of precision and absolute stability. A year later the 916 was joined by a smaller-engined model, the 748, which combined near-identical shape and chassis parts with a more rev-happy personality all of its own.

Right: Taiwanese firm PGO stirred up interest with this 1600cc prototype at the Cologne Show in 1992, but it did not reach production.

Left: Wealthy Italian enthusiast Giancarlo Morbidelli's dream of producing an exotic 850cc V8 tourer was dashed when Pininfarina's styling work was so heavily criticized that the project was first delayed, then abandoned.

Below: Few bikes have captured the imagination like visionary Kiwi engineer John Britten's V-1000, pictured here on the Daytona start grid. The hand-built V-twin racer was fast, futuristic and utterly beautiful.

Gilera halts production

While Ducati celebrated the 916's success, another famous Italian name sunk to a new low. Gilera had made a big push in the early '90s, under Piaggio's control, with an unsuccessful 250cc grand prix racing team and several new roadsters including a retro-styled 500cc four-stroke single called the Saturno. More spectacular was the CX125, a racy single-cylinder two-stroke with single-arm suspension at both front and rear. But sales were disappointing, and in 1993 Piaggio closed the factory at Arcore, outside Milan, keeping the Gilera name only for use on sporty scooters.

The scooter market was booming, as convenient and inexpensive 'twist-and-go' machines were sold all over the world. European firms including Piaggio, Aprilia and France's Peugeot benefited. So did firms in Asian countries including Taiwan and China, which produced a huge number of machines for sale in their own markets, and increasingly for export too. Few were interested in big-bike production, although China's Chiang Jiang produced flat twins based on the 1950s BMW R71. Taiwan's PGO displayed a promising 1600cc V-twin prototype sportster at the Cologne Show in 1992, but it did not reach production.

Another still-born project was the Morbidelli 850 V8, an exotic sports-tourer created by wealthy Italian businessman Giancarlo Morbidelli, whose racebikes had won several world titles in the 1970s. Morbidelli's 847cc liquid-cooled transverse V8 engine was a work of art. But the bike's styling, by famed car house Pininfarina, was a disappointment when unveiled in 1994. The bike was restyled, and tuned to increase peak output to 120bhp. But by the time the revised V8 was ready, the project had lost momentum, and Morbidelli abandoned plans for small-scale production after only a handful of bikes had been built.

Such disappointments were put into context by the death in 1995 from cancer of John Britten, the brilliant 44-year-old New Zealander whose V-twin racebikes had been universally admired. Few bikes have combined elegance and innovative engineering as successfully as the V-1000, a liquid-cooled, dohc V-twin that produced over 170bhp in an early 1108cc form. Britten and his small team made almost everything by hand, including the girder front forks and the rear

Above: Honda's 750cc RC45 did not match the impact of its V4 predecessor, the RC30, but it did eventually win the World Superbike title.

Above: Kawasaki's ZX-6R was a welcome addition to the 600cc super-sports battle, backing up its powerful 16-valve engine and excellent handling with plenty of character.

Right: Such was the sales success of Suzuki's quick, entertaining and competitively priced Bandit 600 that rival manufacturers replied with unfaired middleweights of their own.

swingarm, both of which were fashioned from lightweight Kevlar and carbon-fibre. The Britten was hugely impressive in winning races at Daytona and elsewhere in the early '90s, when it was timed at over 180mph (290km/h). A handful of V-1000 racebikes were later built and sold. Britten's death robbed the motorcycle world of one of its greatest talents.

Britten had relished pitting his V-1000 against the dominant Ducatis, and in 1994 Honda had unveiled an exotic machine intended for the same job. The RC45, like its RC30 predecessor, was a 750cc V4 derived from Honda's factory racebikes. It produced 118bhp plus strong mid-range power, and its classy aluminium-framed chassis gave excellent handling. As a streetbike the costly RC45 had limited appeal. More seriously for Honda, the RC45 failed to beat the Ducatis in its first three World Superbike seasons. American John Kocinski would finally win the title in 1997, rewarding Honda's huge investment.

Kawasaki's sole World Superbike championship had been won by fellow American Scott Russell on a ZXR750 in 1993. The following year saw the firm further enhance its reputation for rapid straight fours with a new open-class charger, the ZX-9R. This was an 899cc 16-valve missile whose 139bhp peak output provided neck-wrenching acceleration towards a top speed of over 165mph (266km/h). The ZX-9R's styling was sharp, but this was a heavier and less extreme machine than its super-sport rivals. Its aluminium-framed chassis gave good handling, and the way the ZX-9R delivered performance in comfort made it a worthy successor to its illustrious forebear, the GPZ900R of ten years earlier.

Kawasaki suffered a blow in January 1995 when its home city of Kobe was hit by a devastating earthquake that left more than 5000 people dead and disrupted production. The year was also marked by the launch of the ZX-6R, a super-sports 599cc four designed to take on Honda's CBR600F, which had sold more than 100,000 units since its introduction eight years earlier. The ZX-6R's 16-valve engine, a higher-revving development of the ZZ-R unit, gave a top speed approaching 160mph (257km/h). The Kawasaki's rigid aluminium frame, taut suspension and racy looks completed a fiercely competitive machine.

Naked fours streak in

Another outstanding middleweight was Suzuki's Bandit 600, a cheaper naked four offering lively performance. The Bandit was an instant hit, and was joined a year later by a more practical and only slightly more expensive half-faired model. Suzuki's success inspired other manufacturers. Over the next few years, quick and capable fours including Yamaha's Fazer 600 and Honda's Hornet would make the budget middleweight class one of motorcycling's most crowded.

The Japanese firms also produced a host of bigger naked fours. Suzuki's Bandit 1200 was the most popular, thanks to its blunt styling, flexible 16-valve engine, light weight and competitive price. Honda's CB1000 was styled to resemble the CB1100R production racer of the early '80s, but lacked excitement until uprated to create the CB1300. Yamaha's XJR1200, powered by a detuned version of the FJ1200 sports-tourer's air-cooled engine, combined muscular looks with 140mph (225km/h) performance to match.

Triumph had confirmed its growing confidence in 1993 with a fully-faired four, the Daytona 1200, whose peak output of 145bhp defied the UK industry's self-imposed 125bhp limit. Although its tall, steel-framed modular chassis was dated, the 160mph (257km/h) Daytona was Triumph's fastest and best sportster yet. But most people preferred the more distinctive triples. Triumph's response in 1994 was the naked Speed Triple, which backed-up its 885cc engine's storming performance with low bars and plenty of attitude.

Although the Speed Triple owed its name to the 1930s Speed Twin, John Bloor had been keen to establish his firm as a modern manufacturer, so had avoided retro machines. By 1995, Bloor was ready to exploit Triumph's heritage with a classically styled model, the Thunderbird. This held a softly tuned, 69bhp version of the 885cc triple engine in Triumph's first non-modular frame. New bodywork incorporated details including a '50s-style Triumph 'mouth-organ' tank badge. The T-bird's blend of modern performance and traditional style went down well. It became Triumph's best-selling model, and led the firm's move into the US market, which proved difficult to crack due to its cruiser bias and the country's huge size.

Above: Like its predecessor the CB1000 'Big One', Honda's CB1300 was styled to resemble the all-conquering CB1100R of the early '80s. Peak power output remained just under 100bhp, but the CB1300's liquid-cooled 16-valve engine had huge reserves of mid-range torque.

Left: Yamaha gave its retro-styled musclebike some extra grunt when the original XJR1200's air-cooled engine was enlarged to 1250cc to create the XJR1300. An uprated chassis incorporated Öhlins rear shocks.

Above: Triumph's Daytona 1200 four produced 145bhp, exceeding the unofficial UK limit.

Below: Harley introduced fuel-injection in 1995 on its Ultra Classic Electra Glide, which celebrated 30 years of the big touring V-twin.

Below right: Revitalized Triumph's first retro model was the Thunderbird triple, with 'mouth-organ' tank badge and 'peashooter' pipes.

Meanwhile, Harley-Davidson continued to make the most of its heritage. In 1995, Harley celebrated the 30th anniversary of its biggest and most famous model with the Ultra Classic Electra Glide, a US-market special edition of the giant tourer that was notable for introducing fuel-injection. The 1340cc V-twin engine was mechanically unchanged, but the injection gave sweeter low-rev running and improved fuel consumption. Even Harley didn't claim much in the way of improved performance from the Heritage Springer Softail that followed in 1997. But with its eye-catching springer front suspension system, allied to a hardtail-look rear, the new Softail was strikingly reminiscent of a 1940s Panhead.

The Japanese firms had tried to match Harley over the years with V-twin cruisers, with varying success. One of the better attempts had been Yamaha's neatly styled XV535 Virago, which had become especially popular with female riders due to its low seat. For 1997 it was joined by the Drag Star 650, with wide-spaced forks, forward-set pegs and hardtail-look rear suspension to give some extra 'custom' style.

Honda's Shadow 1100 and Kawasaki's Vulcan 1500 had gained credibility with some potential buyers by being built at the firms' US factories. Honda showed even more determination to match Harley in 1995 with the Shadow ACE, short for American Classic Edition. Designed by American Honda, this had a revised version of the 1099cc liquid-cooled V-twin engine, with both conrods mounted on a single crankpin in Harley style, instead of spaced at 90 degrees. The result was a more 'American' feel and exhaust note. Harley's attempt to patent its 'potato-potato' exhaust sound would be abandoned years later, after much had been spent on legal fees.

Yamaha used its US base to create the XVZ1300 Royal Star, launched in 1996. Despite looking like an air-cooled V-twin, the Royal Star was a liquid-cooled V4. Its 1294cc dohc engine was a much detuned, 74bhp version of the V-Max's 140bhp unit. Performance was predictably modest, given the bike's 671lb (304kg) of weight. Despite disappointing sales Yamaha continued with plans to develop its Star line as a 'sub-brand' in the way that Lexus is an offshoot of Toyota, the car giant with which Yamaha had developed links.

The most improbable US success story was that of the Boss Hoss, the giant bike powered by a Chevrolet V8 car engine. Tennessee-based Monty Warne built his first V8 bike for fun, but so

Left: Harley-Davidson's dedication to giving its modern bikes a traditional look reached a new level in 1997 with the Heritage Springer Softail, which featured old-style springer front forks, a hardtail-look rear, and 16-inch wire wheels with big fenders and white-wall tyres.

Below: Yamaha's line-up of cruisers saw the Drag Star 1100 joined by a smaller V-twin, the Drag Star 650. While big cruisers were popular mainly in the US and a few European countries, notably Scandinavia, middleweights had wider appeal, especially for female riders.

many people were interested that in 1991 he began selling chassis kits, then complete machines. A typical early-'90s Boss Hoss (the name was Boss Hog until Harley objected) featured a six-litre Chevy motor that produced 300bhp and gave a top speed of over 160mph (257km/h). Only the brave attempted it, given the scary handling that resulted from 1100lb (500kg) of weight and a square-section car back tyre.

Warne refined the Hoss, adding an automatic gearbox (early models had just one gear: 'fast forward') and a round-section rear tyre that improved handling. Before long he was selling several hundred per year, at $30,000 or more each. By 1997 Warne had built more than 1000 bikes, and had introduced a slightly lighter and cheaper 4.3-litre V6 model, the 'ladies' bike', which produced a mere 200bhp.

Honda produced a unusual big bike in 1996: a 1520cc flat six that was called the Valkyrie in the US and the F6C in Europe. Its Gold Wing-derived engine delivered 100bhp, good for a top speed of 125mph (201km/h), plus so much low-rev torque that the rider required strong arms but rarely the gearbox. For a bike weighing almost 700lb (318kg) the six cornered and braked well too, thanks to a strong steel frame, firm suspension and big triple discs. Honda billed the Valkyrie as the world's first 'performance cruiser', and few who rode it disagreed.

The year's other big Honda was a performance machine of a more familiar variety. The CBR1100XX Super Blackbird, named after the US spy plane, was intended to recapture the unofficial world's fastest motorcycle title from Kawasaki's ZZ-R1100. That it did, reaching a top speed of 180mph (290km/h) thanks to a powerful and refined 1137cc 16-valve engine, allied to bodywork that was aerodynamically efficient but which left the monotone Super Blackbird looking decidedly ordinary.

The key to the Honda's wind-cheating shape was its piggy-back headlamp, with twin lenses one above the other. This allowed a sharp, narrow fairing whose low screen was also ideal for maximum speed, if not for the Blackbird's intended sports-touring role. Despite that and its unexceptional low-rev power delivery, the CBR made a comfortable and entertaining long-distance blaster, and was popular in many European markets.

The once dominant 750cc class, which had lost importance over the years, was enlivened by the 1996 arrival of Suzuki's GSX-R750T. The racy four had been given a liquid-cooled engine four years earlier, in place of the original oil-cooled design. Now the 749cc unit was tuned and fitted with a ram-air system, and bolted into a twin-spar aluminium frame, in place of the taller traditional design. The resultant 126bhp, 394lb (179kg) Suzuki was a stunningly fast, focused and fine-handling bike that stole the limelight from Kawasaki's stylish, but heavier and less powerful, new ZX-7R. A year later Suzuki produced an even more manic four, the GSX-R600, which combined similar looks and layout with an even revvier 104bhp engine, and screamed to a top speed of 155mph (249km/h).

Italian firms struggle

While the Japanese manufacturers were developing ever-faster sports bikes, several Italian firms were struggling. In 1993 Moto Guzzi, hindered by the ill-health of owner Alejandro de Tomaso, had built just 3000 bikes. The following year the firm was taken over by a Milan-based merchant bank, which by 1996 had doubled production, posted a modest profit and introduced a handful of new models. The 1100 Sport Injection and Daytona RS were revised versions of existing sporty V-twins. The new Centauro was a naked 992cc V-twin with curious styling and rather crude suspension, but at least Guzzi was showing signs of life.

Laverda had gone into receivership in 1987, and several attempts to relaunch it since then had ended in failure. In 1994, local entrepreneur Francesco Tognon took control, moved Laverda from its Breganze base to a new site at nearby Zané, and began production of a sporty parallel twin called simply the 650. This consisted of a 668cc 70bhp air/oil-cooled engine, derived from an old

Above: Honda's 1995-model Shadow ACE, short for American Classic Edition, was notable not for its typical Japanese cruiser styling, but for its 1100cc V-twin engine's use of a single crankpin, in order to replicate the offbeat exhaust note popularized by Harley-Davidson.

Right: The Royal Star was the first of what Yamaha intended would be a new family of cruisers, aimed mainly at the US market and based on the V-Max's liquid-cooled V4 engine.

Left: An early-'90s Boss Hoss was a huge brute of a bike that held a 300bhp six-litre Chevrolet V8 engine in a crude chassis, with square-section car rear tyre. The Hoss was impractical but it looked wild and was exciting to ride.

Above: The second Boss Hoss model, the V6, incorporated a new transmission, purpose-built forks and improved brakes. Its 4.3-litre engine produced 200bhp, making this merely the world's second most powerful production bike.

'70s design, in a new twin-spar aluminium frame. The first 650 was an agile and torquey bike that was let down by inconsistent build quality. A string of new 668cc twins over the next few years led in 1997 to the 750S. This had a bigger 747cc liquid-cooled engine producing 82bhp. With sleek, fully-faired looks plus the traditional fine handling, it was Laverda's best twin yet.

Cagiva's financial problems came to a head in 1996, when production ground to a halt. In September of that year Claudio Castiglioni, Cagiva's President, sold a 51 per cent controlling stake in Ducati to Texas Pacific, a US investment group that owned three airlines plus numerous other businesses. TPG's new management team, led by Federico Minoli, paid 700 suppliers more

Left: Honda's Valkyrie, known as the F6C in Europe, was a 'performance cruiser' powered by a slightly modified 1520cc flat six engine from the Gold Wing. It looked ungainly but handled and braked surprisingly well.

Honda CBR1100XX (1996)

Engine:	Liquid-cooled dohc 16-valve four
Capacity:	1037cc (79 x 58mm)
Maximum power:	162bhp @ 10,000rpm
Transmission:	Six-speed, chain final drive
Frame:	Aluminium twin spar
Suspension:	Telescopic front; single shock rear
Brakes:	Twin discs front; disc rear
Weight:	491lb (223kg) dry
Top speed:	180mph (290km/h)

Above right: Aerodynamics-led styling and dull paintwork ensured that the Super Blackbird was not particularly attractive, but its top speed of 180mph (290km/h) meant that it was the world's fastest production bike in 1996.

Below: Arguably the most important update in the life of Suzuki's GSX-R750 came in 1996 with the 750T, which featured a ram-air induction system, plus a twin-spar aluminium frame design that was more rigid than its predecessor.

Right: Moto Guzzi, apparently recovering under new ownership, unveiled a pair of updated V-twin sportsters, the 1100 Sport Injection (left) and the Daytona RS.

than $50 million, restarted production, overhauled the Bologna factory to improve efficiency and quality control, and began a three-year programme to invest a further $70 million in new equipment. An exciting new era had begun.

By 1997 production was up to a record 26,000, double the previous year's stoppage-hit figure, and Ducati had launched the sports-touring ST2 that had been under development for some time. Shaped as much for comfort and practicality as for style, the ST2 was powered by a 944cc 83bhp liquid-cooled version of the familiar sohc desmo V-twin. The ST2 was good for 140mph (225km/h), handled well, and its relatively upright riding position and long-travel suspension were welcome on long trips. Ducati had a way to go to match the build quality of Honda's VFR750F, but the ST2 was a promising start.

While Ducati was challenging Honda with a new sports-tourer, Honda and Suzuki were hitting back with V-twin sports bikes, both with 996cc, liquid-cooled, dohc eight-valve, 90-degree engines. Honda's VTR1000F Firestorm was a quick and capable machine that shared some of the VFR's practicality, thanks to a carburetted motor tuned for mid-range response rather than top-

Left: *The 750S was by far Laverda's best parallel twin so far, thanks largely to a new 747cc liquid-cooled engine that was smoother and more refined than its air/oil-cooled 668cc predecessors, as well as more powerful.*

Below: *Ducati's ST2 was important because it was the first of a new line of sports-tourers, but the 944cc V-twin's real significance was that it was the Bologna brand's first new bike since the take-over by US group Texas Pacific.*

end power. Despite that, the 110bhp twin was capable of almost 160mph (257km/h), and handled well thanks to an aluminium beam-framed chassis.

Suzuki's TL1000S had an exciting specification based on a fuel-injected V-twin motor that produced 123bhp – more than both the Firestorm and Ducati's 916. The aggressive, half-faired Suzuki's tubular aluminium frame incorporated a unique rear suspension system consisting of a single spring and separate rotary damper. The TL1000S was a star in almost every respect. Its motor was wonderfully torquey, with enough top-end power for a top speed of 160mph (257km/h), and its handling was light and precise.

But the TL's blend of acceleration and quick steering resulted in occasional instability, and bad publicity concerning crashes resulting from 'tank-slappers' prompted Suzuki to recall it for fitment of a steering damper. The TL1000S's sales never recovered. A year later it was joined by the TL1000R, with full fairing and more conventional beam frame. The R model was faster but heavier, and lacked the S model's mid-range punch.

The other outstanding sports bike of 1997 signified the second phase of Triumph's recovery. The T595 Daytona was a sleek, fully-faired triple that abandoned the British firm's modular concept, and was launched to confront the Japanese opposition head-on. The Daytona's 955cc engine, based on the original 885cc unit, was fuel-injected, and tuned with the help of Lotus Engineering to produce 128bhp. Its frame was an innovative design of twin oval-section aluminium tubes, which held an equally striking single-sided swingarm.

Triumph unveiled the Daytona at the 1996 Cologne Show to an enthusiastic response. The triple lived up to its promise, as its powerful and flexible motor sent the T595 surging towards a top speed of over 160mph (257km/h). Handling was excellent too, as the rigid frame and well-damped suspension gave unshakeable stability and neutral steering. The triple did not quite match the pure pace and agility of more focused Japanese super-sports bikes, but as a rapid roadster it was hugely impressive.

At the same time Triumph launched the T509 Speed Triple, an updated version of its naked streetfighter complete with bug-eyed twin headlamps, more powerful 885cc engine, and the Daytona's aluminium-framed chassis. The Triple's unique, stripped-down streetfighter style struck a chord, and the model became a big hit. The T595 and T509 names, taken from the factory code-

Above: Suzuki's TL1000S provided thrilling performance from its torquey eight-valve V-twin engine, but was criticized after its innovative chassis gave stability problems.

Below right: Triumph took a big step forward with its impressive new-generation three-cylinder machines, the super-sports T595 Daytona (left) and naked T509 Speed Triple.

Triumph T595 Daytona (1997)	
Engine:	Liquid-cooled dohc 12-valve triple
Capacity:	955cc (79 x 65mm)
Maximum power:	128bhp @ 10,200rpm
Transmission:	Six-speed, chain final drive
Frame:	Tubular aluminium perimeter
Suspension:	Telescopic front; single shock rear
Brakes:	Twin discs front; disc rear
Weight:	436lb (198kg) dry
Top speed:	165mph (265km/h)

names in Triumph tradition, would later be dropped because many people found them confusing. But the new-generation triples confirmed Triumph's growing status.

BMW also unveiled two dramatic new bikes in 1997. With the R1200C, the firm's design chief David Robb – ironically, an American – proved that it was possible to create a stylish cruiser without copying Harley-Davidson. More than that, the R1200C flaunted its BMW heritage with a 1170cc boxer engine, and a Telelever front suspension with polished aluminium arm. The softly tuned 61bhp twin was flexible, handled well and incorporated clever details including a pillion seat that hinged to become a backrest.

The more conventional K1200RS was another bold step for BMW because the four-cylinder sports-tourer's maximum output of 130bhp blew open the self-imposed 100bhp limit that had handicapped the German marque for years. The 1171cc 16-valve BMW shot smoothly to 150mph (241km/h) and was very stable, although at 573lb (260kg) it was also heavy. In 1998 BMW followed the four with a very different high-performance model, the R1100S flat twin. Its 98bhp 1085cc air-cooled motor was a tuned version of the R1100RS sports-tourer's unit. With distinctive styling, a flexible motor, 140mph (225km/h) top speed and sound handling, the R1100S gave BMW its most competitive sportster since the R90S of two decades earlier.

Aprilia's superbike debut

The other outstanding twin-cylinder newcomer of 1998 was also eagerly anticipated. Aprilia's RSV Mille was powered by a 998cc dohc V-twin that produced 128bhp, and whose cylinders were arranged at 60 degrees, instead of the familiar 90 degrees, because this gave a more compact unit. Twin balancer shafts cancelled the resultant vibration. Styling was shaped in Aprilia's wind tunnel; the strong aluminium twin-spar frame was designed in the firm's race department.

Predictably, Aprilia's first superbike proved to be superbly fast, stable, agile and reliable. The RSV was rather tall, and despite some neat touches its styling lacked a little Italian glamour. But the V-twin thundered towards a top speed of 165mph (266km/h) in thrilling fashion, and delivered superb handling and roadholding. Thoughtful details included a high-tech instrument panel containing a lap timer and racer-style gearshift warning light. With one model, Aprilia had established itself as a major-league superbike manufacturer.

Left: The 1997-model K1200RS confirmed a significant change of heart at BMW. The big 16-valve sports-tourer's peak output of 130bhp far exceeded the self-imposed 100bhp limit that the German marque had observed in the past.

Below: BMW's R1200C cruiser was a distinctive and innovative bike that emphasized the marque's heritage. This R1200C Independent version added new paintwork, extra chrome and a tinted screen to the basic format.

Even the RSV had to take second billing in 1998 to the bike whose vital statistics alone suggested that the superbike status quo had shifted again – and whose performance very much confirmed it. Yamaha's YZF-R1 produced 150bhp, weighed a mere 389lb (177kg) and had a wheelbase of just 54.9in (1395mm). That meant it was the most powerful, lightest and shortest open-class sports bike yet. The R1's sharp, twin-headlamp fairing and bodywork helped give an aggressive look that perfectly matched its personality.

The new bike was a development of the 1996-model Thunderace, itself a fast and fine-handling 1002cc four. Yamaha's new 998cc 20-valve engine was more powerful and also more compact, thanks to a novel 'stacked' gearbox. The motor's extra stiffness meant it could form part of the chassis, allowing a lighter aluminium Deltabox II frame. The R1 backed up its 170mph (274km/h) top speed with a wonderfully broad power band, excellent brakes, and superb handling that let it scythe through bends with more poise than any 600cc sports bike.

A year later Yamaha broadened the YZF range with a similarly styled and focused 599cc model, the YZF-R6. The R6 used ram-air to reach a claimed peak output of 120bhp, and weighed

Left: More than two decades after the seminal R90S of the mid-'70s, BMW's fast and stylish R1100S proved that the air-cooled flat twin engine layout was still very viable as the basis for a high-performance superbike.

Aprilia RSV Mille (1998)

Engine:	Liquid-cooled dohc eight-valve 60-degree V-twin
Capacity:	998cc (97 x 67.5mm)
Maximum power:	128bhp @ 9250rpm
Transmission:	Six-speed, chain final drive
Frame:	Aluminium twin spar
Suspension:	Telescopic front; single shock rear
Brakes:	Twin discs front; disc rear
Weight:	416lb (189kg) dry
Top speed:	165mph (266km/h)

Above: The Aprilia RSV Mille was an instant hit.

Below right: Yamaha's R1: fast, light and sharp.

Yamaha YZF-R1 (1998)

Engine:	Liquid-cooled dohc 20-valve four
Capacity:	998cc (74 x 58mm)
Maximum power:	150bhp @ 10,000rpm
Transmission:	Six-speed, chain final drive
Frame:	Aluminium twin spar
Suspension:	Telescopic front; single shock rear
Brakes:	Twin discs front; disc rear
Weight:	389lb (176kg) dry
Top speed:	170mph (274km/h)

a class-lowest 372lb (169kg). It quickly became established as the hardest and fastest of the 600cc race-replicas. But when the Supersport world championship for 600cc fours and 750cc twins began in 1999, the first winner was Frenchman Stephane Chambon, riding Suzuki's GSX-R600. Yamaha's exotic, limited-edition 750cc four, the YZF-R7, would also fail to make the hoped-for impact in World Superbikes.

In 1998 Honda celebrated its 50th anniversary by building its 100 millionth motorbike, and by giving its VFR sports-tourer a new 108bhp fuel-injected V4 engine to create the VFR800FI. A less happy anniversary was that of Norton, which reached its centenary in 1998. The firm's recovery had foundered in the mid-'90s. Several former directors were convicted of financial irregularities, and hundreds of enthusiast shareholders lost the money they had invested in the company. The marque's new Canadian owners put little money either into new models or into the dilapidated factory at Shenstone, which was left producing small quantities of spare parts.

In spring 1998 the Aquilini Group, Norton's latest owner, held a reception at the Dorchester Hotel in London's Park Lane to announce a stunning range of new models. The flagship, unveiled in prototype form, was a futuristic 1500cc V8 superbike called the Nemesis, which Norton claimed produced 280bhp and had a top speed of 225mph (362km/h), making it by far the world's fastest production motorcycle. The range would also include two large-capacity fours, a V8 cruiser and a 600cc single.

The Nemesis, which incorporated advanced features including active suspension, perimeter disc brakes and a push-button gearchange and clutch, had been designed by Al Melling, head of Yorkshire based Melling Consultancy Design. Melling's claim that the radical, untried bike would be produced at Shenstone in six months' time was at best hopelessly optimistic, but many people accepted it. Positive media coverage would keep the Nemesis saga going for several years until the project's inevitable abandonment amid a flurry of solicitors' letters.

Ironically the only Norton produced in 1998 was the relatively humble C652SM, powered by the single-cylinder engine from BMW's F650. The single was devised by Joe Seifert, whose

Grands Prix versus Superbikes

The rise of the World Superbike championship during the '90s meant that motorcycling gained two rival series fighting for prestige and attention. The established grand prix championship offered the excitement and technical interest of pure-bred racing prototypes. The Superbike series for production-based machines put strict limits on which parts could be changed, resulting in close racing from bikes resembling standard showroom models.

Superbike's format made the series very relevant for manufacturers, encouraging much works team participation – plus

development of racy 'homologation special' roadsters such as Honda's RC45 and various limited-edition Ducatis. The organizers tried to ensure fairness by pitting 750cc fours against 1000cc twins, with varying additional weight penalties over the years. Despite this, Ducati's red V-twins dominated the decade by winning eight of the ten titles, including two for Texan Doug Polen and four for Englishman 'King Carl' Fogarty, whose hard-riding style and abrasive personality did much to make Superbikes popular.

The 500cc grand prix championship was ruled throughout the '90s by the two-stroke V4, although Yamaha's YZR500 differed from Honda's NSR500 and Suzuki's RGV500 by using twin contra-rotating crankshafts rather than one. By the end of the decade, peak power outputs had risen to almost 200bhp, and Honda's NSR500 had been timed at 200mph (322km/h). Californian Wayne Rainey won a hat-trick of titles for Yamaha before his career was ended by a 1993 crash that left him paralysed. Australian Michael Doohan

recovered from a serious leg injury to become grand prix racing's outstanding figure with five consecutive championships for Honda, before a crash ended his career in 1999.

While the Superbikes and 500cc grands prix battled for supremacy, and fans debated the merits of Doohan and 'Foggy', the other racing classes were largely overshadowed. The 250cc grand prix twins, once almost as important as the 500s, declined in importance along with the 125cc singles. By the end of the decade the once popular but increasingly irrelevant sidecars had lost their world championship status, and were no longer part of the grand prix scene.

Above left: Ducati's eight-valve V-twin took Carl Fogarty to four World Superbike titles.

Above: Michael Doohan on Honda's NSR500 V4.

Left: The racy Yamaha YZF-R6 produced 120bhp.

Below: Honda's VFR800FI sports-tourer.

Above: Norton's stylish and futuristic Nemesis prototype was unveiled at a London press conference in 1998, making a claimed 280bhp from its 1500cc V8 motor. Any intent the firm's owners had to produce it came to nothing.

Above: The V92 was not the most stylish cruiser on the block, but it was a creditable first attempt at a big V-twin by Victory, the newly created motorcycle division of US firm Polaris.

Right: Many enthusiasts were critical of reborn Indian's use of Harley-based S&S engines, but there was no denying that the Limited Edition Chief was a stylish and imposing machine.

Norton Motors Deutschland firm owned rights to the name in most of Europe, and built by British specialist Tigcraft, who supplied its tubular steel frame. The agile single's straight-line performance was modest and only a few were sold, none of them in Britain because Seifert did not own Norton rights there.

The issue of marque ownership had generated bitter fighting in the US over the Indian name. In the early '90s Harley's revival prompted claims to Indian ownership by two individuals, both of whom seemed more keen to sell Indian-branded merchandise than to build bikes. Philip Zanghi ended up in prison for fraud; Wayne Baughman disappeared from the scene after extracting several million dollars from investors.

In 1996 the Indian issue was controversially settled in a Colorado court, when the receiver awarded rights to a Canadian-based consortium. The winning Indian Motorcycle Company paid the receiver almost $20 million, which was used to reimburse creditors, and took over the California Motorcycle Company, the leading maker of 'Harley clone' V-twins.

Return of the Chief

In 1999 Indian began production of its first bike, the Limited Edition Chief: a giant cruiser, powered by a 1442cc S&S V-twin engine, and with classic Indian features including huge fenders. Its price was high, quality was mixed, and many enthusiasts were unimpressed. But at least Indian was finally back in business. Kawasaki, which had recently launched a pair of Drifter models by revamping its VN800 and VN1500 V-twin cruisers with big fenders, was forced to pay the receiver $75,000 for hijacking Indian's trademarked feature.

Two other US firms had also launched high-profile V-twin cruisers. In 1998 Polaris, the snowmobile and watercraft giant, had begun production of the first bike from its new Victory motorcycle division. The V92C was not the most stylish of machines. But its 1508cc (92 cubic inches, hence the name) fuel-injected sohc V-twin produced a healthy 75bhp, and by cruiser standards the Victory handled and braked very well. It was also competitively priced.

The Super X from Excelsior-Henderson, launched in January 1999, was a heavier and more expensive machine, powered by a 1386cc dohc V-twin engine which, like the V92C, was air/oil-

Harley-Davidson FXDX Super Glide Sport (1999)

Engine:	Air-cooled ohv pushrod four-valve 45-degree V-twin
Capacity:	1450cc (95.3 x 101.6mm)
Maximum power:	68bhp @ 5400rpm
Transmission:	Five-speed, belt final drive
Frame:	Steel twin cradle
Suspension:	Telescopic front; twin shocks rear
Brakes:	Twin discs front; disc rear
Weight:	661lb (300kg)
Top speed:	110mph (177km/h)

Left: Harley took a big step forward with its powerful and refined Twin Cam 88 engine, and the Dyna Super Glide Sport added to the appeal with very respectable chassis performance.

Below: Seven Harley models were initially updated with the 1450cc Twin Cam 88 motor in 1999, including the laid-back Dyna Wide Glide (left) and more traditionally styled Road King.

cooled and held its cylinders at a 50-degree angle. The old name had been revived by brothers Dave and Dan Hanlon, who had raised $90 million to develop the bike and create a purpose-built factory in Minnesota. The Super X produced plenty of low-rev power, and had a distinctive look from its leading-link front suspension.

Harley-Davidson responded to its new challengers with its first new engine in 15 years. The Twin Cam 88 got its name from its twin camshafts and capacity of 1450cc, or 88 cubic inches. Although most engine parts were new, the format of air-cooled, pushrod-operated, 45-degree V-twin remained. Peak output was increased from 50 to about 68bhp, cooling was uprated and numerous parts were made more robust. The new motor gave notably more lively performance. It was especially impressive in the all-new Dyna Super Glide Sport, a lean and sweet-running roadster that combined effortless cruising ability with very respectable handling.

Harley was also keen to diversify, and in 1998 took control of Buell, having bought a 49 per cent stake in the firm five years earlier. Under Erik Buell's control the company had produced some quick and cleverly engineered models, notably the 1996-model S1 Lightning with its mean, bikini-faired styling, tuned 91bhp Sportster 1200 V-twin engine and innovative, quick-steering chassis. With Harley's help Buell increased production, started exporting to several countries, and developed new models. The X1 Lightning, launched in 1999, kept Buells' quirky character, increased the V-twin motor's output yet again to 95bhp, and improved some cosmetic details including the notoriously large airbox. Buell still had some quality control issues to address, but with Harley's resources behind it the future looked promising.

Ducati was reaping the benefit of its new management and its run of World Superbike success. In 1999 the Bologna factory's production hit a record 33,000, with the company increasingly profitable. Ducati, by now fully owned by TPG, had taken control of some key importers,

Top: The S1 Lightning, Buell's first naked roadster, had a tuned 1200cc Harley motor.

Above: Ducati's ST4 sports-tourer used a 105bhp eight-valve V-twin engine from the 916.

MV Agusta 750 F4 Serie Oro (1999)	
Engine:	Liquid-cooled dohc 16-valve four
Capacity:	749cc (73.8 x 43.8mm)
Maximum power:	126bhp @ 12,500rpm
Transmission:	Six-speed, chain final drive
Frame:	Tubular steel and cast magnesium
Suspension:	Telescopic front; single shock rear
Brakes:	Twin discs front; disc rear
Weight:	406lb (184kg) dry
Top speed:	165mph (266km/h)

Right: The long-awaited F4 750 Serie Oro was a suitably stunning bike for MV Agusta's return.

established high-profile 'Ducati store' dealerships, and launched lucrative sidelines in tuning parts and accessories. New bikes in 1998 had included the ST4 sports-tourer, essentially the ST2 fitted with the 105bhp dohc eight-valve engine from the 916; and the restyled, fuel-injected 900SS sportster. In March 1999 Ducati, its recovery seemingly complete, was floated on the Italian and New York stock exchanges.

Moto Guzzi was less healthy, its lack of direction emphasized when the management arranged to move production from the traditional Mandello del Lario base to a new factory in Monza, outside Milan. The workers had other ideas, and Guzzi stayed put. But the firm was boosted in 1999 by the introduction of the V11 Sport, a neat naked roadster with a punchy 91bhp V-twin motor and plenty of retro style.

Bimota's two-stroke disaster

The situation was far worse at Bimota, after a promising few years. Between 1994 and '96 the firm had sold a record 1100 units of the Pierluigi Marconi-designed SB6, which wrapped Suzuki's GSX-R1100 engine in a sturdy aluminium frame that also enclosed the swingarm pivot. In 1997 Bimota hoped for even greater success with the revolutionary 500 V-due, with its 'clean-burning' direct-injection two-stroke V-twin engine. The stylish V-due was in huge demand but when deliveries began, it became clear that the direct-injection did not work reliably. Bikes were returned, payments refunded, and the factory was closed for much of 1998. Production eventually recommenced in 1999 under the control of former Laverda boss Francesco Tognon, but Bimota's situation remained precarious.

Cagiva had survived numerous financial scares during a decade spent developing its four-cylinder sports bike. But when, at the 1997 Milan Show, Claudio Castiglioni pulled the covers from the bike by then renamed the MV Agusta 750 F4, nobody doubted that the effort had been worthwhile. For the famous old marque's return, Massimo Tamburini had created a two-wheeled

sculpture to rank with his Ducati 916. The F4 was brilliantly engineered and utterly gorgeous, from the tiny twin headlamps in its fairing's nose, all the way to the four cigar-shaped tailpipes that emerged from beneath its tailpiece.

The F4's 749cc 126bhp liquid-cooled motor held 16 radial valves, and incorporated a grand prix-style removable cassette gearbox. An innovative chassis combined ladder-like steel tubes with cast pieces. On the limited-edition F4 Serie Oro (Gold Series) these and the single-sided swingarm were magnesium, instead of the standard bike's aluminium. In either specification, the F4 was magnificent. It raced smoothly to a top speed of over 160mph (257km/h), emitting a glorious induction howl, and delivered precise, agile handling and powerful braking. But even in its hour of triumph, MV suffered the familiar problem of production delays.

If MV's F4 was one of the most beautiful motorcycles of all time, then Suzuki's GSX-R1300R Hayabusa was arguably one of the least attractive, but there was a good reason for that. The Hayabusa, named after a fast-flying Japanese peregrine falcon, had been given its drooping fairing nose, large front mudguard and bulbous tailpiece to improve its aerodynamic efficiency. Suzuki's aim was to create the world's fastest bike, and the Hayabusa's 190mph (306km/h) top speed meant they had succeeded.

The Hayabusa's 1298cc motor was an enlarged and tuned version of the dohc 16-valve unit from the GSX-R1100. Fuel-injection and ram-air helped give 173bhp, a record for a production bike. The chassis, based on a twin-spar aluminium frame, was unexceptional. What was special was the Hayabusa's performance, which was not just mind-blowingly strong, but also remarkably well-controlled. Its power delivery was crisp and flexible; its handling neutral and stable. Its brakes, tyres and ground clearance were excellent.

So stunningly, addictively fast was the Hayabusa that its rider needed only a relatively short straight to see 200mph (322km/h) on its slightly optimistic speedometer. Whether that was entirely a good thing for a standard production streetbike in 1999 was another matter entirely.

Above: The V11 Sport used Guzzi's traditional 1064cc V-twin engine. Its lime green paintwork and red frame echoed the V7 Sport of the 1970s.

Above: Bimota's 500 V-due: brave but flawed.

Left: Suzuki's Hayabusa: ugly but seriously fast.

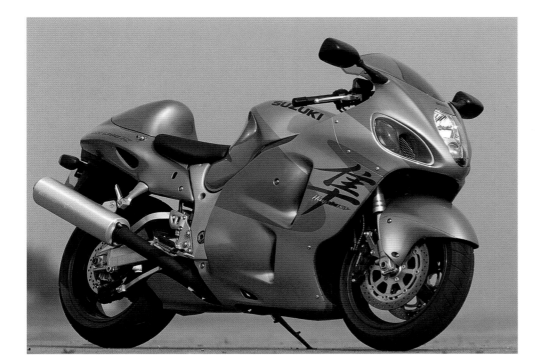

Suzuki GSX-R1300R Hayabusa (1999)	
Engine:	Liquid-cooled dohc 16-valve four
Capacity:	1298cc (81 x 63mm)
Maximum power:	173bhp @ 9800rpm
Transmission:	Six-speed, chain final drive
Frame:	Aluminium twin spar
Suspension:	Telescopic front; single shock rear
Brakes:	Twin discs front; disc rear
Weight	473lb (215kg) dry
Top speed:	190mph (306km/h)

Towards the Limit

21st Century

Ducati MH900e (2000)	
Engine:	Air/oil-cooled sohc four-valve 90-degree V-twin
Capacity:	904cc (92 x 68mm)
Maximum power:	75bhp @ 8000rpm
Transmission:	Six-speed, chain final drive
Frame:	Tubular steel ladder
Suspension:	Telescopic front; single shock rear
Brakes:	Twin discs front; disc rear
Weight:	409lb (186kg)
Top speed:	130mph (209km/h)

Above: Ducati's limited-edition MH900e combined retro style and modern engineering in unique fashion, and was great fun to ride.

Right: Harley's Fat Boy and the rest of the Softail range gained balancer-shaft equipped Twin Cam 88 engines for the 2000 model year.

Previous page: In 2002 the sharpened VFR800FI sports-tourer became the first motorcycle to use Honda's VTEC variable valve technology.

Motorcycling's new millennium began in suitably forward-looking fashion when, at one minute past midnight on 1 January 2000, Ducati's MH900e went on sale via the Italian firm's web site, becoming the first vehicle to be sold in this way. The initials stood for 'Mike Hailwood Evoluzione', and the Ducati was an ideal bike to span the old and new eras, as it blended classical influences with modern features in unique fashion.

The MH900e also highlighted several key trends in motorcycle design. Its focus was on performance; it exploited a new marketing niche with limited-edition production; and it combined high technology with traditional engineering themes – in this case, Ducati's desmodromic V-twin engine and tubular steel ladder frame. Many other bikes had used some of those elements but few had combined them all so neatly.

Ducati's design chief Pierre Terblanche had begun planning the MH900e years earlier, inspired by Hailwood's Isle of Man TT win in 1978, when 38-year old 'Mike the Bike' had come out of retirement to ride a Ducati to a famous victory. Although it didn't look much like Hailwood's fully-faired racer, the MH900e had a '70s feel emphasized by its chrome-rimmed headlamp, period graphics and the engine's large dummy sump. The prototype's rear-facing camera (instead of mirrors) did not make it into production, but the final bike included a stylish rev-counter and digital speedometer, and a single-sided swingarm made from tubular steel instead of the more familiar aluminium.

Public response was so positive that the planned 1000 bikes sold out in a few hours, and double that number would eventually be built. With a peak output of 75bhp from its 904cc air/oil-cooled V-twin engine the Ducati was not especially fast, but it rumbled to 130mph (209km/h), had plenty of character, and handled well. As a riding experience the MH900e was merely good; as a marketing exercise and a piece of design, it was brilliant.

Harley-Davidson, still the masters of retro styling, introduced a 2000 model range that looked almost unchanged but incorporated significant updates. Harley's six Softail models, including the ever-popular Fat Boy, were fitted with the 1450cc Twin Cam 88 engine, reworked to include twin balancer shafts to reduce the solidly-mounted V-twin's vibration. At the other end of the capacity scale, Harley's subsidiary Buell launched the Blast, a 492cc single-cylinder roadster aimed at converting new riders, especially women, to motorcycling.

Tough times ahead

Harley's continued success contrasted with the difficulties faced by many other manufacturers as major markets took a downturn in the new millennium, following faltering global economies. Italy, where recent legislation requiring riders to wear crash-helmets was an added factor, saw a dramatic drop in scooter sales, leaving manufacturers with a problem of over-supply. Piaggio was particularly badly affected, and so postponed plans to relaunch Gilera with 600cc four-cylinder and 850cc V-twin superbikes.

European scooter and small bike manufacturers were also facing increasing competition from countries including China, whose fast-growing industry was producing more than ten million machines per year, mainly for domestic sale but increasingly also for export. By contrast the biggest threat to large capacity bikes was from politicians, as governments' plans to reduce road casualties made superbikes, with their increasing power and speed, an easy target.

That situation came to a head in 2000 with the arrival of Kawasaki's ZX-12R, a high-tech 1199cc powerhouse which, with a top speed approaching 190mph (306km/h), was designed to challenge Suzuki's Hayabusa for the title of world's fastest motorcycle. Amid confusion surrounding the four-cylinder Kawasaki's precise power output came confirmation that it had become the first bike affected by a Japanese manufacturers' agreement to limit top speed to 186mph (300km/h), for fear of more severe government-imposed restrictions.

The Kawasaki's output was eventually confirmed at a ram-air assisted 176bhp. But its 16-valve fuel-injected engine was not the bike's outstanding feature. The ZX-12R was more notable for its innovative monocoque (one-piece) aluminium frame, inspired by that of Kawasaki's unsuccessful KR500 grand prix racer of the 1980s. The hollow frame incorporated the airbox; fuel lived under the seat. The lack of external frame spars allowed slim, aerodynamic bodywork that contributed to the Kawasaki's searing speed.

Despite being quite big and heavy, the sharply styled ZX-12R handled well, and made a capable sports-tourer thanks to a roomy riding position, reasonable wind protection and powerful brakes. It restored Kawasaki's reputation for brutal four-cylinder performance but the firm still lacked a super-sports model to challenge Yamaha's revised YZF-R1 and Honda's FireBlade, which was redesigned for 2000.

Kawasaki ZX-12R (2000)	
Engine:	Liquid-cooled dohc 16-valve four
Capacity:	1199cc (83 x 55.4mm)
Maximum power:	176bhp @ 11,000rpm
Transmission:	Six-speed, chain final drive
Frame:	Aluminium monocoque
Suspension:	Telescopic front; single shock rear
Brakes:	Twin discs front; disc rear
Weight:	462lb (210kg) dry
Top speed:	186mph (300km/h)

Above: Kawasaki's ZX-12R looked relatively conventional, but was notable both for its electronically limited 186mph (300km/h) top speed and its monocoque aluminium frame.

Left: Honda's 2000-model FireBlade (right), called the CBR929RR in the US, echoed the original CBR900RR of 1992 with its highly competitive blend of power and light weight.

Above: Honda's SP-1 was a rapid roadster, and the basis for a Superbike world title winner.

Below: Bimota created the cleverly engineered SB8K around Suzuki's TL1000 V-twin engine, before hitting more financial problems.

Below right: The new millennium's craziest bike was Louisiana firm MTT's Y2K, powered by a 286bhp gas turbine helicopter engine.

Following its sensational arrival in 1992, the CBR900RR had been updated every two years, remaining popular while losing a little of the original bike's raw excitement. That changed in 2000 with an all-new 'Blade, known as the CBR929RR in the US due to its increased engine capacity. The Honda's other figures were equally important because it produced 150bhp, equalling the R1's unchanged output, and at 375lb (170kg) was even lighter than the racy Yamaha. The revamped RR was just what Honda needed: a faster, lighter, more agile, better braked bike that was right back on the pace.

Another model Honda had needed urgently was one that could challenge Ducati's long-standing dominance of the World Superbike championship, and in 2000 the Japanese giant finally swallowed its pride and joined in with a big V-twin of its own. The SP-1, known as the RC51 in the US, was a fully-faired machine with a powerful 999cc dohc eight-valve motor and a high quality chassis, though it was closer to a normal production streetbike than a limited edition race replica like its V4 predecessor, the RC45.

The racy SP-1 made a fast and uncompromising roadster, with plenty of character and performance from its fuel-injected, 136bhp engine. On smooth roads the firmly suspended, aluminium beam-framed V-twin handled superbly, too, despite being quite heavy at 431lb (196kg). Honda's effort was rewarded when Texan ace Colin Edwards rode the factory SP-1 to the World Superbike title in its debut season.

Even Honda's V-twin was almost ordinary in comparison with the year's most outrageous motorcycle: the gas turbine-engined Y2K produced by Louisiana firm Marine Turbine Technologies. With an output of 286bhp and a claimed top speed of 250mph (402km/h), Y2K was the most powerful and fastest bike ever to go into series production, albeit in very small numbers. The price of $150,000 meant it was also one of the most expensive.

MTT specialized in building boats and fire pumps using 'timed-out' aero engines; Y2K's Rolls-Royce Allison 250 turbine had previously powered a Bell Jet Ranger helicopter. For motorcycle use the turbine was heavy and impractical, but MTT's strong aluminium frame gave

Left: Cagiva's V-Raptor combined sharp styling and a neat steel frame with Suzuki's TL1000S V-twin engine. Peak output was rated at 105bhp instead of the TL's 123bhp, only because Cagiva measured at the rear wheel, not the crankshaft.

Below: France gained its first superbike manufacturer with the arrival of Voxan, whose V-twin range was headed by the quick and charismatic Café Racer. After going bust in 2001, the firm was reborn two years later.

the long, fully-faired bike good stability to go with its awesome straight-line performance and unique, high-pitched sound.

Bimota, Italy's best known builder of exotic superbikes, received an unexpected boost when Australian star Anthony Gobert won a rain-affected World Superbike race on the firm's new SB8K, powered by the 996cc V-twin engine from Suzuki's TL1000S. But racing success proved short-lived, the firm's financial fortunes plummeted once again, and production in Rimini was abandoned for much of 2000. MV Agusta, too, was in trouble, with production suspended due to the collapse of merger talks with Piaggio, whose financial health had declined because of the scooter market crash.

Claudio Castiglioni had renamed his group MV Agusta, and had begun the year by launching the first Cagiva-branded superbikes, both of which also used the eight-valve TL1000S V-twin engine. The Raptor and V-Raptor were stylish roadsters designed by Miguel Galluzzi, the creator of Ducati's Monster. The sportier V-Raptor, in particular, was a striking bike with a sharp beak and dramatic fake air-scoops. With crisp acceleration, 150mph (241km/h) top speed and fine handling, the Raptors looked set for success. But no sooner had Cagiva unveiled smaller 650cc versions, powered by the V-twin engine from Suzuki's impressive new SV650, than the Varese production lines ground to a halt because of the company's financial difficulties.

Another firm with a range of V-twins was Voxan, an ambitious new manufacturer, based near Clermont-Ferrand in central France and run by industrialist Jacques Gardette. Voxan's modular three-bike range was based on a 996cc eight-valve engine with cylinders at 72 degrees. In 2000, the initial naked Roadster model, launched a year earlier, was joined by the half-faired Café Racer, featuring similar 100bhp output to comply with French law, and the same steel frame. The Voxans combined 140mph (225km/h) performance with good handling plus plenty of character, and sold well in France. But they were not profitable and, after a Scrambler dual-purpose model had been launched in 2001, the firm ceased production. It would return in 2003, under new ownership, with a smaller workforce and a revamped range of V-twins.

BMW had hoped that one face of motorcycling's future would be the C1, a curious egg-shaped commuter machine. Much more than simply a scooter with a roof, the innovative C1 incorporated a crash-resistant safety cell to protect the rider, who wore car-style seat belts, and in

Above: BMW earned top marks for imagination with the enclosed and crash-resistant C1, but drawbacks including high price and higher centre of gravity ensured that sales were slow.

Suzuki GSX-R1000 (2001)

Engine:	Liquid-cooled dohc 16-valve four
Capacity:	998cc (73 x 59mm)
Maximum power:	161bhp @ 11,000rpm
Transmission:	Six-speed, chain final drive
Frame:	Aluminium twin spar
Suspension:	Telescopic front; single shock rear
Brakes:	Twin discs front; disc rear
Weight:	374lb (170kg) dry
Top speed:	180mph (290km/h)

Right: Suzuki moved the open-class super-sports fight to a new level in 2001 with the GSX-R1000, whose 161bhp engine and ultra-sharp chassis made an unbeatable combination.

most European countries required no crash-helmet. A 125cc 15bhp single-cylinder engine gave a top speed of 60mph (97km/h). BMW claimed the C1 was the world's safest bike. But it was also top-heavy and expensive, and few people bought one even when BMW offered a more powerful 200cc engine.

A more successful new style of commuter machine was the giant scooter. Most of the major manufacturers created variations on the theme. Suzuki's Burgman 400 was joined in 2001 by Piaggio's X9 500, whose 460cc single-cylinder engine sat on the swingarm in scooter style. Honda's Silver Wing and Yamaha's Tmax were more advanced twin-cylinder machines, of 582cc and 499cc capacity respectively. Their frame-mounted engines gave sharper handling to match their lively straight-line performance. The following year would see the appearance of Suzuki's Burgman 650 twin, whose gearbox offered both manual and automatic operation.

Suzuki also provided the high-performance highlight of 2001. The GSX-R1000 stormed onto the scene with a maximum output of 161bhp that gave it a 10bhp advantage over its super-sport rivals. The GSX-R1000 was heavily based on the GSX-R750, itself updated to good effect a year earlier. As well as looking almost identical, the new bike even shared most of its cylinder head with the smaller motor, and at 374lb (170kg) was only 9lb (4kg) heavier than the 750.

The GSX-R1000's savage performance was enough to send it straight to the front of the open-class superbike battle. Its 998cc 16-valve motor delivered massively strong mid-range response, and enough top-end power for a maximum speed of 180mph (290km/h). Handling and roadholding were outstanding, thanks to a rigid aluminium frame and high-quality suspension parts.

In typical GSX-R style the new bike was firm and uncompromising, but it made a thrilling street bike and an all-conquering racer. The Isle of Man TT was cancelled in 2001, due to movement restrictions in the UK introduced as a response to foot-and-mouth disease. In 2002, Yorkshireman David Jefferies would lap the Isle of Man circuit at over 127mph (204km/h) in winning the Senior TT, and at over 124mph (199km/h) on a near-standard GSX-R as he raced to victory in the Production event.

New triples from Triumph

Triumph produced its best sports bike yet in 2001: the Daytona 955i. The comprehensively revamped, 147bhp triple was good for 170mph (274km/h) and handled superbly, though it had lost its predecessor's distinctive styling and single-sided swingarm. The British firm also used a detuned version of its new 955cc 12-valve engine to update the Sprint ST, an aluminium beam-framed sports-tourer that had been very competitive since its launch in 1999.

Triumph's most eagerly awaited model of 2001 was the firm's first twin, for which was reserved the most famous name of all: Bonneville. Unlike its illustrious predecessor, this Bonnie was not a high-performance bike but a gentle, retro-styled roadster designed to appeal to riders who remembered the old Triumph twins. It was styled to resemble the 650cc T120 Bonneville of the late '60s, and its 790cc dohc eight-valve air-cooled parallel twin motor was so softly tuned that its 61bhp output gave a top speed of 115mph (185km/h), similar to that of the old model.

The new Bonneville's performance was nothing special, but it looked good, was competitively priced and sold well. Ironically the British bike found a rival in Kawasaki's W650, a 50bhp retro twin that had been launched in 1999, inspired by the Japanese firm's own W1 and W2 twins of the 1960s. Triumph would soon follow the standard twin with spin-off models, the Bonneville America and Speedmaster, whose cruiser look was aimed at the US market. But the firm's plans would be hit in April 2002 by a fire that destroyed most of the Hinckley factory and cost much of that year's production. Triumph, whose annual sales had risen above 30,000 units, took the opportunity to rebuild its production lines in a larger building on the same site, in anticipation of further growth.

Ducati was another firm to appreciate the value of cheap and softly tuned twins, as the Monster 600 had been its best-selling bike of recent years. By 2001 the Bologna firm had produced 100,000 Monsters, more than half of them the smallest V-twin, and marked the occasion with the Monster 620ie, featuring an enlarged 618cc engine, fuel-injection, more rigid frame and twin front discs. The 60bhp motor gave a top speed of 115mph (185km/h), and the Ducati handled well, especially in M620Sie form, with uprated chassis and handlebar fairing.

Above left: Triumph's updated and renamed Daytona 955i was faster, lighter and more competitive than its T595 predecessor, but had lost a little of the old triple's distinctive style.

Above: Yamaha's Tmax giant scooter had much in common with motorbikes, including a 39bhp dohc twin-cylinder engine that bolted to the frame, not to the swingam in scooter style.

Below: The 2001-model Triumph Bonneville looked like its namesake from 1968, and despite having a 790cc dohc engine its performance was similar to that of the old 650cc twin.

Above: Kawasaki beat Triumph to production of a retro parallel twin with the W650, which was a pleasant bike although few people had heard of the 1960s W1 and W2 twins that inspired it.

Below: Ducati's Monster 620Sie, the upmarket version of the revised naked middleweight, backed up its extra power with extras including a headlamp fairing and aluminium swingarm.

Meanwhile the big Monster was gaining muscles, by being fitted with the dohc eight-valve, liquid-cooled engine that had previously powered the mighty 916 sportster. The resultant Monster S4 was a wild 101bhp machine that snarled to 150mph (241km/h) and more than lived up to its name. Ducati's policy of using old super-sports engines for other models also produced a new sports-tourer, the ST4S, whose 996cc eight-valve engine produced 117bhp, and was matched by an uprated chassis with Öhlins rear suspension. The ST4S faced a capable new rival in Aprilia's first purpose-built sports-tourer. The Futura combined a 998cc V-twin engine, detuned slightly from RSV spec to give 113bhp, with distinctive, angular styling and a single-sided swingarm.

Yamaha's long-running, air-cooled FJ1200 had been one of the outstanding long-distance bikes of the '90s, and in 2001 Yamaha introduced a worthy successor with the FJR1300. This had a similar look to the old FJ, but had a new liquid-cooled 1298cc 16-valve engine that produced 145bhp, and an aluminium beam frame that helped keep weight down to a reasonable 521lb (237kg). Unlike the old FJ, the FJR13000 was a purpose-built sports-tourer with shaft final drive. It was comfortable and fast, with generous low-rev torque and a top speed of 150mph (241km/h).

Yamaha also produced a versatile big four of a more basic variety with the FZS1000 Fazer, called the FZ1 in the US, which combined a YZF-R1-based motor with a tubular steel frame. Despite being detuned, the 998cc 20-valve engine produced 143bhp, enough for a top speed of 160mph (257km/h). A neat, twin-headlamp half-fairing, efficient steel-framed chassis and excellent brakes helped make the big Fazer popular.

Left: Bolting the legendary 916's dohc eight-valve V-twin engine into the Monster chassis created the Monster S4, a snarling naked roadster with arm-wrenching performance.

Below: Aprilia broadened its V-twin line in 2001 with the Futura sports-tourer, featuring smooth and torquey 113bhp V-twin engine, aluminium frame and distinctive, angular bodywork.

Honda caused some confusion by introducing two new versions of its long-time favourite, the CBR600F. Alongside the standard model was the CBR600F Sport, with identical 110bhp power output and very similar chassis, plus a few internal engine differences designed to facilitate race tuning. The CBR's versatility had long been an asset on the road, but a handicap in Supersport racing against more single-minded rivals such as Suzuki's GSX-R600. Ironically Australia's Andrew Pitt would win the 2001 world championship on Kawasaki's ZX-6R, which had been updated a year earlier but remained a practical all-rounder.

Honda also unveiled the GL1800, a revamped version of its long-distance legend, the Gold Wing. A biggest yet 1832cc version of the flat-six motor produced 117bhp and required valve adjustment only every 32,000 miles (51,000km). Other features included uprated fuel-injection, a twin-spar aluminium frame with single-sided swingarm, and a more aerodynamic fairing with a six-way adjustable screen. The Wing was still a huge motorbike, but it was faster, more refined and more agile than ever before.

The most surprising arrival of 2001 was Harley-Davidson's V-Rod. The long, low, silver machine was a radical departure for Harley, both in its jaw-dropping styling and its 1130cc liquid-cooled 60-degree V-twin engine, whose 115bhp output was almost double that of previous Harley cruisers. The dohc eight-valve 'Revolution' motor was developed with the help of Porsche Engineering of Germany, and based on the V-twin unit of Harley's VR1000, which had been uncompetitive in US Superbike racing since its debut in 1994.

Above: Unlike the old FJ1100 model that it resembled, Yamaha's FJR1300 was a purpose-built sports-tourer whose four-cylinder engine delivered its 145bhp via shaft final drive.

Above: Yamaha's FZ1000 Fazer, known as the FZ1 in the States, was conceived as a steel-framed budget roadster but its 143bhp engine delivered plenty of speed and entertainment.

Below: Honda attempted to have the best of both worlds with its middleweight four in 2001, when this standard CBR600F was joined by a 600F Sport model with extra tuning potential.

Right: Kawasaki's fast and versatile ZX-6R was arguably the pick of the 600cc fours in 2000, and would gain an improbable edge two years later when its engine was enlarged to 636cc.

Style and performance

Visually the V-Rod was inspired, with its kicked-out forks, aluminium radiator shroud, slash-cut silencers and solid disc wheels. Performance was thrilling, too. The Harley thundered away from the line, revving to its 9000rpm redline through the gears as it headed for a top speed of 140mph (225km/h). Its chassis was good by cruiser standards, especially the powerful twin-disc front brake. The V-Rod thrilled almost everyone who rode it, following its launch in mid-2001 as a 2002 model (in Harley tradition). But sales were disappointing, at least by Harley standards. Most Harley customers still preferred their bikes to come with a heavy dose of nostalgia.

Ducati's 999 was another distinctive V-twin that drew a mixed response from the public. By 2002, eight years had passed since the arrival of the iconic 916, during which time Ducati's eight-valve flagship had retained its look while evolving into the 998 via numerous capacity increases. Trying to improve on Massimo Tamburini's original design was comparable to repainting the Sistine Chapel ceiling, and Pierre Terblanche's 999 did not please every Ducati enthusiast. With its tiny, stacked headlights and single under-seat silencer, it looked different and suitably aggressive, while keeping many family features.

The 999 retained its predecessor's 998cc eight-valve desmo engine, known as the Testastretta ('*narrow-head*') due to its valve design, and weighed an almost identical 438lb (199kg). But the new bike was slimmer and much more refined, designed for added practicality as well as performance. It had a lower seat, adjustable ergonomics, sophisticated CAN line digital electronics, a longer swingarm for improved traction, and used 30 per cent fewer components. Straight-line performance matched that of the 998, handling was slightly sharper, and the 999 was a more comfortable and rider-friendly machine. So too was the 749, which combined a 748cc Testastretta V-twin engine with near-identical chassis and bodywork.

Aprilia's Tuono, the other outstanding V-twin of 2002, was also long awaited. A naked Aprilia superbike had seemed inevitable ever since the RSV Mille's introduction in 1998. When the Tuono – *Thunder* in Italian – finally arrived, it combined its high bars and upright riding position

with a small fairing, complete with trademark triple headlights. Aprilia said this was necessary to ensure stability because the 998cc dohc V-twin RSV motor was not detuned, and its 130bhp output gave a top speed of over 150mph (241km/h).

That was doubtless true, and most who rode the Tuono were glad of its fairing because this was a wonderfully fast, charismatic and entertaining machine. The big, flexible 60-degree V-twin engine was ideal for a high-barred bike, and the Tuono's chassis, based on the RSV's twin-spar aluminium frame, gave superb handling. Styling was suitably aggressive, and included round plastic crash-protectors for the frame. Few bikes came close to matching the Tuono for providing high-speed thrills with a reasonable level of comfort and practicality.

Aprilia followed a trend with the Tuono by first introducing a limited edition model, the Tuono R, shortly followed by the mass-produced standard machine, the Tuono Fighter, which had less exotic suspension parts. MV Agusta had pioneered this approach with its F4, initially hand built in ultra-limited Serie Oro ('Gold Series') form. The Varese firm did the same thing with its naked Brutale, which was again unveiled in standard Brutale S form, and as the Brutale Serie Oro with frame castings and swingarm in magnesium instead of the S model's aluminium.

In either form, Massimo Tamburini's latest creation was another remarkable motorbike, with its uniquely shaped headlight and a squat, pugnacious look for which the name Brutale was entirely appropriate. Its 749cc radial 16-valve engine was slightly detuned from 750 F4 specification but still produced 127bhp, along with a tuneful note from slash-cut silencers. The MV's racy geometry, taut suspension and weight of just 407lb (185kg) gave superb handling, too.

The Brutale was not a practical, sensible roadster, it was a hugely enjoyable naked sports bike that rarely failed to put a smile on its rider's face. But MV's financial problems, which followed the collapse of a proposed agreement with Piaggio, resulted in the debt-laden firm being placed in a state of 'controlled administration' to protect it from creditors. Full production would belatedly begin in 2003, ironically the centenary year of similarly troubled Husqvarna, part of Claudio Castiglioni's MV Agusta group.

Above: *Honda's naked GL1000 Gold Wing of the '70s seemed a distant memory on the arrival of the GL1800, with its 1832cc flat six motor, aluminium beam frame, adjustable screen, built-in luggage compartments and other luxury features.*

Below left: *Harley began a bold new era with the stunning V-Rod, which looked as though it had been hewn from a solid lump of aluminium, and delivered tarmac-wrinkling performance from its 115bhp liquid-cooled V-twin engine.*

Harley-Davidson VRSCA V-Rod (2002)

Engine:	Liquid-cooled dohc eight-valve 60-degree V-twin
Capacity:	1130cc (100 x 72mm)
Maximum power:	115bhp @ 8500rpm
Transmission:	Five-speed, belt final drive
Frame:	Tubular steel
Suspension:	Telescopic front; twin shocks rear
Brakes:	Twin discs front; disc rear
Weight:	594lb (270kg) dry
Top speed:	140mph (225km/h)

Ducati 999 (2002)	
Engine:	Liquid-cooled dohc eight-valve 90-degree V-twin
Capacity:	998cc (100 x 63.5mm)
Maximum power:	124bhp @ 9750rpm
Transmission:	Six-speed, chain final drive
Frame:	Tubular steel ladder
Suspension:	Telescopic front, monoshock rear
Brakes:	Twin discs front, disc rear
Weight:	438lb (199kg)
Top speed:	170mph (274km/h)

Right: *Ducati's 999 couldn't match the beauty of the 998, but was a better all-round motorbike.*

Above: *The 749S was at its best in fast corners.*

Below: *Aprilia's Tuono: naked V-twin thrills.*

Benelli's three-cylinder rebirth

Another glamorous Italian marque to start with a limited-edition model was Benelli, which had been reborn in the late '90s under the control of Andrea Merloni, a youthful bike enthusiast whose family controlled the huge Merloni group that owned white goods brands Indesit and Ariston. While gaining experience by producing scooters, Benelli had been developing a three-cylinder superbike, the Tornado. The 898cc 12-valve triple had bold styling, by British designer Adrian Morton, and an innovative chassis based on a frame of steel tubes and aluminium sections, held together using glue as well as bolts.

The Tornado's most unusual features were its under-seat radiator and pair of fans, set into the tailpiece. Benelli's relatively low-budget race team was not competitive in World Superbike. But the 143bhp Tornado roadster was a powerful and fine-handling replica of the factory racer, especially in initial Tornado Limited Edition form, with Öhlins suspension and other lightweight chassis parts. Those initial 150 hand-built bikes were quickly followed by the mass-produced Tornado Tre, also with 160mph (257km/h) top speed and excellent handling, while Benelli developed an equally distinctive naked triple, the TNT, for production in 2004.

While Benelli had been struggling to develop its own engine, Mondial, another famous old Italian name, was making a comeback with a sleek superbike called the Piega, powered by the 999cc V-twin engine from Honda's SP-1. The Piega was a stylish, fully-faired sportster that wrapped a Ducati-style tubular steel frame around the standard dohc, eight-valve SP-1 engine, whose output was raised slightly to 140bhp with new airbox, injection system and exhaust. Mondial succeeded in selling small numbers of the Piega, despite its high price, and followed Benelli in developing a naked model, the Nuda, for launch in 2004.

Honda had also launched a naked version of its popular super-sports bike in 2002. But despite being essentially an unfaired version of the mighty FireBlade, the Hornet 900 lacked the imagination and attitude of the Italian machines. Rather than use its latest 954cc FireBlade motor, Honda detuned the 1998 model's 918cc unit to give just 108bhp. With styling similar to that of

The Movie Star's Accessory

Just as motorcycles have become popular in recent years by providing fun rather than essential transport, so their portrayal in the movies has followed suit. Bikes are frequently used in Hollywood productions, not as a central features of the film, as in *The Wild One* or *Easy Rider*, but generally as just one of a number of vehicles to be used, and often crashed, by the star.

Some bikes have made more of an impression, dating back to the '80s when Richard Gere rode a Triumph T140 Bonneville

in *An Officer and a Gentleman*, and when Tom Cruise's Kawasaki GPZ900R proved almost as exciting as his F-14 Tomcat fighter in *Top Gun*. The theme continued into the '90s with a varied two-wheeled cast. Arnold Schwarzenegger's character rode a Harley Fat Boy in *Terminator II*. Pierce Brosnan, as James Bond, gave BMW's R1200C cruiser valuable publicity in the 1997 film *Tomorrow Never Dies*.

Triumph has frequently benefited from exposure in the movies. Pamela Anderson

rode a Thunderbird triple in the 1996 production *Barb Wire*. In 2001 Tom Cruise was back on two wheels aboard a Speed Triple, in *Mission Impossible 2*. More recently, *How to Lose a Guy in 10 Days* featured a Bonneville, and Colin Farrell rode Triumph's America twin in *Daredevil*.

Ducati made the most of its opportunity after its 996 sportster was used for a dramatic chase sequence in the 2003 release *The Matrix Reloaded*. At that year's Milan Show the Italian firm unveiled a limited edition 998 Matrix Reloaded replica V-twin, finished in the movie bike's dark green paintwork.

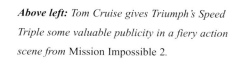

Above left: *Tom Cruise gives Triumph's Speed Triple some valuable publicity in a fiery action scene from* Mission Impossible 2.

Top right: *The two-up chase sequence from* The Matrix Reloaded *prompted Ducati to produce a special-edition V-twin in matching colours.*

Left: *Massimo Tamburini takes a break from riding his latest creation, MV Agusta's Brutale Serie Oro. The influential Italian design genius co-founded Bimota before shaping bikes including the Ducati 916 and MV Agusta F4 750.*

Above: Benelli re-entered the superbike market with the sleek Tornado Limited Edition, an innovative 898cc liquid-cooled triple based on the Pesaro firm's World Superbike racer.

Above right: Mondial, another famous old Italian marque, returned with the Piega, a glamorous sportster powered by the 999cc V-twin engine from Honda's SP-2.

the Hornet 600, the new bike had neither performance nor visual impact, but its rider-friendly nature and competitive price were some compensation.

The peak output of Honda's revamped VFR800 was also 108bhp, but the V4 sports-tourer was a very different bike. Its 782cc eight-valve engine was modified to incorporate VTEC variable-valve technology, as used by the firm's cars to give improved low-rev response. Sharper styling and a new high-level exhaust system added to the refined sports-tourer's appeal.

Yamaha also uprated an old favourite with the TDM900, a new version of the versatile parallel twin that had sold almost as many units in Europe as the VFR since its debut in 1991. Aggressive, bug-eyed styling was combined with a more powerful 897cc 86bhp engine and a lighter, aluminium-framed chassis that made the TDM feel notably more lively.

Right: Honda followed a popular format by using its FireBlade engine to power a naked roadster. The Hornet 900 was cheap but its severely detuned motor marred the fun.

Honda trumped Yamaha in the battle to create the biggest V-twin cruiser, with the arrival of the VTX, powered by a gigantic 1795cc 107bhp engine. The VTX out-cubed not only Yamaha's Drag Star 1100, but also the Wild Star, which was powered by a 1602cc air-cooled engine with pushrod valve operation. Meanwhile Kawasaki was taking a more aggressive approach with its Mean Streak, whose 1470cc V-twin motor was held in a sportier chassis incorporating upside-down forks and twin front disc brakes with six-piston calipers.

The emerging 'performance cruiser' category was enlivened by the arrival of Yamaha's Road Star Warrior. Powered by a Wild Star engine enlarged to 1670cc and tuned with hot cams and lighter internals, the Warrior delivered 80bhp with massive low-rev torque. Its chassis featured a tubular aluminium frame plus upside-down forks and twin discs borrowed from the racy YZF-R1. With its laid-back riding position and long wheelbase, the Warrior was much more of a cruiser than a sports bike. But it was a hard-accelerating, surprisingly sweet-handling machine, and good fun to ride.

While the Japanese giants were attacking the cruiser market with renewed enthusiasm, some of the US cruiser manufacturers were struggling. Excelsior-Henderson had been first to suffer, as slow sales of the Super X had forced the Minnesota firm to close its smart new factory by the end of 2001, having spent around $100 million. Reborn Indian's financial worries were temporarily eased in 2001 when a Boston-based investment group injected over $40 million. The following year Indian launched a new Chief, powered by a V-twin engine of the firm's own design, though the 1638cc 45-degree unit was still based on the old S&S powerplant. But in September 2003, Indian's revival stalled when its backers pulled out. The factory in Gilroy, California was closed with the loss of almost 400 jobs.

Victory had also failed to meet early sales targets, partly due to the V92C cruiser's bland looks. But parent company Polaris had the financial clout to continue. In 2003 Victory hit back with a much more stylish cruiser, designed in consultation with legendary custom builder Arlen Ness and his son Cory. The Vegas retained the V92C's 1507cc air-/oil-cooled V-twin engine, but almost everything else was new. A classical custom shape and a host of neat details made the Vegas an attractive bike, and stronger sales rewarded Victory's commitment.

Harley-Davidson's most important new models of 2002 were not cruisers but an innovative pair of new generation Buell sports bikes, the XB9R Firebolt and XB9S Lightning. The sportier

Above: Yamaha's 2002-model TDM900, a comprehensively reworked version of the firm's familiar parallel twin roadster, gained performance with a more powerful 897cc engine and lighter, aluminium-framed chassis.

Left: In an attempt to meet US market demand for 'performance cruisers', Kawasaki created the Mean Streak by fitting its VN1500 V-twin with a sportier chassis featuring upside-down forks and six-piston brake calipers.

Above: *In 2002 Indian finally produced a Chief powered by the firm's own 1638cc V-twin engine, but in the following year the company suddenly folded after its backers pulled out.*

Above right: *Yamaha's Warrior had laid-back cruiser looks but its 1670cc V-twin engine was held by a tubular aluminium frame, and its forks and front brake came from the YZF-R1.*

Firebolt, in particular, was a dramatic machine, with an aggressive glare from its sharp twin-headlamp fairing. But the Buells' key feature was their innovative chassis. The frame's hollow aluminium spars doubled as the fuel tank, leaving the space between them for the airbox. The aluminium swingarm carried oil in similar fashion. And the front brake was the first perimeter disc seen on a production streetbike.

Buell's frame, which incorporated the familiar Uniplanar method of rubber mounting, was very compact, and combined with steep steering geometry to give light and precise handling. Although their new 984cc V-twin engine produced 92bhp, impressive for a unit based on Harley's humble air-cooled Sportster motor, the Buells were not particularly fast, with a top speed of about 135mph (217km/h). But they were stylish, agile and distinctive enough to make an impact, and were joined in mid-2003 by visually similar XB12 models whose 1203cc engines produced notably more mid-range punch.

Right: *Victory's Vegas, styled with the help of custom legend Arlen Ness, was a stylish bike that could be personalized by US customers via the firm's innovative custom paint programme.*

Buell XB9R Firebolt (2002)	
Engine:	Air/oil-cooled ohv pushrod four-valve 45-degree V-twin
Capacity:	984cc (88.9 x 79.8mm)
Maximum power:	92bhp @ 7200rpm
Transmission:	Six-speed, belt final drive
Frame:	Aluminium twin spar
Suspension:	Telescopic front; single shock rear
Brakes:	Single perimeter disc front; disc rear
Weight:	385lb (175kg) dry
Top speed:	135mph (217km/h)

Harley's happy birthday

Harley itself had no major new models in 2003, but the year was significant as it was the firm's centenary. Having struggled for many of the previous 100 years, Harley reached the landmark in remarkable health, with the year's production approaching 300,000, following 18 consecutive years of increased sales and profit. Not bad for a firm that had built just 32,000 bikes in 1986. The centenary was celebrated with a variety of events and parties, centred in August on a series of organized rides to Milwaukee from points across the US and beyond.

Shortly afterwards Harley also introduced four new 2004 models in the one remaining family of bikes that had not recently been overhauled: the Sportsters. The new XL1200R Roadster and XL1200C Custom models had new, more powerful engines producing 70bhp, but the most important feature of those bikes, plus the two 883cc models, was the addition of rubber mounting, which made their performance far more usable.

While Harley had been growing fast, Kawasaki had been falling behind, and had announced an R&D agreement with Suzuki that suggested reduced investment in the future. But at the Munich Show in 2002, the firm's president Shinichi Morita made an unusually bold speech. 'We at Kawasaki are aware that over the past few years our machines have not fully met the expectations of our customers,' he admitted. 'We view this situation with great seriousness. Our stunning new 2003 models represent a re-confirmation of Kawasaki's reputation as a builder of high-performance, high-quality machines.'

Morita's words were backed up by two exciting bikes. The Z1000 was a striking musclebike with a twin-headlamp handlebar fairing, and a 953cc four-cylinder engine developed from the ZX-9R's 16-valve unit. Style was deemed as important as performance, so the Z1000 had an eye-catching four-silencer exhaust system even though it did not benefit the engine's 125bhp output. Even so, the Kawasaki was a lively, hard-charging bike with a top speed of 150mph (241km/h), good handling and plenty of streetfighter attitude.

More impressive still was the ZX-6R, a middleweight missile that put Kawasaki right in the thick of the super-sports action. The new ZX-6R shared its name and 636cc capacity with its predecessor, but this was a much more aggressive bike that produced 116bhp (123bhp with ram-

Above left: Buell's XBR9 Firebolt was an aggressively styled sportster whose innovative features included fuel-carrying aluminium frame spars and a perimeter front brake disc.

Below: The naked Buell XB12S Lightning produced a respectable 100bhp and had agile handling thanks to its compact and light chassis, racy steering geometry and excellent suspension.

Right: Harley's new generation Sportster 1200 came in two versions: the XL1200C (left), with lower seat and wire wheels, and the XL1200R with retro-style paint and twin front discs.

Below: Kawasaki's Z1000 led the firm's fightback, living up to its famous name with suitably aggressive styling and storming performance from its 16-valve engine.

Opposite centre right: Honda's CBR600RR was powered by a straight four rather than a V5, but its style and chassis design were closely based on the mighty RC211V MotoGP racer.

Opposite bottom right: Yamaha's 2003-model YZF-R6 was less dramatically updated than its rivals, but featured a more powerful 123bhp (with ram-air) engine and a more rigid frame.

air), weighed just 354lb (161kg), handled brilliantly and howled to a top speed of 165mph (266km/h). The ZX-6R also had lean, sharp looks, race-derived radial front brake calipers, and other neat details including an on-board lap-timer. It was arguably the year's outstanding bike, and confirmed Kawasaki's return to form.

Honda had the perfect response in the CBR600RR, a rapid 16-valve four that abandoned the CBR600's traditional versatility. Instead, the RR was a pure-bred super-sports charger that revved to 15,000rpm and produced 115bhp. Its chassis, inspired by that of Honda's all-conquering RC211V MotoGP racer, featured a high-level exhaust system and an aluminium frame that held fuel below the seat. The RR's speed and fine handling were not surprising, for Honda had reversed its normal design process for the first time, by firstly creating a racing prototype from which the roadster had been developed.

In an outstanding year for new middleweights, Yamaha's updated YZF-R6 featured fewer high-tech features, but was right up there with its 600cc super-sports rivals. And Triumph, which had found little success three years earlier with its TT600, handicapped by dull looks and poor fuel-injection, tried again with another in-line four, the Daytona 600. This British challenger was much more stylish, thanks to new, angular bodywork. Its 16-valve motor produced 110bhp, good for a top speed of about 160mph (257km/h), and its TT600-based, aluminium-framed chassis gave agile handling of the highest standard.

Among the most popular middleweights of recent years had been Suzuki's naked SV650 and half-faired SV650S V-twins. For 2003 Suzuki launched updated versions of both, and also introduced a pair of similarly styled SV1000 models, powered by a detuned 115bhp version of the 996cc V-twin engine from the discontinued TL1000S. The SVs couldn't match the TL's raw performance, but their more conventional aluminium frame design gave stable handling.

Arguably the best new V-twin of 2003 was Aprilia's RSV1000R. For all its pace and poise, the original RSV had not been the sleekest of superbikes, and the new model, although less distinctive, had a more streamlined look. Its 998cc 60-degree V-twin engine was tuned to give 139bhp, an increase of 9bhp, and the new, more compact chassis gave slightly lighter and more

Kawasaki ZX-6R (2003)

Engine:	Liquid-cooled dohc 16-valve four
Capacity:	636cc (68 x 43.8mm)
Maximum power:	116bhp @ 13,000rpm
Transmission:	Six-speed, chain final drive
Frame:	Aluminium twin spar
Suspension:	Telescopic front; single shock rear
Brakes:	Twin discs front; disc rear
Weight:	354lb (161kg) dry
Top speed:	165mph (266km/h)

Left: Kawasaki's racy ZX-6R handled superbly.

precise handling. Alongside the standard RSV was a higher spec model, the RSV1000R Factory, featuring Öhlins suspension, radial brake calipers and some carbon-fibre bodywork parts.

Moto Guzzi was showing increased vitality under Aprilia's control, having been bought by Ivano Beggio in September 2000. Beggio invested heavily in upgrading the old Mandello del Lario factory, increasing production to over 10,000 bikes, and in developing new models. The first of these was the Breva 750, a fairly simple roadster powered by a softly tuned 48bhp version of Guzzi's familiar air-cooled transverse V-twin engine.

The Breva's upright riding position, low seat and shaft final drive made it a very practical bike. Its 105mph (169km/h) top speed and all-round performance were modest, but handling and braking were good, and the Breva made a useful entry-level machine. For 2004 the Breva would be joined by an 1100cc model, with 84bhp output and similar styling.

Guzzi was also working to develop the MGS-01, a handsome sports machine powered by a tuned 1225cc version of the Daytona model's eight-valve V-twin engine. The MGS-01 was developed as a prototype by Giuseppe Ghezzi of Ghezzi & Brian, a specialist firm with links to the factory. After the prototype was displayed to enthusiastic reaction at the Munich Show in 2002, Guzzi announced that the MGS-01 would be put into production, initially as a 125bhp limited-edition racebike, the Corsa, and with a roadgoing model to follow. A similarly striking naked roadster, the Griso, was also on the way.

Aprilia had also bought Laverda, another famous old Italian marque, and unveiled a new SFC1000 model for production in 2004. A long-term return to three-cylinder superbikes seemed likely but in the meantime the SFC was powered by a 998cc 141bhp Aprilia V-twin engine, to which it added a frame of tubular steel and aluminium, plus bodywork in Laverda's traditional orange. The Laverda would face a multi-cylinder Italian rival from MV Agusta, which unveiled its long-awaited F4 1000. Alongside the standard 998cc radial-valve four was the F4 1000 Tamburini, featuring innovative adjustable intake trumpets for a broader spread of power, and peak output increased to 173bhp. MV's financial future appeared to have been secured by an agreement with the Malaysian car firm Proton, backer of Kenny Roberts' MotoGP race team.

Right: Triumph's Daytona 600 was slightly down on power compared to its Japanese super-sports rivals, but the British marque's 16-valve four had the style and handling to become a success.

Above: The RSV1000R Factory was the upmarket version of Aprilia's revamped V-twin, and handled even better than the standard model thanks to Öhlins suspension front and rear.

Below: Laverda's comeback under Aprilia ownership began with the SFC1000, which was painted in the marque's traditional orange but used a V-twin motor from the parent company.

Meanwhile Ducati was broadening its range with the first of a new family of bikes, the Multistrada. Reputedly built to conquer the Futa Pass, a steep, twisty road of varying surface that runs through the Apennines between Bologna and Florence, the Multistrada combined a torquey air/oil-cooled 992cc V-twin motor with a steel-framed chassis that was typically Ducati, apart from its longer-travel suspension. The Multistrada's tall, un-aerodynamic styling was controversial, but most who rode the Ducati were impressed by its blend of flexible power delivery, easy handling and long-legged comfort.

Austrian firm KTM had achieved an impressive rise during the '90s, based on its success with off-road competition bikes. A string of Paris-Dakar wins, backed up by motocross and enduro

Right: Revitalized Moto Guzzi promised much with the MGS-01, which the Mandello firm planned to build in this Corsa racing form before production of a roadgoing version.

Left: Ducati's Multistrada lacked the sleek style of the firm's sports bikes, but the 992cc V-twin's comfort, versatility and agile handling impressed most people who rode it, boosting Ducati's plans for a family of similar bikes.

success, confirmed KTM's prowess, as did sales of over 65,000 bikes in 2002. The firm's ambitious plan to become Europe's biggest manufacturer was boosted the following year with the arrival of the Adventure 950, its first twin-cylinder model.

The dual-purpose V-twin was powered by a new 942cc dohc eight-valve engine with cylinders set at 75 degrees. The Adventure was quick, with lively acceleration to a top speed of 130mph (209km/h). Although it wasn't as smooth or comfortable as some big trail bikes, the KTM's excellent suspension and relatively light weight made it an outstanding off-road machine. Meanwhile, the Austrian firm was developing the V-twin motor to power a naked roadster, the Duke 990, plus a super-sports bike for eventual World Superbike racing.

With annual bike production having risen to almost 100,000, BMW was also enjoying its most successful period, and in 2004 introduced a new version of its best-selling model of all. The R1200 GS was the latest in the long line of dual-purpose boxers stretching back to the R80 G/S that had established the big trail bike class in 1980. The R1200 GS was a completely new bike whose 100bhp peak output was 15bhp up on its R1150 GS predecessor, and which was a substantial 66lb (30kg) lighter, at just 438lb (199kg) dry.

Below: Given KTM's background in off-road competition, it was no surprise when the Austrian firm's long-awaited Adventure 950 V-twin was much happier on the dirt than most of its rivals in the twin-cylinder trail bike class.

The air/oil-cooled, high-cam motor also gained a balancer shaft, which made the 135mph (217km/h) performance more usable. The GS was brilliantly versatile, as happy cruising at 100mph (161km/h) as negotiating a bumpy dirt track. It was also stylish, comfortable and well equipped, with ABS brakes and adjustable ergonomics. With BMW also rumoured to be developing a large-capacity, four-cylinder superbike with radical front suspension, the German firm's old reputation for dull touring bikes was now a distant memory.

Yamaha's trio of new dual-purpose bikes included the XT660X, the first purpose-built Japanese model inspired by the increasingly popular sport of supermoto. Essentially a cross between road-racing and motocross, supermoto had led to dirt bikes with stiffer suspension and fat, sticky tyres being produced by European firms including Britain's CCM and Italian-based Husqvarna, which had built its first TD610E Super Motard several years earlier. When Yamaha

BMW R1200 GS (2004)

Engine:	Air/oil-cooled ohv eight-valve high cam flat twin
Capacity:	1170cc (101 x 73mm)
Maximum power:	100bhp @ 7000rpm
Transmission:	Six-speed, shaft final drive
Frame:	Tubular steel; engine as stressed member
Suspension:	Telelever front; single shock rear
Brakes:	Twin discs front; single disc rear with ABS
Weight:	438lb (199kg) dry
Top speed:	135mph (217km/h)

Below: BMW's brilliantly versatile R1200 GS, considerably lighter and more powerful than its predecessor the R1150 GS, was an outstanding performer both on- and off-road.

Right: Ducati tested market reaction to its 1970s-inspired SportClassic models by displaying the prototypes. The positive reaction convinced the factory to put all three into production.

launched a new single-cylinder trail bike, the XT660R, the firm also created the 660X by combining the same 48bhp liquid-cooled engine with stiffer suspension, roadgoing wheels and tyres, and a bigger front brake.

Another 2004-model Yamaha was even more revolutionary. The WR450F 2-Trac was the first production bike to use two-wheel drive. Yamaha's system, developed with Swedish suspension specialist Öhlins (which it owned), used hydraulics to transfer some drive to the front wheel when the rear wheel broke traction. As well as being tested successfully in off-road competition, 2-Trac had also shown promising results in tests with large-capacity road bikes. Although the WR was initially destined for very limited production, two-wheel drive looked to have a promising future.

A more immediate trend in roadster development was towards sporty models with classical styling. Ducati followed the MH900e by unveiling three SportClassic prototypes, including a silver, half-faired bike inspired by Paul Smart's famous 1972 victory in the Imola 200 road race. Triumph introduced the Thruxton, a sportier version of the Bonneville parallel twin featuring an enlarged 865cc engine producing 69bhp, plus café-racer styling including low bars, rearset footrests and humped seat.

Meanwhile, old rival Norton was set for another comeback, albeit in small numbers. The Commando 952 was a parallel twin in Norton tradition; a modern bike with much of the old models' familiar style. It was developed by Kenny Dreer, a leading Norton restorer and specials builder, based in Oregon, USA, who had raised several million dollars to buy the Norton name from its previous owners, both in Canada and Germany. With 85bhp from its 952cc air/oil-cooled engine, and a lightweight steel-framed chassis, the new Commando promised lively performance. Dreer reported strong interest at the projected $15,000 price, although the failure of Indian and Excelsior-Henderson gave warning that re-establishing Norton would not be easy.

While old British rivals Triumph and Norton prepared for a revival of hostilities, the first of the new breed of sporty parallel twins to reach the streets came from Germany, in the distinctively angular shape of MZ's 1000S. The tubular-steel-framed twin, initially intended to be boosted by a supercharger, had undergone lengthy development since being unveiled in 2000. With an output of 114bhp and dry weight of 462lb (210kg), the 1000S was not particularly powerful or light. But it handled well and confirmed the arrival of MZ, now under Malaysian ownership, in the large capacity market.

MotoGP's Four-stroke Takeover

Grand prix bike racing was transformed in 2002 when the 500cc class was replaced by MotoGP, which was open to four-strokes of up to 990cc. Although the 500cc two-strokes had provided memorably close racing in recent years, they had little in common with roadgoing bikes. By contrast the four-stroke MotoGP bikes would provide valuable development for production machines, and the class soon attracted interest from most major manufacturers.

Although the 990cc capacity limit was fixed, bikes with fewer cylinders were given a weight advantage, which encouraged a variety of different engine layouts. Honda considered a V6 before basing its RC211V on a 20-valve V5 with cylinders set at 75.5 degrees. Yamaha's YZR-M1 and Kawasaki's ZX-RR were transverse fours, Suzuki's GSV-R was a V4, and Aprilia's RS3 Cube was a transverse triple.

The racing was spectacular and loud, but the Honda was simply too fast for all the rest. Italian superstar Valentino Rossi, who had won the previous year's championship on

Honda's two-stroke NSR500, dominated the first two MotoGP seasons on the RC211V, whose engine revved to 14,000rpm, produced over 220bhp and gave the bike a top speed of over 200mph (322km/h). Only fellow Honda riders Alex Barros, in 2002, and Sete Gibernau, in 2003, put up a consistent challenge to the charismatic Rossi.

Predictably the lighter but less powerful 500cc two-strokes, several of which joined in during the first season, lacked the sheer horsepower needed to be competitive. Suzuki's and Kawasaki's four-strokes were also well off the pace. Even Yamaha managed only one rostrum place in 2003, though the firm's hopes were boosted by the signing of champion Rossi for 2004. By contrast Ducati's Loris Capirossi won a race in 2003, the debut year of the powerful Desmosedici ('Desmo 16-valve'), and was timed at a record 206.7mph (332.6km/h) on the thundering Italian V4 at the Italian GP at Mugello.

MotoGP's success was confirmed by the increasing number of factories considering involvement, and contrasted with the fortunes of the World Superbike championship. Ducati's British ace Neil Hodgson rode a works 999 to a convincing win in 2003. But controversial rule changes then resulted in most works teams abandoning the Superbike series, whose status was greatly diminished.

The future of real road racing was even more bleak. A succession of fatal accidents in Irish road racing was followed in July 2000 by the death of 26 times TT winner Joey Dunlop, the greatest road racer of all, at a minor meeting in Estonia. At the Isle of Man in 2003, multiple TT winner and lap record holder David Jefferies was killed when he crashed his Suzuki GSX-R1000 at high speed. Many riders still loved to pit themselves and their machines against the famous 37.73-mile (60.7km) Mountain Circuit and the roads of Northern Ireland's North West 200. But others were wondering how long these historic events could continue.

Foggy's new challenge

Malaysian oil giant Petronas had undertaken a high-profile project to produce and race a 989cc three-cylinder superbike, the FP-1, in conjunction with British former World Superbike champion Carl Fogarty. During the World Superbike 2003 season the Foggy Petronas team had struggled to make the hastily created racing version of the triple competitive against the dominant Ducatis. Development of the production FP-1 also took longer than planned, but Petronas appeared to have the financial resources to see the project to completion.

Above left: Valentino Rossi on Honda's RC211V.

Top centre: Northern Ireland's North West 200 is one of the most spectacular real road races.

Above right: TT racing lost its brightest star when David Jefferies was killed in 2003.

Above: MZ's angular 1000S parallel twin finally entered production after years of development.

Right: The Thruxton 900 added performance and café-racer style to Triumph's parallel twin.

Above: The stylish, American-built Commando 952 gave hope of a genuine new Norton at last.

Below: Hyosung's Comet 650 owed much to Suzuki but was designed and built in Korea.

Another rising Asian force was South Korean firm Hyosung which, after beginning by producing small-capacity bikes in conjunction with Suzuki, was growing in size and confidence. While Daelim, another Korean firm, continued to build obsolete Honda models, Hyosung introduced 650 and 1000cc V-twins of its own design and construction. With increasing numbers of Comet roadsters and Aquila cruisers heading for export markets including Europe and the US, Hyosung looked set to emulate Korean car firm Hyundai by establishing a reputation for high-quality machines at competitive prices.

The outstanding new bikes of 2004, however, had more familiar origins. Kawasaki's impressive recovery gathered pace with the ZX-10R, an outrageously aggressive 998cc 16-valve super-sports four. The ZX-10R shared the lean, angular styling of the ZX-6R, had an even shorter wheelbase, and weighed just 374lb (170kg). Its peak output of 172bhp was increased to over 180bhp by the ram-air system, giving a power-to-weight ratio of well over one bhp per kilogram.

Those statistics suggested a stunningly fast, racy motorbike, and the ZX-10R did not disappoint. It screamed to over 100mph (161km/h) in first gear, lifted its front wheel under hard acceleration in thrilling fashion, and scorched to a top speed of over 180mph (290km/h). The Kawasaki also had handling so responsive that it verged on the nervous, plus superb braking thanks to radial front calipers and lightweight, wave-pattern discs.

Few bikes had ever come close to bringing such vicious, adrenaline-charged performance to the street, although one that had was Suzuki's GSX-R1000, which weighed just 370lb (168kg) following a 2003 update that also incorporated radial brake calipers. Yamaha joined in by comprehensively updating the YZF-R1 for 2004. Its revised 20-valve engine's 172bhp output matched that of the ZX-10R, and the Yamaha's new chassis incorporated a high-level exhaust system for the first time.

Honda faced the growing challenge with the fastest FireBlade yet. The CBR1000RR followed the CBR600RR by inheriting styling and chassis design from the RC211V racer. The 'Blade's new 998cc 16-valve engine produced 170bhp, and breathed out through a high-level exhaust system. At 394lb (179kg) the FireBlade was slightly heavier than its closest rivals, but it handled superbly thanks to its race-derived chassis, whose key feature was mass centralization. Ironically the FireBlade followed the RC211V in delivering its performance in relatively controlled, undramatic fashion, aided by a sophisticated steering damper. That arguably made it faster but less exciting to ride than some of its rivals.

Honda's most spectacular newcomer was the Valkyrie Rune, an innovative giant cruiser powered by the GL1800 Gold Wing's flat six engine. The Rune had begun as a concept machine designed by American Honda, and made it into limited production, with features including trailing-link front forks, enormous curved radiator and a collection of striking bodywork shapes. Honda planned to build just 1200 units during 2004, all for US sale at over $25,000 each. The Rune's introduction sparked hopes that another futuristic American Honda prototype, the New American Sports, would one day lead to a production model too.

Even Triumph's Rocket III couldn't match the visual impact of the Rune, but the British firm's three-cylinder cruiser had an even larger capacity as well as much more performance. The gigantic 2294cc in-line triple produced 147bhp and delivered its maximum torque at just 2500rpm. Triumph claimed the Rocket III out-accelerated Suzuki's Hayabusa to 100mph (161km/h) – provided a pillion passenger was in place to help keep the enormous rear tyre gripping the road.

Whatever the truth of that, the Rocket III showed the motorcycle world one new direction in which high-performance bikes might develop. With the latest crop of racy super-sports machines arriving just as motorcycling in some countries was under siege from rising accident rates, increased calls for legislation, record numbers of prosecutions for speeding, and even spiralling costs of track day insurance, any alternatives were welcome.

Kawasaki ZX-10R (2004)	
Engine:	Liquid-cooled dohc 16-valve four
Capacity:	998cc (76 x 55mm)
Maximum power:	172bhp @ 11,700rpm
Transmission:	Six-speed, chain final drive
Frame:	Aluminium twin spar
Suspension:	Telescopic front; single shock rear
Brakes:	Twin discs front; disc rear
Weight:	374lb (170kg) dry
Top speed:	185mph (298km/h)

Above: Kawasaki belatedly joined the open-class super-sports war with the ZX-10R, which boasted sharp styling, light weight, a rev-happy 172bhp engine, and neat details including wave-pattern front disc brakes.

Left: Yamaha overhauled its fearsome YZF-R1 to good effect for 2004. A more powerful 172bhp engine was angled forward in a slimmer and more rigid frame; and a new high-level exhaust system ended with an under-seat silencer.

Index

Page numbers in *italics* refer to illustrations

ABC 31-2, 34
Adler 18, 70
Aermacchi 69, 95
Agostini, Giacomo 76, 90
AJS *48*, 58, 59, 71
AMC 40, 58, 66, 70-1 *see also* AJS;
    Matchless; Norton
Aprilia
    Futura 174, *175*
    RS250 *146*, 147-8
    RSV Mille 158-9, 160, 184
    RSV1000R 184-5, *186*
    Tuono 176-7
Ariel 18, 58, 66, 67
    Red Hunter 49, *50*, 66
    Square Four 40-1, 54-5, 66

Benelli 34, 95, *96*, *97*, 106, 123, 178
Bianchi 17, 34
Bimota 105-6, *123*, 124, 143, 145, 164,
    165, *170*, 171
    YB6 EXUP *128*, 130
BMW 32, 37, 45, 70, 84, 133, *159*
    C1 171-2
    F650 Funduro *145*, 147
    K100 114-15
    R50 49, *50*, 70
    R75/5 87, *88*
    R80G/S 129, 187, *188*
    R90S 87-8
    R100RS 99, *100*
    R1100RS *145*, 146-7
    R1200 GS 187, 188
    R1200C 158, *159*, 179
Boss Hoss 152-3, *155*
Bridgestone 350 GTR *60-1*, 78
Britten V-1000 149-50
Brooklands 19, 37, 47
Brough Superior 7, 37, 39-40
BSA 31, 44, 62, 67, 73, 80, 89
    A7 46, 75
    A10 Road Rocket 58, 75
    Bantam *47*, 73
    Gold Star 47-8, 49, 68
    Golden Flash *47*, 57-8
    Rocket Three 80-1, 84-5
    Spitfire *73*, 75
    Thunderbolt *73*, 75
Buell *130*, 132-3, 163, 168, 181-2, 183
Bultaco 88, *89*

Cagiva 122, 131, 145, *146*, 148, 155, 164,
    171
Crocker *38*, 39
Curtiss V8 *17*, 21
customizing 69-70, *79*, 90, *136*
Cyclone 27, 28

Daimler Einspur 7, 10-11, 13-14, 16, 121,
    191
De Dion-Bouton *12*, 16-17, 19
Depression 35, 36-9
DKW 32, 33, 45, 49, 70, 87
Douglas 28, *29*, 45-6
Ducati 51, *53*, 79-80, 111, 122, 155, 168, 179
    750 Sport 92, *93*
    851 130, 131, 145-6
    900SS 92, 93, 114, 131-2, *134-5*, 145,
      164
    916 147, 148, 165, 176
    999 176, 178
    GT860 93, *94*
    M620ie Monster 173, *174*
    M900 Monster 145, 146
    Monster S4 174, *175*
    Multistrada 186, *187*
    Pantah *113*, 114
    racing 92, *93*, *113*, 146, 150, 161, 163
    SportClassic 188

ST2 156, 157
Duke, Geoff 46, 47, 59

Excelsior 17, 19, *21*, 22, 27, *35*, 36-7, *39*, 44

films, motorcycles in 41, 56, 79, 104, 179
Flying Merkel 19, *22*, 23, 28
FN Four 15, 18, 20-1
forkless motorcycles 143
Francis-Barnett 58, 71

Garelli 34, 88
Geneva *11*, 12
Gilera 37, *147*, 169
    Saturno 52, *53*, 59
Guggenheim Museum 7, *11*

Hailwood, Mike 63, 76, 114, 168
Harley-Davidson 14, 20, 23, 40, 45, 84,
    111, 121-2, 136
    61E 38-9
    Dyna Super Glide Sport 163
    Electra-Glide 69, 104, 122, 152
    Fat Boy 140, 168, 179
    racing *19*, 22, 37, 95
    Softail 152, *153*, 168
    Sportster 1200 *139*, 140
    Super Glide 90, *91*
    V-Rod 7, 175-6, *177*
    V-twin *21*, 23
    World War I *26*, 29
    XL Sportster 57, 69
    XL1200C 183, *184*
    XL1200R 183, *184*
    XLCR1000 Café Racer 95, 96, *97*
    XR750 96-7, 98
Henderson *21*, 22-3, 36-7
Hesketh V1000 124-5
Hildebrand & Wolfmüller 12, 14-16
Holden *13*, 18-19
Honda 88, 140
    CB72 63, 64
    CB450 74, 76-7
    CB500 *84*, 85, 95
    CB750 *6*, 7, 81, 84-5, 87, 101, 104
    CB750 Nighthawk *136*
    CB900F 104-5, 113, 123, 124
    CB1100R 112, 117, 151
    CBR600F *127*, 138, 174, *176*
    CBR600RR 184, *185*
    CBR900RR FireBlade 142-3, 169-70,
      190
    CBR1000RR FireBlade 190, 191
    CBR1100XX Super Blackbird 153-4,
      156
    CBX1000 *82-3*, 106-7
    CX500 *100*, 103, 115, 116
    GL1000 Gold Wing 99-101, 127
    GL1100 Gold Wing 111-12
    GL1500 Gold Wing *126*, 127-8, 153
    GL1800 Gold Wing 175, *177*, 190
    Hornet 900 178, 180
    NR750 *142*, 144-5
    NSR250 *138*, 139-40
    racing 62-3, 76, 85, 104, *105*, 113, 123,
      129, 130-1, 170
    RC30 *128*, 129, 130-1, 133, 150
    RC45 150, 161, 170
    Shadow ACE 152, *154*
    ST1100 Pan European 138
    Super Cub 50-1
    Valkyrie F6C 153, *155*
    Valkyrie Rune 190, *191*
    VF750 115-16, 126
    VF1000R *116*, 117
    VFR750F *108-9*, 110-11, 126-7, 130
    VFR800FI *166-7*, 180
    VTR1000F Firestorm 156-7
Husqvarna 55, 122, 177, 187

Indian *13*, 19-20, 26-7, *36*

Chief 38, 55-6, 162, 181, *182*
Four *36*, 38, 55, *56*
Model 741 Military Scout *44*, 45
Powerplus *26*, 27
racing 37, 38
Scout 38, 55, 56
V-twin 22, 27, 38
World War I *26*, 29
Isle of Man Tourist Trophy Race 16, 19,
    29-30, *34*, 35, 62-3, 74, 172
    Ducati 114, 168
    Norton 46, 47

James 58, *59*, 71
JAP 16, 26, 37, 40, 53

Kawasaki 64, 76, 84, 86, 88, 101, 112, *136*,
    152, 169
    GPZ900R 117, 179
    Mean Streak 181
    racing 117, 133, 150
    W650 173, *174*
    Z1 90, 91, 117
    Z1-R 103, *105*
    Z1000 183, *184*
    Z1300 107, 110
    ZX-6R 150, 175, *176*, 183-4, 189, 190
    ZX-10R 189, 190
    ZXR750 *132*, 133, 150
    ZZ-R1100 (ZX11) 137-8
Knievel, Evel 96-7
KTM 186-7

Laverda 91, 111, 124, 154-5, *157*
    Jota 94-5, 96
    SFC1000 185, *186*
Lawson, Eddie 118, 123, *146*

Matchless 16, 17, 19, 26, *56*, 58, 66, 71, 126
Megola *32*, 33
Michaux-Perreaux *10*, 11, 13
Moto Guzzi 34, 52, 59, 78-9, 93, 111, 122-3
    Daytona 145, 154, *156*
    Le Mans 850 94, 95
    MGS-01 185, *186*
    V11 Sport 164, *165*
Moto Morini 93, *94*, 122
Motor Manufacturing Company (MMC) 17,
    18
MTT Y2K 170-1
MV Agusta 53, 59, 63, 76, 80, 98, 106,
    179, 185
    750 F4 164-5, *177*
    750 Sport 91, 92
MZ/MuZ 49, 64, *146*, 147, 188, *189*

Neracar 33, 34
Norton 29-31, 44, 70, 160
    Classic *131*, 133
    Commando 72, 75, 97, 188, *189*
    Dominator 46, 47, 58, 65-6, 67
    F1 *140*, 141
    Manx 46, 47, *48*, 67
    racing 46, 47, 59, *131*, 133
Norton Villiers Triumph 70, 89, 97
NSU 18, 29, 30, 33, 49-50, 62, 63, 70, 88

Panther *24-5*, 31, 70, 71
Pierce Arrow 15, 21
Pope Model L *8-9*, 22, 23, 28
Puch 18, 29

Quasar 98-9

Roberts, Kenny 98, 123
Royal Enfield 18, *31*, 44, 49, 68, 71-2, 73
Rudge 22, 35, 54
Rumi 52-3

scooters 51, *52*, 71, 72, 73, *148*, 169, 172,
    173

Scott 17, 21-2, 45, *46*, 98
Sheene, Barry 89, 98, 119
sidecars 26, *28*, 29, *50*, 71, 84, 161
speed records 37, 54
steam power *10*, 11-12, 14, 26
Sturmey-Archer 26, 33
Sunbeam *18*, 26, 31, 45, *46*
Surtees, John 53, 59
Suzuki 64, 88, 111, *138*
    Bandit 600 *150*, 151
    GS750 102, *103*, 106
    GS1000 102, 103
    GSX-R750 119, 120, 133, 140, 154, *156*
    GSX-R1000 172
    GSX-R1300R Hayabusa 165
    GSX1100S Katana 112, 113-14
    GT750 86-7
    racing 98, 119, 160, 161, 172
    RG500 Gamma 118-19, 123
    T500 *75*, 77-8
    TL1000S 157, *158*, 171, 184

trail bikes 129, 186-7, *188*
tricycles *12*, 14, 17, 26
Triumph 26, 28-9, 44, *71*, 73
    Daytona 151, *152*, 157, 158, 173, 184,
      186
    racing 74, 89
    Rocket III 190, *191*
    Speed Triple 151, 157-8, 179
    Speed Twin 40, 41, 46, 57
    T120 Bonneville 59, 65, 66, 67, 74, 173
    T140 Bonneville 97-8, *99*, 125, 126,
      179
    T150 Trident 80-1, 84-5
    T160 Trident 97, *99*
    Thruxton 188, *189*
    Thunderbird 56, 57, 151, *152*
    Tiger 41, 46, *47*, 57, 65, 67
    TR7 Tiger *124*, 125-6
    Trophy *140*, *141*
    X-75 Hurricane 89-90
turbocharging 115

Velocette 35, 48-9, 72-3
    Viceroy *71*, 72, 73
Vespa 51, *52*
Victoria 32, 33, 49, *51*, 70
Victory 162, 181, *182*
Villiers 26, 54, 58, 70, 71 *see also* Norton
    Villiers Triumph
Vincent *42-3*, 53-4

Werner Motocyclette *13*, 17-18
World War I *23*, *26*, 28-9
World War II 41, 44-5

Yamaha 64, 88, 98, 102, 103, 110
    Drag Star 650 152, *153*
    FJ1200 118, 133, 174
    FJ1300 174, *175*
    FZ750 120, *121*, 128
    FZR1000 *127*, 128, 143
    FZS1000 Fazer 174, *176*
    racing 98, 123, 160, 161
    RD350LC 111, 112
    RD500LC 118, *119*
    Road Star Warrior 181, *182*
    TDM900 180, *181*
    V-Max 120-1, 122
    XS-1 *75*, 77, 85
    XS1100 102-3, *104*
    XVZ1300 Royal Star 152, *154*
    YZF-R1 159, 160, 169-70, 181, 189-90
    YZF-R6 184, *185*

Zenith 18, 22, 37
Zweirad Union 49, 70